V.P. 179

Fulgencio Batista rose from abject poverty, made incredible sacrifices to gain an education and regarded Abraham Lincoln as his idol. His story of Cuba under his leadership is told here in order to keep the record straight.

Written with restraint and a remarkable absence of personal bitterness, the Batista years, as presented by their creator, offer a sharp contrast to the Castro era which has followed. There can be no question about which offered more opportunity or security to the average man and woman in Cuba.

The book is a heavily documented, highly factual record of the slow and successful struggle of the Cuban people to advance from backwardness to becoming the most advanced nation in Latin America with the highest per capita standard of living and the lowest rate of illiteracy.

Pro-communist propaganda has depicted President Batista as a brutal and dictatorial spokesman of reaction and his regime as one callous to the needs of the Cuban people. Readers of his book will learn that his government engineered a revolution in public health and popular education, aided free trade unions, protected the Cuban masses with a farflung social welfare system and radically transformed the institutions of the island so as to open wide the gates of opportunity for all Cubans.

FULGENCIO BATISTA was born January 16, 1901 at Banes in Orienta Province. He worked as a cane cutter, mechanic and scales foreman in the sugar fields; as a fireman, brakeman and conductor on the railroad; then as a store clerk until he passed examinations as a stenographer-staff sergeant. Attaining his education at nights, he opened a private tutoring school, dealt in real estate and farm produce. In 1931 he joined a patriotic organization opposed to United States intervention in Cuba under the Platt Amendment and on Sept. 4, 1933, he led the "Revolution of the Sergeants," and turned over government control to a civilian Junta which subsequently appointed him Chief of Armed Forces. In 1939 Batista's government lost the election under the new constitution and he resigned from the Army to become a presidential candidate. He won the elections, but in 1944, his party lost to Dr. Ramón Grau San Martín. Batista was not a candidate because the President could not be reelected under the provisions of the 1940 Constitution. After inaugurating the President Elect, in October 1944, he left Cuba for a tour of Latin America. He then lived in exile at Daytona Beach, Florida until he was elected senator in absentia in 1948 and returned to Cuba. Then, 1952, he led a bloodless coup. He won the elections held in 1954. Before inaugurating the winning candidate in February 1959, he was forced to resign in favor of the Dean of the Supreme Court Justices and immediately thereafter Castro forces took over.

THE GROWTH AND DECLINE
OF THE CUBAN REPUBLIC

Translated from the Spanish
by Blas M. Rocafort

THE GROWTH AND DECLINE
OF THE CUBAN REPUBLIC

Fulgencio Batista

THE DEVIN-ADAIR COMPANY
New York   1964

"You can fool all the people some of the time, and some of the people all the time, but you can not fool all the people all the time.

—ABRAHAM LINCOLN
Speech at Clinton, 8 September 1858.

Preface

The purpose of this book is to present a truthful and factual account of the economic, social and political development of Cuba during the quarter of a century between the overthrow of the Machado Administration in 1933 and the conquest of my country by Communist guile in 1959.

During seventeen of those twenty-five years (between 1933 and 1944 and again between 1952 and 1959), I had the privilege and great responsibility of serving as the *de facto* or *de jure* Chief of State.

For readily understandable reasons, this era has been consistently maligned. Although public opinion in the United States is deluged with statements about Cuba, it is misinformed concerning the progressive, forward-looking, socially conscious and democratic society which Castro and his Communists assaulted and eventually destroyed.

The study of history is not a useless pastime, but a means of using the past as a guide to the future. Eventually, my countrymen will win freedom from their Communist oppressors and they will then face the task of rebuilding a free and progressive society on such firm foundations that it can never again be subverted. To achieve this, it is imperative that they understand that past, not through the veil of propaganda, but as it actually was: *"Ich will bloss sagen wie es eigentlich gewesen ist,"* as the great German historian, Leopold Ranke, once put it.[1]

[1] "I will merely state how it actually was."

This book is based, wherever possible, on official documents and other unimpeachable sources. Although no Cuban can be emotionally indifferent to the Calvary of his country, I have tried in these pages to suppress emotions and rely on facts to persuade.

I trust that this work will show clearly that the fundamental orientation of Cuba under my leadership was toward the welfare of the people and particularly its underprivileged elements. I shall show that the social legislation which we introduced, implemented and enforced was, in many respects, the most progressive and advanced of its kind in the Western Hemisphere. I shall point out in detail how we established free clinics and free hospitals throughout the Island, thereby almost entirely eliminating the scourge of tuberculosis which had previously been rampant, reducing infant and general mortality to minimum levels, vastly improving the general health of the people and ameliorating public health standards to such an extent that we were recognized as outstanding by such entities as the World Health Organization.

The official records will also reveal the vast number of schools and other educational institutions constructed which transformed my countrymen from a sadly illiterate people into one of the best educated in Latin America. By presenting easily verifiable statistical data and other facts, I shall show that, although our opponents predicted that my social welfare program would bring financial ruin to Cuba, the Island reached new peaks in industrial output, mining, agriculture, gold and foreign exchange reserves, per capita national income and the other basic indexes of economic stability and progress. Largely because of faith in the stability and integrity of government, hundreds of millions of dollars of foreign capital were invested in Cuba in the 1950s, creating new industries and new jobs for skilled Cuban workers.

Both in war and in peace, we always collaborated with the United States in its struggles to preserve freedom against the twin totalitarian challenges of nazism and communism. Although Cuba is a comparatively small country, we became one of the largest importers of United States products in the world. Today, all this has been changed. Cuba is ranged with the totalitarian bloc dedicated to burying America and the Cuban market is closed to United States goods. The irony of it is that the United States Government bears a large measure of responsibility for feeding the cancer that is today killing Cuba and menacing the United States.

Without being too immodest, let me point out that, as early as 1952, I sounded a solemn warning to all the nations of the Western Hemisphere concerning Communist penetration of the New World, but unfortunately that warning went unheeded. In that year of 1952, I severed diplomatic relations with the Soviet Union and thus my Administration and I became the special targets of Communist hatred and Communist destructive force.

In the sphere of political thought, an amazing, almost unbelievable, transformation began to occur, to gather momentum and finally to sweep all opposing ideas out of its path. My Administration, which had been correctly characterized as one that combined democratic institutions and support of free enterprise with bold and continual advances by the State in the areas of social welfare and support of the just demands of organized labor, was labelled as a cruel, reactionary, semi-feudal despotism,[2] notorious for its "indifference to the needs of the people for education, medical care, housing, for social justice and economic opportunity . . ."[3]

The Communists had decided to employ, in Cuba as elsewhere, the technique of the big lie. To justify the Castro assault on free institutions, it was necessary to falsify recent Cuban history *in toto* and to impose upon world opinion a characterization of Cuba's Government and social institutions thoroughly at variance with the facts. This was achieved by repetition, by the planned utilization of the gullible, the ignorant, the naïve, the unscrupulous, the perennial sympathizers with leftwing causes, the thwarted, the psychic and physical cripples, the men of resentment—choosing, of course, only those who sat in high places. And as these lies were repeated, in some cases in innocence, in others with guilt, the truth dissolved like a mirage. In the "enlightened" literary and political circles of the United States, a time came when everybody "knew" that Cuba was a backward country and a land of reactionary feudalism; that it frowned on social welfare, suppressed the labor unions and modelled itself on Mussolini and Hitler. The fact that all of this was nonsense, that it was refuted by the published statistics, by the historic record and by the testimony of unimpeachable contemporary witnesses carried little

---

[2] Obviously, a despotism cannot be semi-feudal, because feudalism implies decentralization of power, though decentralization does not mean feudalism, but then the comrades are more learned in villification than in history.

[3] United States State Department, *White Paper on Cuba,* April 1961.

weight. For ignorance and prejudice were in the saddle and had
no desire to look at the record and honestly examine the facts.

It would be fruitful for a competent historian to make a thorough and dispassionate analysis of the successive stages and the
mechanics of this great deception. We would then learn how the
image of free Cuba in the mind of world public opinion was perverted, what forces were brought into action and how they operated. It would be a useful study because the Communists use
basically similar techniques to destroy free societies everywhere.
And to be informed is to be armed.

I end this preface with a sad commentary. In March 1958,
when my Government purchased the military equipment it
needed to defend itself against the onslaught of Castro and his
Communists, delivery of this equipment was denied us by the
United States Government. At the same time, my Administration
and I were subjected to a concerted and savage assault, seemingly coordinated, by some of the most influential publicists of the
press, radio and television of the Free World. A leading correspondent of one of the most powerful newspapers in the United
States praised Fidel Castro to the skies and, by poisoning the
mind of the public, played an outstanding role in placing the
yoke of communism on the shoulders of my people.

The Western World is now reaping the harvest of the years of
sentimental illusions about the true nature of Soviet communism,
which has already brought the world to the edge of nuclear war
and which can destroy civilization forever.

Fulgencio Batista

Estoril, Portugal,
June 1, 1964.

Contents

THE GROWTH AND DECLINE
OF THE CUBAN REPUBLIC

1

The Battle for Cuban Sovereignty

In this work, I deal primarily with economic and social developments and with the legislative work and constructive accomplishments of my various Administrations. This is chiefly a book about laws and stones: *laws* that brought freedom within a framework of order and social welfare within a framework of free enterprise; *stones* that rebuilt a nation.

None of this can be understood in a political vacuum. Accordingly, in the first chapters of this book, I shall sketch the salient political developments in Cuba during the 1933-1959 era. In particular, I propose to explain the rationale, necessity and underlying dynamic forces of our two Revolutions of 1933 and 1952.[1]

The Revolution of the 4th of September 1933 has been characterized as second only to our Independence Day (May 20, 1902) as a milestone in Cuba's advance toward freedom, social justice and order under the shield of law.

On the eve of this Revolution, Cuba was ruled by President Gerardo Machado, who had illegally usurped power in 1928 by manipulating "his puppet Congress into extending his term in the Presidency until 1935." [2] Emil Ludwig, the internationally famous historian and biographer of Napoleon, Bismarck, the Borgias, Kaiser Wilhelm II and many others, wrote:

[1] I have covered this ground in more detail in my *Cuba Betrayed*, Vantage Press, New York, 1962. My personal role in these events is narrated with factual accuracy and in considerable detail in Edmund A. Chester's, *A Sergeant Named Batista*, Henry Holt & Company, New York, 1954.

[2] Chester, *op. cit.*, p. 26.

"On the pretext of wishing to complete an ambitious public works program which could not be finished in his four-year term, he (Machado) devised a formula for maintaining himself in power through an unconstitutional prorogation of his powers. From then on, a vigorous oppositional campaign raged, led by the students of the University of Havana. The Government vainly attempted to smother it by illegal and violent means. However, each new act of repression increased the unpopularity of Machado and the hostility toward his regime spread to certain members of the Armed Forces, who joined secret organizations where they conspired against the unconstitutional Government." [3]

In addition to political repression, Cuba was suffering from the ravages of a world depression which had about reached its nadir by 1933. Cuba, in those days, depended for its livelihood on a single crop—sugar. And in 1933, the value of our sugar exports to the world had shrunk from an all-time high of $1,022,300,000 in 1920 to $45,256,000 in 1933. In other words, our earnings from exports were less than a tenth of what they had been in the past. The Cuban economy was in ruins and the Cuban people lived through dark hours of unemployment, hardship, hunger and hopelessness.

A grave danger that we faced was that the triumph of the revolutionary struggle against Machado would lead to a cycle of chaos, disorder and civil war in which the nation would continue on the downward spiral which had been started by political tyranny and economic disaster. Moreover, the evil forces of communism would do their utmost to spread chaos and intensify social conflict.

In this situation, we had every reason to fear United States intervention under the Platt Amendment, an intervention which would not only do violence to our national sovereignty, but which might again lead to the military occupation of our country by a foreign power. [4]

[3] Emil Ludwig, *Biografia de una Isla*, Editorial Centauro, S.A., Mexico D.F., Mexico, 1948. Since the English version reproduced here and elsewhere is translated from the Spanish, which in turn was probably translated from an original German text, there may be discrepancies between my text and any American or English edition that exists.

[4] The Platt Amendment, so-called because it had been introduced by Senator Orville Platt as an amendment to the Military Appropriations Bill of 1901-02, was subsequently accepted by the Constitutional Convention of Cuba in order to avoid delay in the establishment of the Republic and was

Machado was forced to flee the country by the combined efforts of the revolutionary forces and the pressure of Sumner Welles, who had been sent to Cuba as the personal representative of President Franklin D. Roosevelt to end the prevailing reign of terror and establish a peaceful solution by mediation. Then, to quote Emil Ludwig again:

"The Republic lived through days of despair, in which its very existence was threatened, to such an extent that it could neither guarantee the physical safety of individuals and their families nor the legal rights of institutions. Faced with this chaotic situation, in which the Island functioned as if it were an insane asylum run by its most uncontrollable inmates, on the early hours of September 4th, 23 days after the flight of Machado, the figure loomed on the political horizon of an obscure sergeant stenographer, who had connections with well-known civic figures and who enjoyed a certain prestige among his companions. He was Fulgencio Batista, a former peasant and railroad worker. He assembled the soldiers in Camp Columbia and impressed upon them the necessity of immediate action. Other sergeants and recruits of the different commands, together with some officers, obeyed the orders of the modest stenographer, who, in this meeting and in others which occurred during the day, had assumed the role of commander-in-chief, assuming full responsibility for the movement and gaining the respect of all of the subalterns, the esteem of many of his military superiors and, above all, the support and approbation of the students. The military command, aloof from the soldiery, had no conception of the seriousness of the hour and, when it finally realized it, the eloquent Sergeant Batista had already been carried by circumstances to a destiny which he himself had never expected." [5]

Ludwig goes on to explain how the majority of the officers refused to negotiate sensibly. "The sergeants, satisfied with the triumph of the revolutionary movement," writes Chester, "had no personal interests to appease. Their only desire was to see the

---

later incorporated as an appendix to the Constitution of Cuba. It gave the United States Government the right to intervene in the internal affairs of Cuba in order to insure a government capable of protecting life and property. It violated our national sovereignty in limiting our power to obtain foreign loans. In fact, it imposed upon us a trusteeship under the nation which had helped us win our independence.

[5] Ludwig, *op. cit.*, pp. 332-333.

country returned to peace and normalcy as quickly as possible. In other words, the sergeants, although they held the supreme power in their hands at the time, were willing to allow the deposed officers the right to name the Chief of Staff—the most important figure in any military organization. The only conditions in the sergeants' offer were that a military commission of five be named to direct the work of reorganizing the Army and that the commission be composed of two commissioned officers, Batista, and two sergeants of the Revolution to be selected by the three. All changes in command, all orders, all commissions and all new regulations were to have the unanimous approval of the commission of five." [6]

The reasons for this generous offer were my recognition of the perfectly natural desire of the officers to regain a part of what they had lost in the Revolution. The impotent Government of Carlos Manuel de Céspedes had been swept aside; we had brought an end to the corrupt practices prevailing among the high officers and we had ended the unjust treatment and exploitation of the enlisted men. We had risked our lives to end these corrupt and evil practices and, while we would not tolerate their reintroduction, we were not seeking personal power.

The stiff-necked officers refused to accept our terms. The pentarchy, (that is to say, the directing committee of five civilians that was the Supreme Command of the Revolution), saw that further discussion with them was useless. The pentarchy accordingly promoted me from first sergeant to colonel and ordered me to reorganize the armed forces *in toto*.

From that point on, I became the political authority in Cuba. Emil Ludwig interviewed me and asked how I became the *de facto* Chief of State.

"I told those around me that I was their colleague, but they called me the Chief of the Revolution," I replied. [7]

REBUILDING CUBA

My associates and I made the Revolution of the 4th of September because the Republic had to be saved and because we had to prove to the world that we were capable of managing our own

[6] Chester, *op. cit.*, p. 70.
[7] Ludwig, *op. cit.*, p. 340.

affairs. And we did prove that. A program of the Revolution began to assume shape. Its cornerstones included the establishment of the complete and unconditional independence of Cuba from foreign nations; the defense of the rights of labor; a regime of dignity and justice for the soldiers of the armed forces and, finally, the reconstruction of the national economy.

The poverty of the people, the lack of funds in the Treasury and the alarming collapse of authority caused us anxious hours. Law and order had dissolved as soon as Machado was overthrown.[8] This was a situation in which we would have to move with discretion and skill, but nonetheless swiftly and energetically.

FIGHTING U.S. INTERVENTION

As dawn broke on the fateful day of September 4, 1933, rumors were rife in the Cuban capital, but the American Ambassador was unaware of what was about to happen.[9] By 8:10 of the following morning, however, Mr. Welles was able to telephone his superior, Secretary of State Cordell Hull in Washington, and inform him that a successful revolution had broken out, that ". . . all military officers have been removed and a sergeant named Batista has been installed as Chief of Staff . . ." This must have

[8] Sergio Carbó, editor of *La Semana*, a great revolutionary and one of the outstanding leaders in the struggle against Machado tyranny, recalled many years later: "The demand of the hour, after the overthrow of the tyranny, was the establishment of a sound authority. To do that, it was necessary to reorganize the Army, in which there were still, despite the public scandals and vigorous opposition of the young officers, many of the despised figures who had served as assassins and executioners for the previous (Machado) government. That is why the Army did not have the moral force to clear the streets of shameful spectacles staged by marauders and the killers of *porristas* (Machado secret police), whose cheap exhibitionism contrasted so sharply with the heroic records of the true revolutionaries who had faced death so many times in the difficult days of the fight against the tyrant." Quoted in Chester, *op. cit.*, pp. 72-73.

[9] "Phil told Ambassador Welles about the plot to overthrow the government and was laughed at for his pains . . . Phil came back to the office much provoked. He remarked that if the Ambassador wouldn't listen he would have to take the consequences." Ruby Hart Phillips, *Cuba: Island of Paradox*, McDowell, Obolensky, New York, 1959, p. 57. "Phil" was James Doyle Phillips, *New York Times* correspondent in Cuba and husband of the author. The diary entry from which Mrs. Phillips quoted was dated August 20, 1933.

been rather embarrassing for him as he had reported less than a month previously that "the Army appears completely loyal to the new government." [10]

From then on, Welles technically ceased to be Ambassador and became the Personal Representative of the President of the United States. The leaders of the various revolutionary factions, who had been involved in lengthy discussions with Welles on the ways and means of stabilizing the weak de Céspedes regime which they had set up barely 20 days previously, found it hard to believe that new forces were firmly in control.

When I assumed direct command of the armed forces and leadership of the Government, Ambassador Welles found the situation even more confusing than before and asked his Government to send more warships to Cuba. Accordingly, 29 naval vessels were ordered to neighboring waters in early September; Marine air squadrons were alerted; Marine infantry detachments were assembled at Quantico, Virginia, and Port Everglades, Florida, and Marine pilots were ordered to be prepared to fly south "on a moment's notice." [11]

The next day, Welles reported to his Government:

"I believe that the situation is deteriorating fast. I had a meeting with the political leaders of the Republic[12] in which they expressed that they deemed it advisable for us to land some troops. It is my opinion that in that case part of them could be brought to the American Embassy for protection and others to the National Hotel. This does not mean that they would patrol or anything of the sort. The trouble is that we have only fifty men available on board the *MacFarland* now in port. Please advise if the *Richmond* is arriving tomorrow."

So serious did Welles deem the situation that barely an hour later he sent a dispatch to Washington, urging that troops be landed: "I consider that it is absolutely necessary to bring men to the Embassy now, as we only have the protection of a few police within the Embassy building. I don't know what will happen shortly if we don't have some men here."

---

[10] That is to say, the de Céspedes regime. This dispatch, dated August 13, is quoted in Chester, *op. cit.*, p. 54.

[11] Robert F. Smith, *The United States and Cuba*, Bookman Associates, New York, 2d edition 1962, p. 150.

[12] That is to say, the remnants of the de Céspedes group and other elements opposed to the pentarchy.

Several days after those dispatches had been sent, Mr. Welles and I had a quiet and courteous conversation—a rarity in those troubled days. He revealed the concern of his Government that the anarchy in the country would spread. Sugar mills were still controlled by Communists in some areas. Communist agents were stirring up the masses in the capital itself, threatening to raid American properties and to seize the public utilities.

"In view of this situation," Welles told me, "I fear that the forces of law and order may be unable to control the riots, if they break out, and this would jeopardize the lives of the people."

He went on to remind me that, under the Platt Amendment, the Government of the United States was responsible for the personal safety of the people and their property. In expressing these thoughts, Ambassador Welles avoided making any direct statement about intervention. In this, he was faithfully interpreting the policies of President Roosevelt and Secretary of State Hull, as we now know from the published text of the dispatches between Hull and Welles.

UPHOLDING NATIONAL SOVEREIGNTY

In reply to this, I told Mr. Welles that our revolutionary movement had been prompted by a spirit of nationalism and a demand for full sovereignty. Our armed forces were undergoing reorganization, but, I assured him, they could and would maintain law and order. Moreover, we would see that the lives and property of American nationals in Cuba would have the same protection that would be accorded to others. I reminded him that on September 4th the Civilian Revolutionary Junta had issued a declaration of principles which contained a pledge to honor all treaties and international agreements signed by Cuba with one exception.

That exception was the Platt Amendment. Moreover, any approach based on the Platt Amendment was out of the question.

Welles replied that the United States had no intention of intervening. It merely sought to protect American lives and property. He then revealed his plan to land Marines for the sole purpose of guarding North American properties and homes and suggested the possibility of establishing "neutral zones" to avoid friction. These "neutral zones," he added, would consist of the houses and hotels where American citizens lived, the offices, factories and other enterprises which they owned and the estates and plantations which they possessed. He cited as examples the Cuban Telephone Company, the Cuban Electric Company and several ranches and plantations. In places where Americans lived in widely scattered areas, he proposed that they be temporarily concentrated in hotels which would then be made part of the "neutral zones."

I told him we would not even consider this formula. It would be most dangerous for both countries. It would provoke much greater difficulties than those we were now facing. He was asking us to acquiesce to military intervention.

We have faith in the Cuban people, I added. Since one of the main objectives of the Revolution was the attainment of complete sovereignty, we could never convince the people that they should accept this plan, even if we desired to convince them. *"The smallest landing,"* I emphasized, *"would only result in great loss of life and bring about the collapse of authority."*

In defining my attitude, I reiterated our deep feelings of friendship for the American people and stressed my desire that the relations between our two countries be maintained on a permanent basis of mutual friendship and understanding.

THE GOOD NEIGHBOR POLICY

The impression I got was that Welles had not grasped the significance of my remarks. He expressed his appreciation of my attitude and said that it coincided with President Roosevelt's Good Neighbor Policy, adding that Cuba was of particular interest to him because the United States had helped her win independence and had promised to defend her sovereignty against foreign aggression. Welles promised to report my views to his superiors and wished me good luck.

The days that followed the 4th of September were extremely tense for Cuba and extremely confusing for Welles. Ever since his arrival in Cuba four months earlier (on May 7, 1933), he had been swamped with requests for interviews and had given myriad reports, often tendentious and erroneous.[13]

[13] Welles' instructions as mediator were

"You will . . . regard as your chief objective the negotiation of a definite, detailed and binding understanding between the present Cuban government (that of Machado), and the responsible leaders of the factions opposed to it, which will lead to a truce in the present dangerous

In the Cuban situation of 1933, our hopes for success rested on the new armed forces that we were organizing, despite continuous conspiracies which were breaking out at various points in the Island. The Communists were also doing their utmost to foster chaos. As soon as the new "Army of the Sergeants" established command posts in the key areas, Red plunderings and assaults ceased. Later, the Communists again attempted to create chaos. However, our revolutionary movement was a powerful social force, led by dedicated men. It was dramatically symbolized in *La Semana* of Sergio Carbó by three figures advancing arm in arm: a soldier in uniform, a mechanic and a student.

Meanwhile, the supporters of the mediation negotiations insisted that the only possible solution was for me to resign. They regarded me as unacceptable because I was a newcomer who had climbed to supreme command of the nation from the humble position of sergeant. However, de Céspedes finally conceded that his Administration was incapable of restoring order and that my associates and I were working with all our might to bring the nation back to peaceful and orderly paths. Moreover, he conceded that we were effectively solving the vexatious problem of the deposed commissioned officers, who had refused our moderate terms and had now taken over the National Hotel, where Sumner Welles was temporarily staying.

GUNBOAT CRISIS

During these decisive moments, the mediators plotted to depose me at a meeting with the rebellious officers. Ambassador Welles was advised of this scheme and assured that it would succeed. He sent a dispatch to the State Department, outlining this plot, which had been set for September 7th or some later date. The reply he received from Secretary of State Hull rejected intervention.

"We most emphatically deem," Hull informed him, "that whatever promise was made or even only suggested with reference to U.S. action (i.e. the landing of American troops) would be considered a breach of neutrality in support of one faction over others and that every attempt to form a government under such

political agitation to continue until such time as national elections can be held in Cuba . . ." Secretary of State to Appointed Ambassador in Cuba, May 1, 1933, NA 711.37/178a (*FR*, 1933-V:285).

conditions would be interpreted by the whole world, and particularly Latin America, as an artificial creation by the U. S. Government."

Because the Island was ringed with warships, many Cubans believed that the United States Government was about to intervene. Professors, students, members of the provisional government and supporters of the Revolution, who were gravely concerned with impending intervention, would continuously interrupt me in my difficult tasks. Many Cubans fervently hoped that the Marines would land. Their persistent efforts to bring about the downfall of the pentarchy by any and all means made it necessary for me to plan for our defense and keep our small Army, still in process of reorganization, in a state of alert. At the same time, we sent troops to protect American property and reaffirmed our desire to maintain good relations and close friendship with our powerful neighbor; however, without sacrificing an iota of our sovereignty and national independence.

Until November, we continued to attempt mediation with the former officers, who used violent methods, including bombing my house from the air. Rumors persisted that the United States favored the ex-officers and that it would oppose our revolutionary regime despite the Good Neighbor Policy.

On November 20th, Sumner Welles was recalled to Washington to resume his duties as Assistant Secretary of State. This was necessary because Secretary Hull was proceeding to the Pan American Conference, meeting at Montevideo on December 3rd, and Welles would serve as Acting Secretary during his absence.

Before he left Cuba, Welles let it be known that his opinion of the revolutionary regime had become favorable. This was because of my refusal to allow gangs of radical students and workers to seize the newspapers by violence. Welles stated that the Cuban press was in favor of Batista. Eleven years later, in his book, *The Time for Decision*, Welles endorsed the "Revolution of the Sergeants" and characterized me as an "extraordinarily brilliant figure."

Although he did not relish the firm attitude I took at all times toward the Platt Amendment, Welles informed the State Department during the last weeks of his mission in Cuba that I "seemed to be the only person having authority" and that this "was due partly to his (my) effective action against Communists and extreme radical elements."

On December 18, 1933, Welles was replaced by career diplomat Jefferson Caffery. Ambassador Caffery always respected Cuban sovereignty and avoided interference in our internal affairs.

On January 14, 1934, Dr. Ramón-Grau San Martín, whose provisional Government had not been recognized by the United States or by a majority of the other nations, resigned his office. He was replaced by Carlos Hevia for a period of about 24 hours, who was followed by Dr. Carlos Mendieta, a Medical Colonel of the War of Independence, who took over the Government on January 16th by popular acclaim.

Three months later, the Platt Amendment was repealed by a bilateral treaty signed in Washington on May 29, 1934. This not only abrogated the treaty of May 22, 1903, but modified the right of the United States to lease naval and fueling stations, limiting these privileges to part of Guantánamo Bay.

After five years, Chester wrote, my attack on the Platt Amendment had resulted in its repeal and Cuba had "gained full sovereignty for the first time in its history." [14]

[14] Chester, *op. cit.*, p. 174.

2

Reconstruction and Political Struggles

Small Communist groups sprouted up in Cuba in the early 1920s and in 1925 they united to form the Communist Party of Cuba. The first General Secretary of the Party was Nicanor McPortland, who used the *nom de guerre* of Julio Antonio Mella. He led a political strike among the students at the University of Havana and succeeded in provoking the Machado Government into closing that institution. Shortly thereafter, he was arrested and charged with a bomb plot. Mella resorted to a hunger strike and the Machado Government deported him to Mexico.

Mella became prominent in Red activities there and soon was named General Secretary of the Mexican Communist Party. However, on January 10, 1929, the young Cuban agitator was shot down in the streets and the crime was blamed on the dreaded *porristas* of Machado. More modern historians of the murky origins of Latin American Communism (including two socialist writers notorious for their sympathetic attitude toward Castro) have attributed the crime to a certain Vittorio Vidali alias Carlos Contreras alias Enzio Sarmiento, a man who served for two decades as an executioner for the Kremlin in Spain and Hispanic America and who was then rewarded by leadership of the Communists of Trieste.[1]

[1] The socialist historians in question are Robert J. Alexander, *Communism in Latin America*, Rutgers, New Brunswick, N. J., 1957, and Victor Alba, *Esquema histórico del comunismo en Iberoamérica*, Ediciones Occidentales, México, D.F., 1957, p. 97.

Among the leading Communists grouped around Mella were: Pablo de la Torriente Brau, Juan Marinello (later to become Chairman of the Party), Aureliano Sánchez Arango (who later made a decisive break with the Reds) and Raúl Roa García (who was to become Castro's first Minister of Foreign Affairs.)

Fabio Grobart, "the Russian," a Slavic Comintern agent of unknown nationality and many aliases, was in charge of the Cuban Communist Party from sometime in the 1920s until 1933. When the Revolution of the 4th of September broke out, Grobart tried to capitalize on the events by sending his goons out to provoke riots and armed struggle. His cohorts seized and sovietized numerous sugar mills and provoked bloody street struggles.[2] With the restoration of order and the beginnings of economic recovery, these attempts were beaten back and communism suffered a devastating defeat.

In the course of time, the Cuban political situation and the growing international conflict enabled the Communist movement to come out in the open. World War II made such democratic powers as the United States, under the leadership of President Franklin D. Roosevelt, associate with Russia to save the world from the pressing totalitarian danger from Nazi Germany and her allies.

Cuba had been a traditional ally of the United States. After the attack on Pearl Harbor, we were one of the first nations in the New World to declare war on the Axis. As Soviet Russia had been under massive Nazi assault for the previous six months, the Cuban Communists naturally strongly supported my foreign and domestic policies.

Despite the fact that Roosevelt too had joined hands with Stalin for a temporary common purpose, I was accused of the most sinister intentions when the coalition of Government Parties accepted the support of the Communist Party in 1939. When we made the supreme decision to go to war on the side of the United States, I invited the other anti-Nazi political parties to join with me in the formation of a national government. In other words, on

---

[2] During the brief period of four months when Dr. Grau San Martín first occupied the Presidency (September 10, 1933 to January 18, 1934), however, Communist activities flourished; there was substantial Red penetration of the trade unions, and at the fourth congress of the National Confederation of Workers (CNOC), a Red delegate boasted about how "the first soviet in Cuba" had been set up at his sugar mill.

that occasion, when the stars and stripes and hammer and sickle fought together on the battlefield, a halt was called to ideological differences in order to concentrate on the defeat of the enemy. In 1943, my associates and I brought Juan Marinello, titular leader of the Cuban Communist Party, into the Cabinet. He was a Minister without Portfolio and therefore had no departmental responsibilities and was unable to infiltrate his agents into the Government.[3]

FROM POWER TO EXILE

The accomplishments of my Administrations are discussed topically and in detail throughout the book. At the moment, I want merely to indicate certain salient features of these years and, for that purpose, I prefer to quote others than to try to evaluate my own work.

Describing my first years of *de facto* power, Emil Ludwig wrote:

"A man of the people and of the fields, who understood the needs of the peasants, Batista, working through the National Corporation of Public Assistance and the Center of Child Orientation, courageously faced the grave educational and public health problems of Cuba. He established over a thousand schools, taught by sergeant-teachers, who brought instruction to the most remote parts of the Island. These civic-military schools filled the gaps in the incomplete work of the Ministry of Education. Moreover, a group of doctors, dentists, teachers of trades, home economics instructors and agronomists contributed to the vocational education and redemption of the peasant family, which had been forgotten by previous governments."[4]

One of the most important measures of this era was to provide Cuba with a new Constitution. All the political leaders of Cuba, from Dr. Miguel Mariano Gómez, General Mario García Menocal and Dr. Joaquín Martínez Sáenz, on the right, to Dr. Juan Marinello and Blas Roca, on the extreme left, agreed to the holding

---

[3] A few years later, President Gabriel González Videla of Chile brought three Communists into his Cabinet. He gave them the portfolios of Communications and Public Works, Agriculture and Lands and Colonization. He soon found that, in order to prevent them from taking over his Government, he had to oust them.

[4] Ludwig, *op. cit.*, p. 333.

of elections. Even Dr. Ramón Grau San Martín, who had been engaged in oppositional activities, joined forces. As a result, a Constituent Assembly was brought into being which formulated a new Magna Carta for Cuba, the social and economic provisions of which were among the most advanced in the world. This democratic document became the supreme law of the land on October 10, 1940.

The elections of June 1, 1940, which brought me into the Presidency, were absolutely free and fair. The economic situation of the nation was distinctly unfavorable because of the flagging demand for sugar, low sugar prices and the shipping and export stringencies imposed by war. The United States, our main sugar importer, bought about two million tons annually instead of four. "In reality," wrote Emil Ludwig, "the last two years of his Administration were years of genuinely constructive work, despite Cuba's declaration of war on the Axis immediately after Pearl Harbor, despite the shortage of shipping because of German submarines which besieged the Island, and despite the fact that the nation had to be partially mobilized to protect itself against spies and sabotage." [5]

In 1944, at the end of my four-year presidential term, Cuba had new elections. Unlike those in many other Hispanic American countries, where frauds are habitually perpetrated by the Administration so that it may continue in power, our elections were completely honest. The electorate decided in favor of my opponent, Dr. Ramón Grau San Martín, and the decision of the people was honestly and accurately certified by the Administration and the victory of the opposition conceded.

"I do not know whether Cuba will be a paradise again or blow up with bombings and killings;" wrote Emil Ludwig, "but now that there are no more political prisoners, persecuted and exiled leaders, now that labor is organized and free enterprise flourishes, it seems to me that Cuba is well on the road to that happy state . . .

"As a foreigner, who was unacquainted with Grau San Martín or with Carlos Saladrígas, Batista's friend and former Premier, I maintained a neutral position. I was in no position to determine which candidate would better serve the country. By the afternoon of the second day, it was all over. Batista had forbidden any fraud in the voting, and thereby came away with a moral victory.

[5] Ludwig, *op. cit.*, p. 335.

Cuba's reputation had never been higher and the European opinion of Latin American elections had been profoundly changed. In allowing his Prime Minister to be defeated at the polls, Batista rendered an incalculable service to the prestige of the entire Continent. Yet this was an outcome he could have prevented by violence, through the Army or by guile. For the first time in many decades, it was proclaimed and written all over Europe: 'Yes, there is a true democracy in America. The youngest of her Republics has demonstrated this . . . The defeat of Batista was his greatest victory." [6]

When my Presidential term ended on October 10, 1944, I toured South America at the invitation of its governments. This gave me an opportunity to observe the political, economic and social problems of our sister Republics and to exchange views with political, business and labor leaders.

Upon my return, I bought a house in Daytona, Florida, and lived there with my family. President Grau San Martín took measures to prevent my return to Cuba. It seemed to me that this was poor repayment for the efforts I had made to ensure complete honesty in the elections. Nor could I see how my presence in my own country threatened his power, since, if I had wanted to keep him from the Presidency, I could have refused to recognize his election. However, in order to avoid shaming Cuba by having it ostracize the leader of its 1933 Revolution, I went into what I termed "voluntary exile" in the United States.

AUTÉNTICOS, GANGSTERS AND COMMUNISTS

The Grau San Martín Administration was in an awkward position because it had won the Executive Power, but had lost out in Congress. The Republican-Auténtico coalition had been defeated in all six Provinces in the elections for the House of Representatives and had been defeated in the elections for the Senate in four out of six: Pinar del Rio, Havana, Matanzas and Las Villas.

Consequently, the Cuban people were governed by one of the most unstable regimes in their history. The Government was weak because it lacked popular support, because it had no fixed position on the great issues facing the nation and because it was flagrantly corrupt and notorious for its illicit use of power. To give an instance of the corruption of the Grau Administration, I

[6] Ludwig, *op. cit.*, pp. 213-214, 343-344.

shall quote Ruby Hart Phillips' account of the investigation of alleged embezzlement on the part of Grau by the Government of his successor, Dr. Carlos Prío Socarrás, in 1949:

"Auditors of the government continued to dig into the records. Within a month, Dr. Grau was forced to appear before the Audiencia Court of Havana to hear charges that his government had misappropriated $174,000,000. He pleaded not guilty, alleging that all spending had been carried on legally . . .

"On July 4th, a group of gunmen invaded the court where the case against former President Grau San Martín for misappropriation of $174,000,000 was being investigated and stole all the documents of the proceedings. This was to become the famous Case No. 82 against Grau, but it never came to trial and did not deter Grau from running for President in 1954. No one was ever arrested for the stealing of the documents and none of the documents was ever found." [7]

Under the Grau Administration, the Presidential Palace began to assume the appearance of a country club. Edmund Chester wrote:

"Gangsterism was introduced to Cuba during the Grau regime and there were indications that the government was protecting, if not actually participating in, the hoodlumism which was carried on through the island. One hundred and sixty-four persons were assassinated during the Grau regime, and only a few of the killers were ever apprehended. One of Grau's good friends, a Cabinet Minister named José Alemán, accumulated one of the world's largest fortunes in less time than it takes to count a million pesos, and he did it all on his small salary as a Cabinet Minister. At least that's what people were expected to believe. Alemán not only made money fast, but he converted it into dollars and got it out of Cuba just as fast." [8]

A flagrant source of corruption, gangsterism and subversive activities was the University of Havana. Its autonomy was guaranteed in the Cuban Constitution of 1940. The university police force was responsible only to the Rector of the University and the extreme theory was advanced that the institution enjoyed a status equivalent to that of the Vatican in Italy. What the laws actually provided was that, during a serious disturbance of public order, Congress could suspend the autonomy of the University,

[7] Phillips, *op. cit.*, pp. 250, 253-254.
[8] Chester, *op. cit.*, p. 213.

whereupon the National Police and the Army could enter the campus. Unless Congress took this action, however, the University precincts were barred to Cuban law enforcement agencies.

The University had become an assembly ground for hoodlums, terrorists and murderers and for professionals of dubious standing. It was a discredit to its two-hundred-year-old traditions. It was no longer noted for scientific discoveries or technological contributions of any sort. One of the main troubles was the lack of any rational restrictions on matriculation.

"So inadequate are the entry requirements," Chester wrote, "that it has been a simple matter for gangsters, political agitators, especially Communists, and all sorts of undesirable elements to enroll in the institution and get the benefits of the immunities inherent in the semi-autonomous status of the University . . . The laxity in entry requirements has, over the years, resulted in the enrollment of a number of middle-aged 'students' who have absolutely no interest in scholastic requirements. It has been said facetiously, but perhaps truthfully, that Havana University has the distinction of having more bald-headed students than any university in the world." [9]

The old Alma Mater no longer was representative of Cuban higher education. Some fifteen other colleges and universities appeared on the scene—some of them governmental, others private. These gave courses in modern science and technology which did not exist at Havana University. Their student bodies were interested in education, not agitation.

As for the University of Havana, under the influence of the political elements who had infiltrated into its student body, it had opposed all Cuban Governments ever since 1934. At the same time, the "student leaders" sometimes established surreptitious contacts with the very political leaders whom they overtly opposed in order to get "protection" or for other reasons.

In some Western countries, the zeal to protect the rights of labor has brought about such advanced labor legislation that gangsters and professional criminals enter the trade unions, finding this an area where they can steal, intimidate and kill with impunity. In the case of democratic Cuba, our zeal for academic freedom made us enact legislation which overprotected the University of Havana to such an extent that criminals, terrorists and

[9] *Ibid.*, p. 123.

Communists entered its student body in order to commit murders and other crimes with impunity.

THE RED CONSPIRACY AGAIN

Meanwhile, the Cuban people were being softened up for the great betrayal. The Russian Embassy swarmed with agitators, propagandists, spies, couriers, organizers and secret agents. Havana and Mexico City were the headquarters for the Communist conspiracy for the Northern sector of Latin America.[10]

Grau San Martín was succeeded by President Carlos Prío Socarrás, also of the Auténtico Party. While making a show of opposing Communism, Prío actually favored and abetted it. He was a member of Grau's Cabinet at the time that the Soviet secret representative, Bashirov, planned operational details of the Bogotá insurrection of 1948, which suspended the Ninth Inter-American Conference for several days, caused millions of dollars of property damage, cost hundreds of lives and left Bogotá looking like a bombed city. The further purposes of this first formidable display of Red power in the Americas had been to send the delegates to the Inter-American Conference scurrying away for their lives, to overthrow the democratic government of Colombia and substitute a Red regime and to assassinate the chief of the American delegation, General of the Armies George C. Marshall.

Miss Frances Damon, Treasurer of the World Federation of Democratic Youth, a Communist front, arrived in Havana in February 1948 under orders to create a hostile atmosphere among the students, intellectuals and workers toward the Inter-American Conference which was to meet in Colombia two months later. After visiting the Communist newspaper, *Hoy,* and the Federation of University Students, she held a lengthy meeting with Fidel Castro, Enrique Ovares, the Red student leader, Alfredo Guevara, and others. She then proceeded to the Soviet Embassy.

Bashirov also had sessions with Castro, Damon and others on the Bogotá operation. His house was under photographic and other surveillance and both Grau San Martín and Carlos Prío Socarrás were informed as to what was happening and what was being planned.

Several days later, Fidel Castro was arrested at Havana Inter-

[10] Mexico, Central America, the West Indies, those Republics of South America which border on the Caribbean Sea plus Ecuador and Peru.

national Airport just as he was about to leave for Central America and thence to Colombia. When searched, Communist literature and a map of the city of Bogotá with all strategic points marked were found on his possession. He was arraigned before the same judge who had unsuccessfully tried to hold him earlier for the murder of the anti-communist youth leader, Manolo Castro. Because of powerful political pressures, Castro was released.[11]

Grau San Martín, with the knowledge of his Labor Minister, Carlos Prío, permitted Castro and his group of student assassins to leave for Bogotá to carry out this terrorist action against a friendly government. The Auténtico Administration did even more. Orders were given the Minister of Foreign Affairs and the Chief of Staff of the Air Force to send a military plane to Bogotá. The Cuban Ambassador to the United States, Dr. Guillermo Belt, who attended the Bogotá conference, was instructed to provide Castro and his fellow Cuban gangsters with protection. Thus, when the insurrection failed and when Castro and his accomplices were wanted by the Colombian authorities for subversion and murder, they flew back to Cuba in an official Cuban plane and under the protection of the Cuban Government. Castro boasted of this at the time in an interview he gave to the official Communist newspaper of Cuba, *Hoy.*

RETURN TO POLITICAL LIFE

As Grau San Martín's four-year term approached its end, the President threw his support to Dr. Carlos Prío Socarrás. Prío was the candidate of a minority faction of the Auténtico Party and Grau was able to impose him on the Auténticos only by resort to an illegal strategem.[12] Allegedly, the main reason Presidential support was given Prío is that the latter represented the BAGA, one of the most corrupt cliques in the history of Cuba which had embezzled untold millions of public funds.[13] The anagram BAGA stood for Bloc of Ramón Grau San Martín and José Alemán.

[11] It might be worth adding that this Communist agent, who would be extolled as a "liberator," a Lincoln of the Caribbean and a man destined to bring justice to Cuba by a certain American foreign correspondent, had been prosecuted for four murders by the time he reached the age of 25 and acquitted only because of political pressures.
[12] See my *Piedras y Leyes*, Ediciones Botas, Mexico City, 1961, pp. 24-25.
[13] This charge was made by Dr. Pío Elizalde in his book, *The Tragedy of Cuba.*

The alliance between Grau and Prío rapidly disintegrated into open enmity and soon each was publicly accusing the other of misconduct and malversion of public funds. Meanwhile, a new political movement appeared on the scene, the Orthodox Party, led by Eduardo Chibás. This group claimed that it was the real representative of the Auténtico movement and was seeking to return the latter to orthodox principles. An enormously accomplished orator, Chibás inveighed against the flagrant corruption and immorality of the Grau Administration over a weekly radio program that became one of the most popular ones in Cuba.

Was Chibás the man destined to cleanse our Augean Stables? The crusade for honesty was urgently needed. However, in his youth as a university student leader, Chibás had been a wild revolutionary fanatic and an ultra-nationalist. He was a demagogue and a firebrand. Probably because of medical reasons, his was a highly unstable personality and his enemies went so far as to claim that he was insane. While Chibás was not personally either a Communist or sympathetic to communism, the powerful movement which he was building became more and more seriously infiltrated with Communists.

For my part, I had decided to retire permanently from politics. As the 1948 elections neared, I was besieged by telephone calls and visitors, urging that my name appear on the ballot so that my supporters could unite against the Administration and for the slates of the Liberal and Democratic parties. Among those who insistently urged that I do this was the distinguished surgeon and Presidential candidate of the coalition, Dr. Ricardo Nuñez Portuondo. Dr. Carlos Saladrígas and others joined him in this request.

I felt that I could not refuse and allowed my name to be entered as candidate for Senator from Las Villas Province. With terrorism and gangsterism rife in Cuba, my friends urged me not to campaign and thus run the risk of assassination. At first, I refused, thinking this a cowardly course. Then my advisors pointed out that my murder would give the Administration a pretext to suspend the elections and install a dictatorship. We were all confident that, in fair elections, a majority of the Cuban people would sweep out the Auténtico rascals and elect our distinguished physician, Ricardo Nuñez Portuondo.

The election was held on June 1, 1948. The campaign had been extremely violent and our speakers and Party workers had been subjected to physical violence by armed gangs. Moreover, the opposition to the Auténticos was split. These factors enabled Prío Socarrás to win the Presidency, although as a minority candidate: he got only 45% of the vote.

Among the six opposition candidates for the Senate in Las Villas Province, I received the largest number of votes. My victory demanded that I return to Cuba to serve in the Senate and on November 19, 1948, I was acclaimed by an enormous crowd at the José Martí Airport which accompanied me on foot and by car in a vast procession to my house "Kuquine" near Havana. The die had been cast and I was back in the maelstrom of public and political life.

3

Rule by Gangsters

After I had been elected Senator without having campaigned for the office, my constituents asked me to visit them in Santa Clara, the Provincial capital of Las Villas. I was told that I would suffer physical harm if I went there. The young men who organized my reception had been beaten up and my life threatened.

The Prío Administration had announced that any gathering in my favor would be broken up, but nevertheless crowds lined the road from the suburbs into the heart of the city. After an enthusiastic meeting, I returned to Havana with my party. On the road back, we had to disarm some of Prío's gangsters who had been sent out to molest us.

"Prío inherited Grau's gangs," I wrote in *Cuba Betrayed*,[1] "and the security of his Government depended on them. They were used for what were no longer mysterious bloody actions. Teenagers went around with pistols. They walked the streets with arrogance and murdered their rivals in broad daylight."

GRAFT AND SMUGGLING

"When Prío took over the country on October 10, 1948," wrote Chester, "the people were crying for an honest and efficient administration and he faced the greatest opportunity ever offered a Cuban President. Had he taken advantage of it, he would have become one of the great leaders of his day. But the government

[1] Fulgencio Batista, *Cuba Betrayed*, Vantage Press, New York, 1962, p. 221.

of Prío was no better than the government of Grau. In fact, many Cubans believe it was worse.

"The Prío administration was a government of 'deals'. The functions of government were important to a number of officials only because they provided contacts for the transaction of private deals which enriched them personally. The interests of the people were subordinated to the self-interest of government functionaries, and the criterion in government seemed to be 'How much can I get out of it?' instead of 'Is this good for Cuba?' As a result, all sorts of illegitimate and semi-legitimate operations were carried on with official tolerance, if not with official sponsorship.

"One of the most profitable sidelines, which eventually became a major industry, was the smuggling racket. This illicit business flourished, without official interference, during the days Carlos Prío occupied the Presidential Palace, and if the men of the Prío government did not know of these operations, they were about the only ones in Cuba who didn't.

"The smuggling business had a violent effect on the nation's economy and the effect was not good. In addition to the fact that the government lost millions of dollars a year in import duties and other revenues through this outlaw operation, the small merchant, a vital factor in the nation's economy, was almost ruined. Legitimate merchants, who paid all import duties and other customs fees, could not, of course, meet the consumer prices offered by unscrupulous traders who dealt in smuggled goods upon which no duties or fees had been paid.

"This particular racket must have been one of the largest contributors to the great personal fortunes accumulated by certain Prío officials while drawing government salaries which were relatively meager.

"Gangsterism in all its forms was practiced during the Prío administration and the breakdown in governmental morality encouraged illicit activities outside the government. There were shakedowns and *chantages*, killings and kidnappings, and little or nothing was done to combat the lawless elements. The alarming thing about the crimes was that their perpetrators were young boys, youths who had fallen into criminal ways because it seemed to be the smart thing to do. Prío apparently did nothing to discourage crime among these juveniles.

"The people of Cuba were to a great extent abandoned by the government of Carlos Prío, and the inevitable result was a complete lack of public respect for his administration and for the men who directed it." [2]

INTIMIDATION

A few days after my return from Las Villas Province, I found that the small estate on which I lived with my family was surrounded by soldiers and Prío secret agents. Friends who came to visit me were regularly stopped a few yards from the gate by these detectives, interrogated and warned that, if I made any more public appearances, I would be sorry. As the weeks passed, this surveillance and intimidation became increasingly brazen. They even had the effrontery to set up mortars which were aimed so they could lob shells into my house.

The United Action Party was organized under my leadership. It consisted of much of the membership of the Liberal and Democratic Parties, which had originally supported Prío, but had become disgusted with him. As soon as our new party was organized, its leaders and active workers became the target of Prío's hoodlums who threatened them and their families with violence. Despite this, I visited every municipality in Cuba and I found that thousands of people always turned out to see and hear me. The Cuban people refused to be browbeaten. As for us, we had to organize defense squads as we could not address peaceful political assemblies without first fighting our way in and disarming the political gangs of the Auténtico Administration.

The first great test was the election for Mayor of Havana. The Administration candidate was one of the President's brothers. This man had been named Minister of Finance, a position for which he was totally unqualified, and in that office had presided over an administration of open and unabashed embezzlement. Private funds, belonging to retired and pensioned people and on deposit at the Ministry of Finance had been looted. Some $42,-000,000 was stolen from the Sugar Workers' Pension Fund alone.

The prospect of having this light-fingered politician Mayor of Havana was unbearable. My United Action Party and the Orthodox Party of Eduardo Chibás united on the candidacy of Nicolás Castellanos for Mayor.

The Prío Administration struck back with terror and corruption. Our party workers were mauled and beaten up. On two oc-

[2] Chester, *op. cit.*, pp. 216-218.

casions, shots were fired at my car. To prevent us from nominating Castellanos, five of our delegates were kidnapped and three others bribed. Nevertheless, we rounded up enough for a quorum and placed our man on the ticket.

Despite the unprecedented use of illegal pressure by the Administration, Castellanos won the elections.

EMBEZZLEMENT AND CHIBÁS

The scandals increased in scope and magnitude. Under orders of President Prío and his disreputable brother, the Minister of Finance, the tax collectors openly took bribes from dishonest businessmen to wink at tax evasion and tax fraud by the latter.

Perhaps the most flagrant scandal of all was the incineration of $47,000,000 of old, worn-out banknotes. The Prío brothers arranged to have packages of old newspapers, cut to the right size, substituted for the notes. This "burned" money was then distributed among the henchmen and hatchetmen of the President.

These scandals were vigorously denounced in the sensational weekly broadcasts of Eddie Chibás over Station CMQ. Since the truth about Prío and his gang was preposterous, Chibás could mix fact with rumor with impunity. He charged falsely, for example, that President Prío had flown secretly to Merida in Yucatán for conferences with leaders of the Caribbean Legion, a powerful international organization of terror, subversion and revolution which was dominated by Communists and Socialists. While this specific statement was untrue, Prío did go to Guatemala later, in violation of the Cuban Constitution, to plot with the Communist President of that country, Jacobo Arbenz.

On one occasion, Chibas accused Aureliano Sánchez Arango, a founder of the Cuban Communist Party and Minister of Education in Prío's Cabinet, of having acquired vast lumber tracts in Central America and of making millions by smuggling these woods into Cuban ports. Sánchez Arango called Chibás a liar and demanded that he produce proofs.

There were violent radio denunciations by both sides; rioting broke out and two of Chibás' supporters were killed by police gunfire.

Chibás promised to appear at his next broadcast with a valise full of proofs of Sánchez Arango's venal activities. He did not produce them, but his tirades became increasingly violent.

While Chibás was gaining steadily in popularity through his dramatic debates with Sánchez Arango, other leaders of his party were seriously considering removing him as an unstable personality.

Finally, on August 5, 1951, Chibás told his vast radio audience that he hoped the sacrifice of his life would arouse the Cuban nation and stir its conscience. He shot himself in the broadcasting studio, without realizing that he was already off the air. He died a few days later.

Prío believed that the Orthodox Party was a flash in the pan which would now disintegrate with Chibás' death. However, the reformer and demagogue now appeared to the people as a martyr and this gave a prestige to his party that put it in a unique position. The people forgot, or had never known, that Chibás had tried suicide before and that these previous attempts had had nothing to do with corruption in high places.

PRÍO AND THE COMMUNISTS

Like other politicians before and since, Prío pretended to be strongly anti-communist, whereas actually and in secret he favored them. It is true that he fought the Communists in the trade unions and broke their control of the labor movement. The reason for this, however, was organizational; it was not a matter of ideology and moral principle.

The Auténticos needed to control the trade unions in order to consolidate their political power and in order to have jobs for their henchmen. As for the Communists, they had become entrenched during World War II when they supported my Administration and worked tirelessly to help Allied (and therefore Soviet) victory. The Grau Administration had been a minority in the Legislature and therefore too weak to wage a war for control of the unions.

The task, therefore, devolved on Prío. It became a duel between two men: Lázaro Peña, the veteran leader of Communist labor, and Eusebio Mujal, an Auténtico and a former member of the leadership of the Communist Party. In this struggle, which was waged on the issue of support for, or opposition to, communism, victory went to the tougher leader. Mujal proved to be a resourceful, intelligent and zealous leader of the labor movement. He continued in that capacity from the time when he won his majority vote under Prío to 1959 when I left Cuba.

Prío's attitude toward international communism was very different. He was an enthusiastic supporter of the Caribbean Legion, which worked day and night to overthrow responsible governments and install ultra-leftist ones. While the Legion had its quota of "socialists," such as José Figueres in Costa Rica, it was primarily an arm of the Kremlin and was backed by international communism. With the blessings of President Prío, the Soviet Embassy in Havana became a vast center of propaganda for the entire Caribbean zone and the meeting place for Havana University students with traveling Communist agents to plot the destruction of Western democracy.

4

Order Through Revolution

Several officers came to see me to ask me to assume command of the Armed Forces and prevent the country from plunging into complete chaos. When I talked to them, I learned that Prío had gone secretly to Guatemala for his meeting with the Red President, Arbenz, and this disturbed me deeply. For the President to have left Cuban soil without the consent of Congress was a violation of law and sufficient reason for his removal.

The officers proposed that we utilize Prío's absence from Cuba to take over the Presidency, but I replied that the forthcoming elections would solve the problem peacefully and in accordance with the Constitution.

A conspiratorial organization among the officers had been in existence for over two years and had twice failed to overthrow the Prío Government. On one occasion, a group of officers learned that the President planned a secret night visit to Army headquarters. They surrounded the building with three infantry companies and a tank company and waited. One group, consisting chiefly of his former students, wanted to install Dr. Roberto Agramonte, who had replaced Chibás as head of the Orthodox Party, in the Presidency. Another group favored me. Since they could not reach agreement, they decided to let Prío go. When the corrupt President left headquarters, he had no realization of what had almost happened.

The Presidential campaign took shape with three candidates: Agramonte for the Orthodox Party, Carlos Hevia for the Auténticos and me for the United Action Party. As the electioneering proceeded, the atmosphere became increasingly violent. Threats and rumors filled the air.

The Orthodox Party proclaimed repeatedly that, if their man were elected, President Prío would be placed in La Cabaña to stand trial for his many illegal acts. Prío's corruptly acquired wealth would be confiscated. Orthodox spokesmen announced that their first act would be to close the ports and airports of Cuba to fleeing politicians and officials. They stated that they would form "people's courts" to try and condemn Auténtico officials.

This not only had the ring of Robespierre, but it suggested the hand of international communism. The agents of Moscow had penetrated deeply into the Orthodox organization, although the Reds did not control the party. In particular, the Orthodox youth, swayed by such Communists as Fidel Castro, was strongly sympathetic to the Kremlin cause. Among the more recognized national leaders, Pardo Llada was outstanding as either a Communist or a willing implement of the great conspiracy.

In February 1952, one of the officers whom I had dissuaded from military uprising told me that Prío had had a meeting with the Army command and other ranking officers at Camp Columbia to discuss a plan to prevent the national elections. He said that, if I were elected, the Auténtico and Orthodox Parties would unite against me and there would be civil war. If the Orthodox candidate won, which he thought probable, a band of fanatics would destroy Cuban institutions and the established order. As far as the Auténticos were concerned, he thought that their candidate, Carlos Hevia, had such an unattractive personality that it was unlikely that he could win. The meeting agreed to re-examine the situation in April with a view to reaching a firm decision.

Shortly thereafter, Dr. Anselmo Alliegro, President of the United Action Party in Oriente Province, came to me unannounced to say that President Prío had run into him, greeted him affectionately and had him come over to La Chata, Prío's villa. Over coffee, Prío discussed the bleak situation which Cuba faced.

He told Alliegro that the Orthodox candidate would probably win. This he found most disturbing because of tapped telephone conversations in which leaders of the Orthodox Parry had spoken frankly and incautiously about their real intentions. He showed his guest transcripts of these taped conversations and it was plain that Agramonte and his people were deeply concerned with wreaking vengeance on their opponents.

The elections were to be held June 1st. One of the phone conversations revealed that the day after the election, the Orthodox leaders, who assumed that they would be victorious, planned to arouse the populace to fury and drive out the Auténticos. President Prío said that part of the plan was to steal his wife's jewels. The Auténtico Chief Executive added that it would be a great stupidity to attempt this on June 2nd, but if the Orthodox candidate won and continued to whip up mob anger, he could get away with it by inauguration day, which was October 10th.

Alliegro told Prío that, if the situation was that desperate, he and the other Auténticos should join forces behind my candidacy. On the contrary, Prío replied, there was no hope of a Batista victory and therefore my people should step aside and back Hevia. "If this added support does not gain victory for Hevia," the President continued, "there is nothing else for me to try but a coup d'état."

I told Alliegro how much I appreciated his reporting this to me, adding that Prío was driving the country to the brink of ruin and would destroy it if he persisted in his headstrong and mistaken policy.

THE REMOS MISSION

Early one morning, my daughter, Mirtha, awakened me to say that Dr. Juan J. Remos, a spokesman for Prío, wished to see me urgently. I arranged to have a conference with him that evening.

Remos reported what I already knew. Prío was in despondency bordering on black despair. He saw no improvement in the prospects of his candidate and considered an Orthodox Party victory, with its modern version of the tumbrils, inevitable. If by April, there was no improvement in Hevia's prospects, he would have to carry out the coup d'état.

In *Cuba Betrayed*, I describe my reaction to this proposal as follows:

"I asked Remos to listen to me as an ordinary citizen and not as an opposition leader or Presidential candidate. I wanted him to carry my ideas to President Prío. It seemed to me that the Administration did not have the support of the people and that it remained in power only through its constitutional legitimacy.

When Prío's term ended, he would no longer have the support of the Armed Forces, even if the military leaders carried out the coup. I explained the gravity of the situation and the violence of the political campaign which was growing progressively worse. If the President carried out a coup d'état, the people would rise and the Armed Forces would split. The Chiefs upon whom he depended would not command attention in such a crisis. The Army and the Navy would split into factions, and collapse. The Chiefs would back up Prío, but without forces or authority. The other officers inclined toward the 'Orthodoxes' or toward me, and there were even a handful who favored the Communist Party. For patriotic reasons, for the welfare of all concerned, I would, as a private citizen, advise President Prío not to commit this stupidity which could only result in a wave of bloodshed and even in the loss of his own life.

"Why were these messages carried to me personally? The only reason that occurred to me was that I might surrender to his wishes, as had some of my men. If the threat of Prío's gangs and their attempts to break up our meetings had compelled me to announce through the press that I preferred physical death to moral death, how could Prío persist in thinking that he might succeed?

"I asked Remos to get in touch with me after giving Prío my opinion. Three days later, he gave me the answer: 'President Prío has not changed his mind.' " [1]

THE BLOODLESS REVOLUTION

When it became quite evident to Prío that I was not going to aid his plan to plunge Cuba into civil war, the threats and violence against me and my party workers were stepped up. There was a plot to attack my home. I was threatened by the press and on the radio. On March 3rd, I went to a meeting at Guanabacoa aware of the fact that Jorgé Quintana, a Prío supporter, had publicly declared that I must not be allowed to return from that political rally alive. The threat strengthened the determination of the people to protect us and, when we approached the meeting, we found ourselves guarded by a crowd of about 30,000 sympathizers, among them armed soldiers, sailors and policemen in civilian dress and organized as an impromptu defense battalion.

[1] *Op. cit.*, pp. 238-239.

At 2:43 A.M. of March 10, 1952, I entered Gate No. 4 of Camp Columbia and took command of the Armed Forces of Cuba. We placed the Chiefs of the Army, Police, Navy and Camp Columbia and the heads of the garrisons in Havana under temporary detention in the homes of my followers, where they were treated as guests. Other leading Auténticos, among them Minister of Education Sánchez Arango, were also arrested. As for President Prío, there seemed to be no need to do anything to circumscribe his activities since he was recovering from a late party at his country estate. Most of his high officials had been enjoying the cabarets and these too could not be considered serious political or military dangers.

By nine in the morning, I was informed that there was shooting at the Presidential Palace. Arriving there, I found that Prío had recovered and gone there. One of his subordinates had lost his head and fired on my emissary when the latter announced that I had taken over the Government. Shortly thereafter, Prío sought and obtained asylum in the Mexican Embassy and then proceeded to Mexico.

The March 10th Revolution had triumphed without spilling a single drop of blood. In this respect, it was an exact replica of the Revolution of the Sergeants of 1933. In neither of these upheavals had any lives been lost. Moreover, in neither case had we imprisoned, executed or otherwise persecuted our political opponents. It was my belief then, and it continues to be my belief today, that a constructive revolution should not exact vengeance of its enemies, but should heal the wounds of strife with magnanimity and should endeavor to unite victors and defeated in work for the benefit of the nation.[2]

[2] On the eve of the 1933 Revolution, I told my forces:

"Each commissioned officer, each soldier, regardless of the offense he may have suffered or the abuses he might wish to avenge, must observe his best behavior toward those who have until today been his superiors and his chiefs. Cuban soldiers are known to be good and generous and now more than ever they have the opportunity to confirm this. This is the request of a comrade. It is the order of the leader upon whom will fall the gravest responsibilities in these moments of supreme decisions. Sergeants in charge of units will be responsible for the physical well-being and safety of these officers, who, for the time being, will be under surveillance—but not under arrest—in their quarters. The families of these officers are Cuban families and whatever the guilt of the officers may be, it does not by any means taint their families. They deserve, and must have, our protection while the

Later, Communist propaganda and the propaganda of Communism's dupes would portray me as a bloodthirsty tyrant. Let me point out simply and briefly that the desire to persecute and kill is a deep-seated trait which almost always becomes visible in a political leader very early in his career. Thus, the fact that Fidel Castro committed four murders before he reached the age of 25 was no accident and was a visible portent of the horrors to come. In my case, by contrast, I avoided persecution and the spilling of blood to the greatest extent possible during the 18 years when I dominated Cuba. This was both because of a belief in justice as opposed to arbitrary violence and because I have a profound personal aversion to bloodshed.

To return to the Revolution of the 10th of March 1952, its swift and bloodless victory was testimony to the fact that neither the Auténtico Administration nor the Orthodox opposition commanded any deep allegiance in the hearts of the Cuban people. To quote Mrs. Phillips again, both because she is a good observer and because, at the time she wrote her book, she was strongly opposed to my regime:

"Within two hours, Batista had made himself ruler of Cuba. Though he had support in other quarters, it was his popularity with the military that had made such a lightning coup possible. Thus, it came as a complete surprise to the people of Havana when the radio stations began broadcasting that General Fulgencio Batista had taken control of the government 'in order to save the country from chaotic conditions which endangered lives and property.' In a nationwide broadcast from Camp Columbia, Batista told the people that President Prío Socarrás had planned to suspend the presidential elections and make himself a dictator. He said, 'I have been forced to carry out this coup because of my love for the people. I shall re-establish public order. I ask the co-operation of all the people in Cuba in this task of peace and cordiality. Shoulder to shoulder we must work for the spiritual harmony of the great Cuban family.'

"The streets of Havana, which had been filled with carnival merrymakers the night before, were deserted. Detachments of police and soldiers appeared in all sectors of the city and tanks moved in to surround the Presidential Palace. Batista suspended

---

situation which we will face after tonight continues to exist." Quoted in Chester, *op. cit.*, p. 62.

constitutional guarantees and canceled the elections scheduled for June. He announced that all international treaties and pacts, as well as obligations assumed by Cuba with the United States, would be respected and fulfilled. *He said that if the United States were attacked by or involved in a war with the Soviet Union, Cuba would fight on the side of the Americans. He promised protection for all United States investments or such capital as might make future investments in Cuba.*" [3]

[3] Phillips, *op. cit.*, pp. 259-260. My emphasis—F.B.

5

Steps Toward Democracy

The seizure of power had been inevitable to avert an attempted coup d'état and civil war. There was not only President Prío's twisted scheme for a coup d'état to worry about, but another consideration. Regardless of who won the June 1st elections, there was reason to believe that Communist agitators and other malcontents would announce that the Auténtico Government had been defeated, would stir up the mobs and call them into the streets. We might then face a Cuban edition of the 1948 Bogotazo, in other words, bombings, lootings, burnings and killings that would gut our capital city, bring us into international disrepute and lead to a possible seizure of power by the extreme left. Additional reason to consider this prospect was that the student murderer, Fidel Castro, had been sent to Bogotá in 1948 by his Soviet masters and had played an important and sinister role in that holocaust. While he had been distrusted by Eduardo Chibás and other leaders of the Orthodox Party, Castro was prominent among the wild Orthodox youth element and was a candidate for Congress in the June elections.

After March 10, 1952, I felt it was necessary to limit the time and scope of the emergency powers that flowed from the bloodless revolution. From the outset, I explained that I had no desire to perpetuate myself in office. We prepared the means for a smooth transition from the extraordinary regime to a normal democratic one. Article 254 of the Constitutional Law enacted on April 4th provided for general elections and required the

Cabinet to specify within 60 days the offices to be filled and their length of tenure.

The Electoral College was assigned the task of proposing revisions in the Electoral Code and of promulgating regulations based upon the Code. The impartiality of that 1943 Code could scarcely be challenged by my opponents since it had governed the 1944 elections in which my political group was defeated by the Auténticos under Grau San Martín.

To give greater scope to political activity and to ensure that the vote of the people would determine the Government, a Constitutional Reform was drafted. This was to be submitted to referendum at the time of the election with the understanding that, if it should be defeated, the 1940 Constitution would automatically be reinstated upon the inauguration of the next President.

These procedures were closely parallel to those we had resorted to during the transition from the revolutionary regimes arising out of the overthrow of the Machado Government to the Administrations elected under the 1940 Constitution. During that interim period, four electoral codes had been enacted and three Censuses carried out so that we would have a complete and accurate roster of eligible voters. Our Revolution summoned the people three times to vote for a President, Governors, Mayors, Senators and Aldermen, five times for Congressmen and once for delegates to a Constitutional Convention.

Within the time set by law, the Government specified the elective offices to be filled. Law #105 of June 2, 1952 defined the procedures for the election of a President, a Vice President, a Senate of 54 members, at least a third of whom must represent minority parties, a House of Representatives with one member for every 45,000 inhabitants and also Governors, Mayors and Aldermen.[1]

The Electoral College submitted a proposed Electoral Code to the Cabinet on schedule. The draft law strengthened our democratic institutions and, by making split-ticket voting impossible in many instances, tended to make parties and programs more important than the personalities of the individual candidates.

The realization of this transition was blocked by the intolerance of the opposition political organizations, which preferred to abstain from the elections to admitting the existence of the revolu-

[1] According to the 1953 Census, Cuba had over 6 million inhabitants, of whom 2,870,678 were voters. Voting was compulsory.

tionary government. Because of this intransigent attitude, we were obliged to move the date of the proposed election forward to 1954. While the motivation for abstention was the well-justified fear by the opposition that it would be defeated at the polls, my associates and I were determined to do everything possible to have an electoral contest in which the voters would be free to vote for the opposition parties as well as for our own.

THE MONCADA ASSAULT

The country was at peace; order reigned; the people enjoyed complete liberty; there seemed to be general support of the Government. At this time, in midsummer of 1953, the people of Santiago de Cuba were enjoying the carnival and had little thought of politics. In this atmosphere of peace, a sudden, unprovoked surprise attack on the soldiers of the Moncada Barracks in the city took place. The assault began in the early hours of July 26, 1953, a Sunday when the troops were either enjoying the carnival in the city or sleeping off their revelries.

The attack was led by Fidel and Raúl Castro and other Communists. It began with the assassination of sick men in their beds in the hospital clinic adjoining the camp. Sentinels and soldiers sleeping in their beds were also murdered. The troops fought back, killed a number of their assailants and easily restored complete control over the barracks.

Fidel Castro, the organizer of the attack, did not appear at the scene of the fighting. Both during, and for several days after, the murders, which he and his Communist superiors had planned, he remained hidden in town. When it was safe to do so, he emerged under the protection of Monsignor Enrique Pérez Serantes, Archbishop of Santiago de Cuba.

Orders were given to respect Castro's life. In accordance with the democratic principles of my Administration, he was tried in an ordinary civilian court before independent judges, at least one of whom was hostile to the regime.

At the time Castro arrived in Santiago to help plan the operation, eight of the top ranking leaders of Cuban communism, among them Lázaro Peña and Joaquín Ordoqui, slipped into Santiago. Later, at the trial, they alleged that they had come to the city to celebrate the birthday of their leader, Blas Roca, the General Secretary of the Party. This was a transparent falsification, both because Blas Roca lived in Havana and because Communist functionaries are not sentimental enough to take a round trip of over a thousand miles because of a birthday party. Moreover, the Party had been outlawed and its leaders had either fled abroad or were in hiding. Under these circumstances, they would only have travelled to Santiago de Cuba for a most important reason. That reason was to plan the attack on the Moncada Barracks.

Castro was sentenced to 15 years in prison. He began to serve his term on the Isle of Pines which, under his dictatorship, has become the worst hell hole in the Western Hemisphere. Under my Administration, however, Fidel Castro, as a political prisoner, was given a pavilion to live in, the use of a jeep with chauffeur, full access to whatever books he chose to read and complete freedom to write whatever he wanted to.

In prison, Castro continued with his monstrous deception. Writing to Dr. Luis Conte Agüero on December 12, 1953 from prison, he observed: "Our triumph would have meant the immediate rise of the Orthodox Party to power . . . Speak to Dr. Agramonte,[2] show him this letter, express to him our loyal sentiments . . ." To his Communist associates, Castro sang another tune. On April 17, 1954, he wrote Melba Hernández, one of those who had used cold steel in the Moncada attack:

"Use guile and smiles with everyone. Follow the same tactics we followed at the trial: defend our point of view without irritating anyone. There will be more than enough time later to trample all of the cockroaches together. Accept any help offered, but remember to trust no one . . ."

RETURN TO THE BALLOT BOXES

The cowardly attack on the Moncada Barracks forced the Government to take exceptional measures and to suspend certain guarantees as provided for in the Cuban Constitution. The elections had to be postponed, but the political parties could carry on their activities at will.

To ensure complete fairness, we invited all the political parties and factions to discuss the new Electoral Code which would govern the forthcoming Presidential elections of November 1, 1954.

A few hours before the polls were opened and at a time when

[2] The successor to Chibás as leader of the Orthodox Party.

all the election boards had been named, Dr. Grau San Martín, the candidate of the Cuban Revolutionary Party, requested a postponement of the ballotting. The matter was debated on television and radio. The Electoral College decided that Dr. Grau's complaints were without foundation and it was generally realized that he was concerned with obstructing the democratic process for the simple reason that he had no chance of winning.

Grau withdrew and ordered the candidates of his party to do likewise. Nevertheless, the people went to the polls in droves. I was elected President of Cuba for the second time and, despite their leader's directive, several Cuban Revolutionary Party (PRC) candidates were elected to Congress.

My inauguration in February 1954 as Constitutional President of Cuba was attended by special envoys from 51 countries.[3] The growth of Cuba's international prestige was clearly evident. For our part, we maintained cordial relations with all the nations of the world with the exception of the Communist countries.

At the end of eight years of persecution, four of which were spent in exile, our second constitutional government began in an aura of peace and work. The fundamental objective was to carry out a great program for economic and social development, one which was already under way. I hoped that Cuba would continue to set an example in advanced social legislation for the Americas.

The opposition was divided into two groups: those who favored attaining power through peaceful and constitutional means and those who refused all compromise, abstained from the polls and were prepared to use conspiracy, assassination, sabotage and terror to win supreme power for themselves.

AMNESTY

The times were not propitious for an amnesty of all political prisoners, but my supporters in Congress and I hoped that an act of great clemency and generosity which opened the prison doors to

[3] These special envoys were from: the Vatican, Federal Republic of Germany, Austria, Belgium, Denmark, Spain, Finland, France, United Kingdom, Greece, Netherlands, Iceland, Italy, Luxembourg, Norway, Sweden, Switzerland, Portugal, Yugoslavia, Argentina, Bolivia, Brazil, Canada, Colombia, Costa Rica, Chile, Ecuador, El Salvador, United States, Guatemala, Haiti, Honduras, Mexico, Nicaragua, Panama, Paraguay, Peru, Dominican Republic, Uruguay, Venezuela, Cambodia, Nationalist China, Egypt, India, Indonesia, Israel, Japan, Lebanon, Pakistan and Thailand.

the terrorists might convince some of them to become normal human beings, to do something useful for society and to confine their political opposition to the channels prescribed by law.

The general amnesty was issued and the Castro brothers, among others, were freed under it. After loudly announcing his intention to repeat his treasonable attack on the State, Fidel Castro proceeded openly to Mexico to prepare there to carry out his purpose.[4]

CONSULTATIVE COUNCIL

Although my Government had been invested with extraordinary powers by the fact of revolution, I did not want to exercise the legislative power without first hearing public opinion. Therefore, as soon as the Revolution had consolidated its power, I created a new organism, consisting of outstanding men and women who represented the manifold activities of the nation. It was called the Consultative Council and was composed of 80 members and 15 alternates.

Among other powers, it had the right to propose laws, to be heard on basic matters of government and to intervene in fiscal matters and international relations through its commissions and its plenary sessions. All of its proposals, once they had been discussed and approved, were submitted to the Council of Ministers for final action. The members of the Council had the untrammeled right to express their opinions and vote as their consciences dictated. They enjoyed a protection tantamount to parliamentary immunity.

The most important organizations of the nation were represented on the Council by their most prominent members. This included, for example, the Presidents of the Associations of Sugar Mill Owners and of Sugar Planters, the Secretary General of the Cuban Confederation of Labor (CTC) and of the National Federation of Sugar Workers (FNTA), the leaders of other federations and labor unions, agrarian leaders, veterans of the War of

[4] It is worth noting that the presiding judge at Castro's trial, Manuel Urrutia, had been so disaffected that he permitted the accused to deliver an interminable harangue, the content of which was pure Marxism and the peroration of which was plagiarized from Adolf Hitler's speech to the court when accused of treason after the Bierhall Putsch of 1923. Urrutia even rendered a dissenting opinion stating that the murder of the soldiers at the Moncada was a lawful act.

Independence, farmers, economists, landowners, industrialists, former Ministers, legislators and mayors. No other deliberative body ever represented the nation as well.[5]

The Consultative Council was called into session on 168 occasions and there were only ten times when it was unable to meet because of lack of a quorum. It met weekly in plenary session, dedicating the rest of its time to the study by its many commissions of the various projects placed before it. The constitutional principle of not passing on any legislation without at least one report from one of its commissions was strictly observed. Before acting on its recommendations, the proposed legislation was discussed in hearings at which interested groups were heard. This system, which was rigorously adhered to, assured that all interested groups would be able to state their case and, on occasion, secure modifications before laws were enacted.[6]

The Council had four Presidents: Drs. Carlos Saladrigas Zayas, Gastón Godoy Loret de Mola, Justo García Rayneri and General of the Armies of Liberation Generoso Campos Marquetti. Each of these men left the Council in order to form part of the Cabinet.

THE CIVIC DIALOGUES

In the beginning of 1956, efforts were made to bring about an agreement or *modus vivendi* between the opposition and the Government. Meetings were organized by the Society of Friends of the Republic, composed of semi-neutrals and opponents of the Administration: the Orthodox Party to which Castro belonged, the Prío faction of the Auténticos, which favored conspiracy and violence, and the Auténticos of Grau who favored a solution at the polls.

[5] Of the 115 people on the Consultative Council over a period of time that was analyzed, 14 were lawyers, 3 farmers, 1 an architect, 2 pilots, a banker, a coffee grower, 5 sugar cane planters, 2 businessmen, a midwife, an economist, 2 students, a cattleman, a pharmacist, 9 sugar mill owners, an industrialist, 4 engineers, an agricultural extension teacher, 3 politicians, 4 doctors of medicine, 18 workers and labor leaders, 12 journalists, a teacher, a landowner, 2 lawyer's assistants, 2 sociologists, 2 tobacco growers, 2 veterans of the War of Independence, 3 former Cabinet Ministers, 14 former Congressmen and 1 former mayor.

[6] In some aspects, the Consultative Council did not replace Congress, nor was the National Capitol used for its deliberations. Senators and Congressmen continued to draw salaries until the expiration of their terms of office.

These conferences were called Civic Dialogues. They were presided over by the eighty-year-old patrician, Cosme de la Torriente, a Colonel of the War of Independence. No agreement could be reached because the radicals insisted, as their first condition, that the Government resign. We did not reject this demand out of hand, but proposed instead that a Constituent Assembly with unlimited power be called to give the people the opportunity to decide whether the Government should resign or serve out its legal term until February 24, 1959. This counterproposal was rejected by the extremists, possibly because they were intimidated by Castro terrorists, and the discussions came to an end.

It is of some interest that, while Prío was negotiating at these Civic Dialogues and simulating a desire for peace, his henchmen made an attack on the Goicuria military camp in the city of Matanzas.

Despite the failure of the Civic Dialogues, we did everything in our power to help the opposition use legal and democratic channels. For example, the National Revolutionary Movement under Pardo Llada did not have enough registrations to qualify as a legal party. To encourage lawful opposition, Law #1307 of February 26, 1954 was passed so that it could qualify. However, when Pardo Llada saw he would not have enough support to win even a single seat for himself or his followers in the House of Representatives, he left for Spain on funds belonging to his party and then announced that he would return via the United States and enter the election campaign. Actually, he proceeded from New York to Venezuela, then appeared suddenly in the Sierra Maestra and served as Fidel Castro's privileged radio propagandist until 1961. In the latter year, on arriving in Mexico on a mission for his Government, he "deserted." The Mexican press was unanimously hostile and labelled him "the Minister of Hate."

ELECTIONS OF NOVEMBER 1958

The elections of November 1958 were held under horribly unfavorable conditions. With the consistent support of the United States Government and a dominant sector of the American press, the Castro movement was gaining strength by leaps and bounds. The American arms embargo on my Government was generally interpreted as a decision by Washington to support Castro's drive for power. Under these conditions, the morally weak, the venal and the opportunistic supported the bearded outlaw. When the State Department allowed Castro's Communist bands to kidnap American citizens without making any effective protest, a further demoralization of those forces in Cuba which believed in democracy and decency inevitably occurred.

A campaign of deceit and lies was unleashed by the men of the Sierra Maestra. Since they were determined to seize power for themselves with no competitors, it was necessary to their purpose that the scheduled elections should either not take place or else be discredited. Law #2 of the Sierra Maestra imposed the death penalty on all urban candidates in the election who refused to withdraw their candidacy. This death sentence could be imposed by members of the Rebel Army or by the so-called Castro militia. It applied to opposition candidates (including the candidates of what had supposedly been Castro's own political group, the Orthodox Party) as well as to my supporters. This law was nothing less than a general license to murder any Cuban who believed in democracy and good government enough to run for public office.

Terrorist attacks increased. Coercion rose toward a zenith. Communications, schools, courthouses and trade union centers were demolished. Candidates, political leaders, party workers and others were murdered in their homes or on their way to work. To give a few examples from hundreds of cases: Nicolás Rivero Agüero, brother of the Presidential candidate of the pro-government forces, and also brother of Rebel leader Luis Conte Agüero, was assassinated; Felipe Navea, Vice President of the National Maritime Union, was killed in the presence of his wife; the teacher-candidate for Congress, Aníbal Vega Vega, was killed on his doorstep; and cattleman Rosendo Collazo was murdered at his ranch in the presence of his wife by a group of outlaws wearing 26th of July armbands and led by his former foreman.

In spite of threats, bombings and murder, the election took place on the announced date, November 3, 1958. Had it not been for acts of violence that sacrificed men, women and children, voting would have been normal. As it happened, from 72% to 75% of the normal number of voters cast their ballots. Since municipal and local officers were also at stake, there was keen interest in the results.

In 1958, under these conditions of intimidation and terror, 54.01% of the eligible electorate voted. This compares with a

voter turnout of about 60% in recent Presidential elections in the
United States.

THE MYTH OF THE 20,000 CORPSES

The real terrorists were those who threw bombs into police stations and crowded streetcars and who murdered candidates for
public office in order to destroy all democratic institutions.

However, the Castro propaganda mill cleverly imputed its own
crimes to its victims. The forces of law and order became the murderers and sadists. These big lies were shrewdly disseminated by
a minority of U.S. publicists who, wittingly or unwittingly, served
the Communist cause with unswerving consistency and consum-
mate guile.

A few days after he had seized power, Fidel Castro charged
my Government with having killed 20,000 Cubans. Even though
this figure was "patently ridiculous—and every informed person
in Cuba knew it—the tremendous surge of popular enthusiasm
for the new dictator swept over the voices of reason and unquestionably accepted Castro's macabre arithmetic." [7]

There were many commonsense refutations of this audacious
lie. In the first days of Castro rule, the refugees from my regime
—voluntary expatriates—began to return from the United States.
There were less than two thousand of them. "Cuban jails were
emptied of political prisoners; and the total liberated did not go
beyond several hundred, all in good condition, hale and well-
fed." [8]

Moreover, every important leader of the Castro movement,
with the single exception of Ernesto (Ché) Guevara had at one
time or another been in the hands of the Cuban Police. These
former prisoners of Batista were living refutations of the Castro
propaganda, imputing atrocities and bestial tortures to my regime. The plain and self-evident fact was that all of these former
prisoners were alive, healthy, unmutilated and untortured.

In January 1959, the weekly magazine, *Bohemia,* published a
list of the supposed victims of the Batista regime. This magazine
was notorious for its fanatical partisanship of Castro and his
movement. Despite its unabashed propaganda, it had flourished
without hindrance in Batista Cuba. After Castro took power, how-

[7] *Cuban Information Service,* editor Carlos Todd, No. 130, page 9.
[8] *Ibid.*

ever, the editors of *Bohemia* were driven into exile because they had the decency to refuse to serve as pliant instruments of Soviet tyranny.

Bohemia's list of victims consisted primarily of saboteurs and terrorists who were killed in gun battles with the authorities or else in immediate and passionate reprisal by soldiers and policemen who were understandably emotional about seeing their friends and comrades blown to bits. The second largest category consisted of innocent bystanders who got killed in these bombings and gun battles.

The most significant thing about the *Bohemia* total, which was generally accepted as accurate at the time, was that it amounted to slightly over 900 people. Not the 20,000 that Castro alleged!

Let me compare the fictitious reign of terror of Batista with the real reign of terror of Fidel Castro. The figures are those compiled by Carlos Todd.[9]

Some 10,717 people had been killed by Castro and his Communists up to June 1, 1963 as follows:

Executed by order of "Revolutionary Tribunals"	2,897
Executed without any trial whatsoever	4,245
Killed in action against Castro forces	2,962
Missing	613
TOTAL	10,717

By comparison, during the seven years of my second Administration, there were no legal executions (because we had no death sentence) and the number of Castro supporters and bystanders killed otherwise is estimated by the hostile source, *Bohemia,* at about 900.

Todd estimated that 965,000 people (over 14% of the Cuban population) had been arrested for political reasons at one time or another and that 81,706 persons were in prisons, of whom 16,-120 were in concentration camps and 2,146 in G-2 torture farms.

Over 6.6% of Cuba's population, 449,450 persons, left the island since Castro took power. Of these, 2,742 left secretly in small boats and it is estimated that over 600 more were killed in the attempt.

Of these refugees, 385,000 were in the United States, 42,000

9 *Ibid.*

in Latin America, 21,000 in Europe and 1,450 scattered else-where. An additional 3,401 gained asylum in foreign embassies. Of these, 3,165 were given safe conduct out of the country, leaving 236 still in the embassies. Castro agents frequently violated the right of asylum, entered the embassies by force and murdered the refugees.[10]

Some 230,000 Cubans on the Island had passports and visa waivers, but could not get transport. Another 385,000 applied for passports and visas. Thus, a conservative estimate would be that 1,067,000 Cubans—almost a sixth of the total population—had left the country or were seeking to leave it.

These figures are necessarily incomplete and understatements because not all the executions, murders, imprisonments and shipments to concentration camps are known. Moreover, the processes at work are continuous. The mills of death continue to grind throughout Cuba.

"The whole story of the crimes of the Castro regime will not be known until Communism is ousted from the Island," Todd writes. "Perhaps it will never be known, for many lie dead and buried without a single record of their demise. But Cuba, the burial ground of thousands, the prison of millions, will go down in history as one of the most brutal examples of the bestial, tyrannical system that is communism."[11]

---

[10] Todd's figures show that the victims of Castro terror are primarily humble people. He breaks down the 10,717 corpses as follows:

Military	3,462	Activists in Catholic or	
Workers	2,677	lay organizations	187
Peasants	2,473	Industrialists	71
Professionals	783	Property owners	63
Students	711	Foreigners	62
Small businessmen	228		

[11] *Ibid.*

6

Pan American Relations

One of the fundamental policies of the new government which assumed power as a result of the coup d'état of March 10, 1952 was to refrain scrupulously from intervention in the internal affairs of other nations. Even under conditions of severe internal emergency, I determined to uphold the right of asylum and to act in strict accordance with our international agreements and the dictates of the Constitution. We always interpreted the right of asylum in a broad and generous fashion, as the diplomatic corps can attest.

In 1956, the Dominican Government created a delicate situation for us. In contrast to our policy of non-intervention, the Dominican dictatorship of General Rafael Leonidas Trujillo had opened its doors to such Cuban insurrectionaries as Carlos Prío Socarrás and Fidel Castro, allowing them to use the Dominican Republic as a base of operations. General Trujillo sought to justify this conduct by falsely alleging that the Chief of Staff of the Cuban Army, General Francisco Tabernilla, had supplied arms to his enemies. Since this pretext was not only false but incredible, the Trujillo government spread the rumor that its hostile policy toward Cuba was a reprisal for the unfavorable comments of the free press of my country concerning the assassination of "Pipi" Hernández, a Dominican labor leader, who had been killed in the city of Havana. I believed this crime was the work of Dominican agents, although diligent investigation by the Cuban police failed to prove it.[1]

My Government requested the Organization of American States to investigate the activities of the Dominican Government against Cuba, describing them as unjust and arbitrary. The OAS probed the affair and declared that the Dominican accusations were completely without foundation.

PANAMA CONFERENCE

In July 1956, the President of Panama invited the Chiefs of State of the 21 American Republics to a conference to celebrate the 130th anniversary of the first Pan American meeting in 1826. I accepted this invitation. Speaking to the Conference, I said that our problem was to consolidate the democratic institutions of the Western Hemisphere and that this could best be done by setting up a permanent organization, representing all the American states, which would plan and encourage closer cooperation in such fields as foreign trade, immigration, education, cultural progress and social reform. I emphasized that this effort would have to be based on full mutual respect for the sovereignty of each of the American Republics.

The Chiefs of State present at the Conference agreed that all of us were affected by the same problems and dangers. They considered that Inter-American economic cooperation to raise living standards, develop new sources of wealth and employment, improve public health, increase the proportion of home owners and advance wage scales would serve as an effective instrument in the struggle against Communist totalitarianism. Progress toward higher living standards, increasing output and new avenues

---

[1] The comments of Jules Dubois in his laudatory and uncritical biography, *Fidel Castro* (Bobbs-Merrill, Indianapolis, 1959) are worth citing since his is the testimony of a hostile witness. He refers to my "feud" with Trujillo (p. 127) and adds that a force of 120 Cuban exiles, many of whom had been recruited by agents of Carlos Prío, were flown into the Dominican capital and given intensive military training by officers of Trujillo's army and air force for the invasion of Cuba. Dubois adds: "It was reported—although definitive confirmation of this could never be obtained—that Trujillo wanted Gerald Lester Murphy, an American pilot from Eugene, Oregon, to bomb Havana; when Murphy refused he was fed to the sharks in the Caribbean Sea." (p. 147)

of opportunity for all the people of the Americas was necessary both to repel the Soviet attack and as a good in itself.

There was a good deal of sentiment, as there generally is at such inter-American gatherings, in favor of U.S. loans and grants as a means of bringing Latin America out of her economic difficulties. My view was that more could be achieved by trade and tariff agreements, measures to control the wild fluctuations of the prices of primary products and other devices of this sort. In the end, more would be achieved by these indirect means since they would create an environment in which our peoples could advance economically by their own efforts, ingenuity and hard work.

Because of my concern as a man of the Americas, I decided to take advantage of the excellent opportunity provided by this top-level conference and try to alert my fellow citizens of the Western Hemisphere concerning the need for close cooperation to preserve democratic institutions in the Americas. I used a press conference as the vehicle for this. What I said there has subsequently assumed importance in the light of world developments. Hence, I will reiterate the most important portions of my statement:

"Whether we like it or not, our way of life is in danger and it would be folly to blind ourselves to realities. Certainly, facing the issue of international communism is disagreeable for all of us, because it involves recognition of the infiltration that has occurred among our peoples. Perhaps, for this reason, we are inclined to try to put off until tomorrow the battle against this formidable threat. The moment has come, however, in which we must face this problem . . . Cuba believes that the quicker we do so and the sooner we take the necessary steps to avert the impending catastrophe, the better it will be for the survival of all the free nations. We can neither avoid nor evade the battle. Nor can we remain apathetic, for history teaches us that the apathy of its intended victims has been one of the main weapons of communism. The men of Moscow have always encouraged apathy among the peoples they menace and in public opinion, for they know that an apathetic people is an easy prey . . . Those of us who have the privilege and the heavy duty of governing must find means to eliminate poverty and misery, for it is on these evils that totalitarian systems, alien to our traditions and national character, thrive.

"Let me say literally that, in the absence of open war, it is hard to convince others of the full extent of the danger facing us. Yet the dangers of cold war are equally real and deadly . . . Whether we choose to believe it or not, the fact is that international communism has infiltrated key areas in the societies of our respective countries . . . Communism has many faces and uses many disguises. Its agents can be charming individuals today in order to become executioners tomorrow. Their real objectives never change." [2]

THE DECLARATION OF PANAMA

At a solemn session of the Conference, the Declaration of Presidents was signed. This is a document of great historic significance, for it states cardinal principles on which the political institutions of the New World partially rest. On this occasion, I indicated that closer inter-American organization should be based on a just social and economic order.

On the economic side, I urged that inter-American credit institutions concentrate on helping the American Republics (particularly the underdeveloped ones) to speed up the development of their own material resources. While covenants and international agreements would help, the chief impetus could not come from outside. It was the responsibility of the peoples of the Americas to raise their own living standards and mobilize their own productive resources. I added that our peoples love their freedom. They have no desire for territorial expansion and they will not allow others to interfere, directly or indirectly, with their sovereignty.

These ideas, I thought, should help unite us and create closer ties in the struggle against Marxism. They could also contribute to creating a solid economic and social structure which would provide a durable bulwark against the attacks of demagogues and Communists.

To achieve these goals, we would have to encourage the investment of private and public capital, to correct major disequi-

2 Unfortunately, this warning was not sufficiently heeded. The danger of Communist penetration was underestimated and, as a result, the enemy today works openly in the Americas with Cuba as its bastion in the Western Hemisphere. And the person whose image was presented to the world as "charming" now has shown his true face as the executioner of his people.

libria in international trade, to lead capital into socially productive channels, to eliminate double taxation on foreign investment, to adopt sound monetary and tariff systems and not to neglect conservation of our resources. I observed that anti-communism by itself is not a program. Rather, the Americas needed a dynamic plan to serve the people, to assure progress and social justice and to foster economic cooperation within the Hemisphere. All this must be based on general respect for the established governments of the Americas and on equal treatment of the large and the small.

I pointed out that the struggle against communism is complex and that it is not enough merely to achieve domestic prosperity.[3] In referring to the Treaty of Mutual Assistance of Rio de Janeiro, which condemns aggression against any American state, I again stressed the menace of communism.[4] I prayed that the Declaration we had just signed would be a guide for the future and, to quote Bolívar, "not mere advice." [5]

PRACTICAL MEASURES

As a result of the Panama Conference, a commission of special representatives of the American Chiefs of State was created to propose concrete plans for economic, social and technical cooperation within the Pan American framework. At the Rio de Janeiro meeting of the Ministers of Finance, the Cuban delegation had expressed interest in achieving results in such basic areas as economic development, commerce, prices and markets, fiscal reform and technical assistance. At that time, our delegation had introduced a motion for an Inter-American Economic Conference to study creation of a special financial institution. This would be "an effective instrument to promote employment and advancing standards of living for the working class, to

---

[3] Cuba is an example. Although it enjoyed unprecedented prosperity and splendid social welfare institutions in 1957, its democratic regime fell victim to a vast Communist conspiracy.

[4] Which treaty Castro repudiated in August 1960 for the original reason that "his" Revolution had not signed it!

[5] In many articles and editorials in the chief Cuban newspapers, favorable comment was made on these economic theses and the impression they made on President Eisenhower and other Chiefs of State. Warm comments were made in *El Mundo, Alerta, Diario de la Marina* and *Avance* by such distinguished writers as Ramón Vasconcelos and Gastón Baquero.

stabilize prices and expand markets, to devise norms for the disposal of surpluses and, in fact, to establish a system of international financing within the American economic system." This motion was approved by the Rio de Janeiro meeting. At the Special Conference held in Chile in February 1955, implementation of this previous Cuban motion was debated.

Following the Panama meeting of 1956, another Inter-American Economic Conference was held in Buenos Aires in October 1957. Here three motions were proposed by Cuba for the creation of suitable Hemisphere instruments for the economic and social development of the Americas.[6] These motions were approved.

As a result of our Cuban initiative, the International Finance Corporation (IFC) was established with a capital of $100,000,-000. It became an institution which was primarily concerned with making investments to finance private enterprise in government-to-government lending. In fact, its *modus operandi* was similar to that of the Bank for Economic and Social Development which we had organized in Cuba. When the Charter of the IFC was presented formally, Cuba was accorded by unanimous vote the honor of being the first to sign as a recognition of our persevering efforts to bring it to life.

[6] These were: (a) to make technical cooperation a regular and continuous activity; (b) to study inflationary pressures, currency problems and balance of payments disequilibria, and (c) to estimate the investment needs of the American Republics and the means of meeting these annual needs.

7

Maritime and Other Agreements

With the expansion of Cuban diplomatic activity, we proceeded to reorganize the Ministry of Foreign Affairs and the Foreign Service. Law #1619 of August 14, 1954 coordinated operations, established badly needed technical departments and set up specialized groups to advise on foreign policy. In addition, urgently needed increases in the pay and allowance of diplomatic personnel were granted.

Cuba participated in numerous international conferences held by the United Nations and the Organization of American States. The Charter of the OAS had been signed in Bogotá in 1948 in the midst of the tragic riots provoked by agitators in the service of international communism (among whom were Fidel Castro and a few other Cubans who would later inundate their country with blood and betray it to a foreign power). My Government ratified this Charter on August 8, 1952.

Cuba participated in the Atomic Energy Conference in Geneva. Her delegation expressed hope that the peoples of the world would agree on the peaceful use of this vast force for the benefit of mankind.

THE RICHES OF THE SEA

All that related to the maritime continental shelf, whether under international or territorial waters, received my special attention. I was concerned with the improvement of fishing and the conservation of our live oceanic resources. In 1951, the year before I took power, the International Bank in its *Report on Cuba* had observed that, despite Cuba's favorable situation from the standpoint of fisheries, she spent 48 million dollars a year importing fish and her "fishing industry is small and unorganized." [1]

Accordingly, the BANFAIC [2] had a floating refrigerator of half a million pounds capacity constructed as a pilot operation in 1953. The following year the National Fishing Institute, which was to do so much to improve fishing methods, was established by Law #1891. In Havana, we built a special fishing terminal that could handle 30 tons of fish every eight-hour shift and that had refrigerated storage space for a million pounds of fish.

Law #1948 of January 27, 1955 proclaimed the waters between the coast and the Cuban keys to be an inner sea. Cuban jurisdiction was established there and in adjacent waters. As for the exploitation of fish in demersal waters, we urged that all interested countries formulate, sign and collectively enforce international treaties for the conservation of marine resources. This principle was applied to shrimp fishing in our relations with the United States.

PAYMENT COVENANTS

We were determined to open and secure export markets for our industry and to diversify production by granting guarantees for the development of new enterprises and industries. At the same time, we wished to avoid creating hothouse industries which could not survive without continuous government subsidy. These considerations motivated our approach to the problems of tariff reform. In our economic policies in the international sphere, our aims were to maintain and expand markets, to further the internal economic development of Cuba and to be able to import our needs at reasonable prices.

Accordingly, we concluded treaties and commercial payment agreements which granted advantages to exporters and at the same time made it possible for Cuban products to compete abroad. We were determined to maintain a basically free enterprise economy with safeguards and controls against abuse.

[1] International Bank for Reconstruction and Development, *Report on Cuba* (Truslow Report), Baltimore, 1951, Johns Hopkins Press, p. 914.
[2] *Banco de Fomento Agricola e Industrial de Cuba.*

THE BATTLE FOR MARKETS

Difficult and often protracted negotiations at the United Nations headquarters, in the OAS and in such subsidiary organizations as the FAO, the ECLA and others brought beneficial results to Cuba in the fields of trade and national economy.

Despite surpluses which hung over world markets, we succeeded in maintaining our traditional markets. We used the trade agreement implement to expand our international intercourse and gain more favorable terms for Cuba. We succeeded in expanding tobacco exports and made sure that our tariff readjustments did not increase the cost of essential foods to the consumer. Within the General Agreement on Trade and Tariffs (GATT), we worked to increase income and employment levels. We encouraged bilateral tariff negotiations to protect our rapidly increasing family of new industries.

RELATIONS WITH THE UNITED STATES

In 1954, my Government initiated talks with Washington to find an equitable solution to the problem of trade imbalance to the disadvantage of Cuba. Trade statistics showed that Cuba's concessions to the United States, particularly in respect to sugar, were not balanced by compensatory advantages. During the period 1950-54, 75% of our imports had come from the United States and it was vitally important to us that our exports to that country increase correspondingly. We were interested in agreements which would assure the export position of Cuba in the American market both in regard to sugar and other commodities.

With rapidly increasing population and the pressing need for greater employment, Cuba had to develop her economy at a swift tempo, progressively industrializing and diversifying her agriculture.

To raise the economic level of the country, we initiated negotiations for a treaty to eliminate the double taxation imposed upon American companies investing abroad. Thus, the flow of American capital to Cuba would be stimulated, we hoped, through the prospect of greater net income.

In these varied negotiations, we secured agreements which revised tariff schedules in our favor, assisted important national industries and thus enabled them to increase output and employment.

TRADE EXPANSION

We were determined to do our utmost to stimulate trade with all countries except those under Communist domination. The first step was to reopen the Legation in Tokyo after the ratification of our peace treaty with Japan on July 25, 1952 and the second to create consular agencies in India, Iran, Ceylon, Japan (whose Legation was later elevated to the rank of Embassy), Egypt, Israel and Lebanon.

My Government concluded a Treaty on Commerce and Navigation with the Federal Republic of Germany and commercial agreements with Austria, Chile, Denmark, Spain, the United Kingdom, Israel, Iceland, Peru, Sweden, Switzerland and Japan.

In addition, Cuba showed her earnest desire to further international economic cooperation by signing a variety of international treaties, conventions, pacts, covenants and instruments.[3] In this as

---

[3] These international instruments included: the basic agreement for the provision of technical assistance to the United Nations of June 1952 and two supplementary agreements signed the same year;

the Convention on Road Transport (August 6, 1952);
the Convention for the Security of Human Life on the High Seas (June 7th, 1954);
Covenant for the Prevention of the Crime of Genocide (December 9, 1953);
Convention on the Political Rights of Women (March 31, 1953);
Protocol for the Regulation and Limitation of the Cultivation of the Poppy, International Traffic in and Use of Opium (March 31, 1953);
By-laws of the International Agency for Atomic Energy (November 20, 1956);
Covenant for the Protection of Works of Art in the Event of Armed Conflict (May 14, 1954);
Covenant on industrial and intellectual property rights, signed with France (July 30, 1952) and with the Federal Republic of Germany (January 22, 1954);
Universal convention on authors' rights (June 8, 1956) and an inter-American covenant on the same (November 29, 1955);
an inter-American agreement on radio communications (July 25, 1952);
International Convention on Telecommunications (December 22, 1952);
Universal Postal Convention (November 26, 1952);

in other matters, our purpose was both to increase the welfare of the Cuban people and to make a Cuban contribution to international understanding.

Air Carrier Covenants with the United States, Spain, the United Kingdom and Mexico;

Passport and visa agreements with Denmark, Sweden and Belgium.

Among the many international instruments signed prior to March 10, 1952 and ratified by my administration, the most important were the Charter of the Organization of American States, the Treaty of Peace with Japan and the International Sugar Agreement.

We also ratified agreements with the United States on technical and economic assistance which were subsequently abrogated by Washington because of the hostile attitude of the Castro dictatorship.

8

Trade Unions and Labor Legislation

The Revolution of the 4th of September 1933 marked the beginning of a quarter of a century of continuous social progress in which the role of the labor movement in Cuba was progressively strengthened. Thanks to the measures adopted and the policies pursued during this era, Cuban labor legislation became one of the most advanced in the world and the Cuban trade union movement one of the strongest and most independent in the Americas.

This proud record of social advance during the two periods in which I bore the primary responsibility for the government of Cuba is a matter of readily ascertainable record. However, under the influence of Communist propaganda, the West has been propagandized into believing the contrary—namely, that my administrations were reactionary in character and opposed to the interests of the working people. This propaganda has gained currency and even authority by constant repetition. It has been insidiously put into the mouths of ultra-liberals and of more or less innocent dupes of world communism, so that today the big lie is accepted as the literal truth and its illegitimate origin is entirely forgotten. This serves to show that, when those who form public opinion forget that they have the duty to investigate facts independently, free institutions are in peril.

In view of this situation, I should like to quote a few American authorities on the condition of labor in Batista Cuba. I have chosen those who cannot by any stretch of the imagination be labelled "reactionary." Writing in 1954, Ernst Schwartz, Assistant Secretary of the Inter-American Regional Organization and Executive Secretary, Committee on Latin American Affairs, CIO, pointed out that the Cuban Confederation of Labor (CTC)

". . . has enabled the Cuban workers to set an example to others of what can be achieved by labor unity and strength. Wages are far above those paid in many other parts of the Caribbean or, for that matter, Latin America. In addition, the eight-hour working day forms the basis for every one of the collective contracts concluded by the CTC's affiliated organizations. Modern types of social protection and insurance are provided in laws, public statutes, or union contracts; while funds maintained and administered in common by labor, employers, and the authorities provide adequate means to put them into practice. The sugar workers union alone, to cite only one example, disposes of such, a fund in the amount of half a billion dollars, and its insurance covers medical attention, sickness, and accidents during and out of work. The CTC, moreover, has taken up a place of full responsibility within the Cuban community as a whole, and at present develops its own economic program to compensate for the seasonal nature of employment and production in the sugar industry. Today, the Confederation counts more than a million members—with its 500,000 sugar workers constituting the most powerful of the thirty-five national federations affiliated with and representing every branch of industry and agriculture on the island. The Confederation has drawn every fifth Cuban into its ranks and has thus obtained a much higher numerical degree of organization in proportion to population than, for example, the much larger movement in the United States." [1]

Commenting on the labor provisions of the Cuban Constitution of 1940, MacGaffey and Barnett point out in a recent book that they incorporated much legislation which had already been enacted during 1933-1940. The authors add:

"The right to work was declared to be 'an inalienable right of the individual' and the maintenance of full employment a national responsibility. Workers were guaranteed a minimum daily wage; fair payment for piecework, to be made only in legal tender; a maximum day of 8 hours and a week of 44 hours;

---

[1] Ernst Schwarz, "Some Observations on Labor Organization in the Caribbean," *The Caribbean: its Economy,* edited by A. Curtis Wilgus, University of Florida Press, Gainesville, 1954, p. 167.

and a month of annual paid vacation. Additional provisions limited the work to be required of minors and women. Social security and protection against disability, old age and unemployment were guaranteed. Workers were granted the right to organize and to strike." [2]

Dr. Aureliano Sánchez Arango, the former Minister of Education in the Prío administration and a man who has been inveterately hostile to me, pointed out that, far from being a backward and exploited country, Cuba, during the last year of my administration, enjoyed a living standard "superior to that of the Soviet Union itself." [3] Dr. José Álvarez Díaz, another former member of Prío's Cabinet, pointed out that Cuba "had a standard of living higher than almost all the American Republics, a large part of the European continent, all the republics of Africa, Asia and in Oceania only New Zealand and Australia had a higher income." Finally, Dr. Felipe Pazos, who was a covert supporter of the Castro movement under my Administration and was briefly President of the National Bank of Cuba under the Communist regime, echoed the same theme as former Finance Minister Álvarez Díaz, adding that the urban workers enjoyed higher living standards "than the figures for average per capita income reflect . . ." [4]

In the sphere of labor legislation, some of the salient accomplishments of Cuban governments during the quarter century between the government of Machado and the slave state of Castro were:

(1) Creation of a Ministry of Labor.

(2) The Nationality of Labor law, which required that in every enterprise at least 50% of the employees and workers be Cubans by birth.

(3) Establishment of a maximum work day of eight hours.

(4) Reorganization and strengthening of the Workmen's Compensation Law.

(5) Creation of a National Minimum Wage Commission.

(6) Legislation guaranteeing collective bargaining, defining

---

2 Wyatt MacGaffey and Clifford R. Barnett, *Cuba: its People, its Society, its Culture,* a volume in the *Survey of World Culture* series, HRAF Press, New Haven, 1962, p. 108.

3 Quoted in Daniel James, *Cuba: the First Soviet Satellite in the Americas,* Avon, New York, 1961, p. 22.

4 *Ibid.,* p. 21.

fair labor bargaining practices and protecting workers against arbitrary and unjust dismissal.

(7) Legislation regulating and protecting trade unions.

(8) Establishment of the National Commission for Social Cooperation.

(9) Legislation stipulating paid vacations based on one month yearly for every 11 years of service and guaranteeing paid sick leave.

(10) Protection of and insurance for female workers.

(11) Legal guarantee of the right to strike.

(12) Establishment of public employment offices.

(13) Protective legislation for juvenile workers.[5]

Our guiding principle was to ensure that labor should participate proportionately in all increases in the value of production I believe that the human factor is paramount in economics.

The social gains of the revolution of September 4, 1933 were subsequently absorbed, consolidated and, in some instances, strengthened by the 1940 Constitution.

SOCIAL SECURITY

Law #781 of December 28, 1934 was amplified as to scope by the law of December 28, 1937, which brought into being a comprehensive insurance system to cover the maternity costs of female workers and of male workers' wives. This system was based on very small contributions by workers and employers. Six months after the establishment of the Central Board of Health and Maternity, income from these contributions was almost $10,000,000. With these funds available, we were able to start immediate construction of a large maternity hospital in Havana with a capacity for 250 expectant mothers and another in Camagüey with

---

[5] The corresponding legal instruments were: (1) Office of the Secretary, Decree #2142, October 13, 1933. (2) Nationalization decree, #2583, November 8, 1933. (3) Eight-hour day law, #1693, September 19, 1933. (4) Workmen's Compensation decree, #223, January 31, 1935. (5) Minimum Wage Law, #727, November 30, 1934. (6) Collective Pacts, Law #446, August 24, 1934, and as implementation decree #2605, April 13, 1938. (7) Trade Unions, Decree #2605, April 13, 1938. (8) Social Cooperation, decree #827, March 13, 1943. (9) Paid Vacations Law, #40, March 22, 1935. (10) Workers' Maternity, Law of December 15, 1937. (11) Strikes, Law #3, February 8, 1934, (12) Employment Offices, Law #148, May 7, 1935 and (13) Child Labor, law #647, October 31, 1947.

beds for 60. By the end of my term, over 100,000 mothers, either female workers or workers' wives, had received benefits from this project.

My administration worked assiduously and continuously to set up a comprehensive system of social security and retirement funds. In my first term, we created the retirement funds for newspapermen, for bank employees and for sugar workers. This last covered half a million Cubans who worked in all stages of the cultivation, transportation and refining of sugar. We also set up a retirement fund for the medical profession.[6]

In my second period in the presidential office, we enacted retirement laws for brewery workers, for workers in livestock agriculture, for construction workers, for chauffeurs and taxicab drivers and for workers in the tannery and shoe making industry. We established social security systems for nurses, stenographers, agricultural engineers, public school teachers, private school teachers, agricultural extension teachers and foresters, doctors of science, philosophy and letters and, in addition, governors, mayors and aldermen.[7]

No less than 50 laws were promulgated between 1952 and 1958 to reorganize or reform the various retirement and social security funds, consolidate their financial operations and ensure that their beneficiaries received the pensions and annuities to which they were entitled. This was particularly necessary in those instances where the funds had been the target of frauds and embezzlement perpetrated during the Auténtico administrations of Grau San Martín and Prío Socarrás.

Supplementary legislation served to strengthen these funds, pro-

---

[6] Journalists, law #172, August 23, 1935, and Social Security, law #1151, October 27, 1935. Bank employees, Law of September 7, 1938. Sugar Workers, Law #20, March 21, 1941; amplified by Executive Decree #3383, November 16, 1943, and consolidated into the social security system by law #1159, January 25, 1955. Medical Profession, Law #2, February 20, 1943.

[7] Brewery workers, law #710, February 27, 1953. Cattle industry, Law #1634, August 14, 1954. Construction workers, Law #1538, July 27, 1954. Chauffeurs and cab drivers, Law #8, October 7, 1957. Shoe workers, Law #1835, December 3, 1954. Social security funds for: Nurses, Law #464, October 14, 1954. Stenographers, Law #1557, August 4, 1954. Agricultural Engineers, Law #2114, January 27, 1955. Public school teachers, Law #10, December 21, 1955. Agricultural extension teachers and foresters, Law #2132, January 27, 1955. Doctors in science and law, Law #2092, same date. Governors, Law #14, December 10, 1956.

vide guarantees against default and give financial solidity to the several social security systems. Thus, Law #2067 of April 27, 1955, created the National Fund for Social Security to give greater solvency to the system. Simultaneously, it provided for the establishment of a governmental commission to prepare the necessary draft legislation for the creation of a State Bank for Social Security.

In one of the last years of our administration, 21 of these funds collected $67,975,404 as against $56,637,851 in 1955. The total income of the retirement and social security funds was $99,004,-036. Deducting payment of benefits and administrative costs, there was a net increase of reserves and capital surplus in that year of $24,870,103. During the period 1952-1955, the increment to reserves and capital surplus was $66,139,723 as against total assets of $212,196,318. Because of the irregularities during previous regimes to which I have already alluded, the funds owed the state $61,806,107 in 1955.

LABOR ORGANIZATION

As a result of the revolution of September 4, 1933, workers were absolutely free to organize unions and employers to organize federations. The Confederation of Cuban Workers (CTC) was legally recognized and endorsed by the Government after its inauguration in 1940. The reason for this recognition was that the CTC embraced the overwhelming majority of the organized workers of Cuba.

Our social policy was to strive to bring the interests of capital and labor into harmony, to combat unemployment, attempt to secure industrial stability and uninterrupted production operations and thus contribute to raising the living standards of the working people of Cuba.

Every demand for wage increases was given immediate attention. The role of Government was to reconcile considerations of social justice with financial realities.

When we considered it beneficial to the domestic economy and to national progress, we decreed wage increases. These included two general raises of 10% and 20%, two special increases in the sugar industry, the first for 25% and the second for 50%, and special increases in the cases of the Hershey Railroad and the Guantánamo and Western. The wages of nurses, waiters, drugstore employees, telephone workers, textile workers and other groups were advanced and there was a wage increase in the printing industry—all as a result of government action.

By fostering labor organization and introducing protective legislation, the 4th of September Revolution and the 1940-44 administration, which consolidated its gains, brought about a continuous, substantial and gratifying improvement in the working and living conditions of Cuban labor. Protection of collective bargaining and fostering of mediation developed a cooperative association between workers and employers, reducing friction between the two classes to a minimum.

By the end of 1958, 33 industrial federations and 2,490 labor union locals were affiliated to the Confederation of Cuban Workers and the Employers' Federation of Cuba had 11 national federations and 215 local ones. In Cuba, 1,500,000 workers, in a total population of 6,500,000 were organized in unions—over 23% of the total. By contrast, in the United States in 1960, unionized labor constituted 17,400,000 Workers—only 21.4% of the total labor force and less than 10% of the total population.[8]

During my second Administration, I worked to extend collective agreements, as they had proved to be an excellent instrument for forestalling and resolving social conflicts. These labor agreements had the force of law and violation of them by either party was punished accordingly. At the close of 1958, some 7,638 collective agreements were in effect in the province of Havana alone. There was not a single industrial area of significance where collective agreements failed to play an important role. The number of these pacts tripled between 1944, the year which marked the end of my first period as President, and 1958, the last year of my second term in that office.

WAGE POLICIES

Our policy was to increase wages and revise minimum wage scales upward with the economic development of the country and to the extent that business conditions permitted. In February 15, 1955, we increased basic pay to $85 a month in Greater Havana, to $80 in other urban zones and to $75 in rural areas. These were merely minimum wages and many collective con-

[8] Figures on union organization in the United States from the *New York Times,* July 9, 1961.

tracts in industry, commerce and agriculture provided for considerably higher pay scales. Prior to this, the minimum wages in force had been those established in 1944, during my first administration—$60 for urban and $48 for agricultural workers.

While I was President, Cuban wages were the highest in Latin America. This was recognized by the workers themselves and was a cause for proud boasts by their trade union organizations. The Cuban Institute for the Stabilization of Sugar published the following revealing comparison of international wage rates in 1958, expressed in dollars:

DAILY WAGES IN 1958 (U.S. Dollars)

Agricultural		*Industrial*	
1. Canada	7.18	1. United States	16.80
2. New Zealand	6.72	2. Canada	11.73
3. Australia	6.61	3. Sweden	8.10
4. United States	6.80	4. Switzerland	8.00
5. Sweden	5.47	5. New Zealand	6.72
6. Norway	4.38	6. Denmark	6.46
7. CUBA	3.00	7. Norway	6.10
8. Fed. Rep. Germany	2.57	8. CUBA	6.00
9. Ireland	2.25	9. Australia	5.82
10. Denmark	2.03	10. United Kingdom	5.75
11. Belgium	1.56	11. Belgium	4.72
12. France	1.32	12. Fed. Rep. Germany	4.13
13. Japan	.90	13. France	3.26

These figures show that the Cuban agricultural worker was better paid than his German or Irish counterpart, earned more than twice as much as the French rural worker and more than three times as much as the Japanese. The Cuban urban worker earned higher hourly pay than his fellow worker in England, Germany or France.

These facts would not prevent writers sympathetic to Communism, such as the late Professor C. Wright Mills of Columbia University, from describing how the workers of Cuba were miserably exploited and how they "squatted on the edge of the road . . . in filthy huts." [9]

Professor Mills spent three or four days in Castro Cuba, spoke

[9] C. Wright Mills, *Listen, Yankee!*, McGraw-Hill, New York, 1960, pp. 13-14.

and understood hardly any Spanish and was subjected to continuous propaganda by Fidel Castro and his Communist henchmen. The thought that he was inadequately equipped either to judge the Cuban situation, or to use it as a pretext for writing an hysterical hymn of hate against his country and its policies, apparently did not occur to the Professor.

To foster the development of unionism, my administration enacted legislation which insured payment of union dues by having them automatically deducted from workers' payrolls. The opposition assailed this measure. However, when it came to power by the ballot in 1944, the Auténtico Party retained the compulsory check-off. The funds deducted from workers' pay envelopes, however, were diverted, under Grau San Martín and Prío Socarrás, for repression of labor organizations, spying on workers' activities and persecution of the workers themselves.

THE EIGHT-HOUR DAY

Establishment of the eight-hour day, which was at the time one of the most cherished goals of the workers everywhere, was achieved by Cuba as one of the fruits of the Revolution of September 4, 1933. This was followed by the introduction of the "English week"—44 hours work with pay for 48 hours.

Following the practice of the more progressive private institutions, we introduced the five-day week for government employees by closing on Saturday (Law #5 of October 27, 1955). Wherever it was economically possible, we encouraged the 6-by-8 formula, that is to say, a 6-hour work day with pay for 8 hours.

PAID VACATIONS

We introduced paid vacations as a matter of law in 1935. This created 300,000 jobs, increasing the labor force of around 1,335,-000 by 23%. However, in the last analysis, sharing the work does not benefit labor or the nation. The fundamental solution is to create and maintain a climate for vigorous economic advance. Social welfare is not a substitute for production and growth. Rather it is a value which can be realized only to the extent that the nation succeeds in creating material wealth.

THE INTERRUPTED PATH

After March 1952, I concentrated on removing the impediments to a healthy economic growth. It was clear that, if the basic conditions were created for sound and diversified private investment in Cuba, both seasonal and chronic unemployment would rapidly approach the vanishing point.

To this end, a continuing, inflationary increase in wages had to be braked and brought to a standstill. To do this successfully, I believed it was necessary that the efforts of all parties concerned be directed toward the same national goals and that the adjustments occur in a climate of peace, mutual understanding and justice. My presence at the head of the government fortunately made this smooth adjustment possible. The labor movement and the workers of Cuba knew that I would not sacrifice the social gains of the Revolution to expediency nor would I under any circumstances tamper with the rights which the workers had won under my previous administration, particularly the right to strike and the freedom of the trade unions. This was recognized by the Cuban Confederation of Workers itself.[10]

THE MYTH OF MASS UNEMPLOYMENT

Communist propaganda claimed that an enormous army of unemployed weighed like a millstone on the Cuban economy during my second Administration. This contention was as mendacious and deliberately deceptive as the allegation that 20,000 persons had been murdered during the Cuban civil struggle of 1956-1958. *The fact is that, as a result of our constructive economic policies and development programs, Cuba had the lowest percentage of unemployment in all Latin America during my second Administration.*

The facts about Cuban unemployment were clearly established as a result of a series of statistical studies conducted by technicians under the directions of the U.S. Bureau of the Census and the International Labor Office. This work was completed in March 1958. It showed that the potential working population of Cuba was 2,204,000 persons as compared with 2,059,659 re-

10 Manifesto of the CTC in Exile entitled "To the Public Opinion of Mexico and America."

ported by the 1953 Cuban Census. Our unemployment rate was 9.17% in 1956 and fell to 7.07% in 1958, the last year of my administration. This was the lowest rate in Latin America at the time.

NEVER BEFORE

No other country in the Americas had better organized, more democratic, more united and more powerful trade unions than Cuba in the late 1950s. The Confederation of Cuban Workers united organized labor. Its strength derived from the devotion of its members, the respect of employers and the support of the Government. It was led by men from every political party and group in Cuba, including those strongly opposed to me and my administration. The single exception was the Communist Party, which has no business in the labor movement because it penetrates it only in order to destroy it and condemn the workers to slavery. Within the CTC and the individual trade union federations, the leadership was chosen by democratic elections in which all non-communist parties and groups freely participated.

The conflicts between management and labor were almost invariably resolved by conciliation and mediation after exhaustive consideration of the claims of both sides. Thanks to this, we had a minimum of strikes. Those strikes which did occur were settled quickly and amicably. This was possible because labor disputes were over economic matters. Despite the fact that the Communists did everything to penetrate and weaken the labor movement, including attempted intimidation of its leadership by terrorist tactics, there were no political strikes. On three separate occasions, the Communist conspiracy, working from its Cuban command post in the Sierra Maestra, called the workers out in general strikes. This occurred in August 1957 and in April and October 1958. Even though the Reds murdered labor leaders who resisted their plans, the Confederation of Cuban Workers refused to support these general strikes and the workers ignored the call of Castro and his Communist henchmen.

CASTRO'S WAR AGAINST LABOR

From the first moment of victory, the Castro movement proceeded to destroy the social achievements of the working class of Cuba and to make its democratically elected organizations mere agencies of the emerging totalitarian state. The independence of the Cuban Confederation of Workers was totally destroyed. Freely elected labor leaders were barred from their offices. Some were furiously pursued and persecuted; others were subjected to never-ending calumnies by the government-controlled press; others were set upon by communist-led mobs; others suffered long terms of imprisonment and still others met death against the execution wall. Naturally, this persecution reached its maxima in intensity where labor leaders known to be hostile to communism were concerned. However, in one form or another, it was levelled against all union officials and militants who refused to become instruments of the police state. When a labor leader was ousted from his post for political reasons, he was almost invariably disqualified from trade union office for decades to come.

THE ASSAULT ON WAGE STANDARDS

In the first flush of victory, Castro announced a series of wage increases which were more or less arbitrary. Then, as his economic difficulties multiplied and the economy sickened, the dictator reduced the real wages of the workers. Labor in public utilities, transportation, financial institutions and most industries suffered.

The construction industry had been flourishing under my administration. The Castro regime, however, imposed rent controls, designed to expropriate the landlords, with the result that stagnation and sudden unemployment struck the construction industry. No less than 150,000 workers lost their jobs in the building trades and more than 300,000 were affected by the repercussions of the slump in collateral industries. All facets of the economy were adversely affected despite the regime's attempts to shore up employment by artificial devices. In the restaurant industry, which had known no unemployment at the end of 1958, the virtual disappearance of tourism caused a 50% reduction in wages in the months following Castro's seizure of power.

Progressive imposition of government controls deprived workers of the right to strike, emasculated the trade unions, held down wages and centralized wage determination in the hands of the central government and its Communist bureaucracy. In August 1962, the Castro government promulgated a decree imposing tighter controls on the wages of Cuban labor, imposing penalties for tardiness and absenteeism which ranged from public reprimand or fine to transfer to distant and primitive places. The decree demanded drastic curtailment of vacation time. Any variation in wage scales had to be approved by the Ministry of Labor.

Statistics on wages under Castro Communism are difficult to obtain or interpret. The dictatorship no longer submits those economic statistics to the United Nations which my Government, and for that matter almost all non-communist Governments of civilized nations, regularly submitted. The reason is obviously a desire to conceal evidence of economic catastrophe and planned impoverishment of the working people of Cuba. Moreover, the presence of inflationary forces, the rapid depreciation of the peso and the paucity of statistics make it difficult to derive real wages from nominal wages.

Monthly payroll deductions were limited to three during my second Administration: Workers' Maternity Insurance, union dues and the contribution to the applicable retirement or social security fund. These averaged 5.15% of wages. Under the new Communist state, some 13.25% of the worker's pay is seized by the State. These new levies do not provide the workers with any compensatory advantages. They include: 5% of wages for the so-called "People's Savings Certificates" or "Industrialization Bonds" and a 3% tax on personal income, which, under my Administration, amounted to only 1% of wages or salaries in excess of $200 per month. Actually, the deductions from workers' wages are much higher, for "voluntary" contributions of a day's work per month are exacted for such purposes as "equipment for the agrarian reform," the "purchase of arms" and even for "cows and pigs." These exactions, voluntary in name only, increase to almost 20% the proportion of wages which are confiscated at the source.

SLAVERY

Barely a year after the seizure of power by the Communists, Cuba's social conquests were merely a memory. Labor was regimented; collective bargaining destroyed; working hours had been increased without any additional pay and arbitrary exactions of money and work were imposed at will.

My Government had been keenly aware of the problem the worker faces of balancing his budget and, at the same time, trying to buy a few special luxuries every year. To make this possible, we saw that workers in both private and public enterprises got Christmas bonuses. We also saw to it that labor received pay for differences between estimated and actual world market prices for sugar. Moreover, there was a yearly payment for sugar production above the established norms. All of these benefits were withdrawn during the very first sugar harvest under Communist rule. The reason given by Castro was so that "inflation would be avoided"—a cruel irony!

Dr. José R. Álvarez Díaz, the Cuban economist who served as Minister of Finance under Prío Socarrás and a source far from friendly to me or my administration, made a careful estimate of the working year under Batista and under Castro.

He found that in 1958, out of a year of 48 working weeks, amounting to 2,496 work-hours, 208 hours corresponded to the 4-hour allowance[11], 72 to sick leave, 190 to vacations, 68 to holidays and 104 to summer vacations. This left a work-year of 1,854 hours.

Under Castro in 1962, the basic work-year of 48 weeks was still 2,496 hours. To this had to be added 312 hours of "voluntary" labor and 96 hours of "voluntary" labor at the end of the week, making a total of 2,904 hours. From this, 190 hours of vacations, 56 of holidays and 104 of summer holidays had to be deducted. This left a work-year of 2,554 hours. *In other words, under the "proletarian dictatorship", the workers had to toil 38% longer!* [12]

OTHER ABUSES AND OUTRAGES

The unemployed and even those at work were called upon to labor without remuneration as "volunteers" under threat of being considered counter-revolutionary with all the sinister conse-

---

[11] That is to say, the worker was paid for a 48-hour week, but actually worked only 44 hours.

[12] Grupo Cubano de Investigaciones Económicas de University of Miami (directed by José R. Álvarez Díaz), *Un Estudio sobre Cuba,* University of Miami Press, Miami, 1963, p. 1,619.

quences that this may entail. This procedure, needless to say, was copied from the U.S.S.R. and other Communist states.

The National Institute of Agrarian Reform (INRA) created "cooperatives", which totally regimented the labor of the peasants and made the promise of land reform a total mockery. The payments made to these peasant members of the "cooperatives" were in scrip which had no value except at the People's Stores. An old law, that of June 23, 1909, banned the payment of wages in any medium except Cuban currency. Its purpose was to ensure that the worker was free to spend his money wherever he pleased. Thus, the Communists have turned back the clock of Cuban history to conditions prevailing half a century ago.

Decree #798 of April 13, 1938 protected Cuban workers from arbitrary or unjust discharge. It was a model of such legislation and was strictly enforced. Under this precept, the worker was entitled to a hearing before being discharged and could appeal, as a last resort, to the Supreme Court.

Under Castro communism by contrast, Cuban workers can be dismissed at will. If they are discharged because of the mere accusation of counter-revolutionary tendencies, they lose all social rights and are blacklisted. By contrast, the law of 1938 protected Cuban workers absolutely from dismissal on political or religious grounds.

Collective bargaining was abolished by the Castro government. The new basic law of the Ministry of Labor places the workers under the total domination of the state. Contracts, firing, change of employment and all similar matters are under the absolute control of the Minister, a hard-core Communist. No Cuban can get a job or change the one he has without the consent of the regime. Merit, ability and seniority no longer count for anything.

To all this must be added the militarization of labor. The Militia serve, not merely to train men and women in the use of arms, but also to indoctrinate the masses and prepare them psychologically for the work of spying, betrayal of their fellow workers and assault or murder of those who resist.

The leaders of the slave Cuban Confederation of Workers wear the uniform of the Militia. This is an organization which has taken over the trade union federations and by means of pressure and terror has imposed blind and abject obedience. The farmer is transformed into a spy and hangman. During the bloody trials of 1961 and 1962, the heinous task of murdering Cuban patriots was given to firing squads formed of the Workers' Militia.

To Cuba's misfortune and that of the entire Western Hemisphere, the transition from freedom to slavery, from prosperity to dearth and progress to retrogression was achieved with sinister thoroughness in the course of a few brief months.

9

The Challenge of Public Education

At the time of the Revolution of September 1933, the public school system in general and rural education in particular were in a deplorable state. The statistics of illiteracy and ignorance were appalling. The immense and immediate task that confronted us was to bring education to the peasant masses so that they could be equipped to improve their miserable living conditions. For the successful accomplishment of this task, it was necessary that we plan the operation very carefully and concentrate on creating the sort of teacher who would blend the art of pedagogy with the discipline and dedication of the soldier.

The state of the budget did not permit offering adequate salaries and, under these conditions, the average schoolteacher shunned the rural schools. Nevertheless, it was necessary to begin and to approach the enormous task without fear of failure. The objective, as stated by Law #620 of February 27, 1936 was "to bring elementary education to places where it had not previously existed and where prospects for its establishment were remote."

From the revitalized Revolutionary Army, we developed cadres of sergeant-teachers. For the most part, these men had high school diplomas, university degrees or at least a teacher's diploma. They represented a real step forward in comparison with the past. In 1899, when the Cuban public school system was initiated under the United States military government, non-professional teachers had been appointed by Frye and Hanna and had set to work without even the benefit of textbooks.[1]

The Rural Civic Schools, as these new elementary institutions were called, spread quickly through the mountainous regions of the island. At the end of my first Administration in 1944, some 2,710 were in operation with an enrollment of 110,725 pupils.

As for elementary schooling in general, there were 11,376 schools in 1944, an increase of 3,172, or 38.6%, over 1933. When I assumed responsibility for the Cuban government, there were 8,663 teachers; when I relinquished it in 1944, there were 12,189, an increase of 40.7%. As budgetary conditions permitted, I saw to it that teachers' salaries were increased so as to attract the ablest people to this nationally vital task.

RURAL CHILDREN'S HOMES

In addition to primary education, I thought it essential to provide peasants' children with useful knowledge concerning their surroundings. As part of the rural educational project, we therefore created secondary centers, which could be considered as more advanced elementary schools, geared to the teaching of trades in general and of scientific agriculture in particular. This new system was adapted to the realities of rural life. It made it possible for the graduates of these schools to cultivate more efficiently, increase crop yields and improve their housing.

We called these centers, Rural Children's Homes. Forty of them were established to serve additionally as headquarters of the Rural Educational Missions and centers of the rural school zones. Each zone was staffed with teachers in specialized subjects to give guidance to the rural school teachers. Each zone contained hundreds of schools and provided medical assistance, dentists, nurses, laboratory technicians, specialists in pedagogy, agronomists, teachers of domestic science and of specialized trades and skills. They were furnished with the equipment they needed. In addition to the basic subjects of the rural educational system, physical education and sports were added.

The educational pattern in rural Cuba was supplemented by

---

1 However, excellent texts were prepared in short order due to the dedicated work of Carlos de la Torre, Enrique José Varona, Esteban Borrero Echevarría, Nicolás Heredia, Vidal Morales and Manuel Sanguily, pioneers in education to whom the Cuban nation owes an eternal debt.

the establishment of a Rural Domestic Science School in the province of Las Villas, that is to say, the geographical center of the Republic, to prepare girls for their future careers as housewives in the countryside.

THE UNIVERSITY OF LIFE

At the apex of this organizational system were the Civil Military Institutes, communities of education. At the end of my first administration, I left three of them blooming in the provinces of Havana, Matanzas and Oriente, with a fourth under construction in Pinar del Rio. Under their roofs, orphans of farmers, workers, journalists and members of the armed forces, who had died prematurely, were housed as if in their own homes.[2]

The first Civic Military Institute opened its doors in 1938 in its Ceiba del Agua campus near Havana. Here some 1,200 girls and boys were comfortably installed, well fed and clothed, given plenty of room for physical exercise and sports, with shops, museums, libraries, excellent medical attention in a first-class hospital, and a competent teaching staff. Later, another 1,200 children were taught similarly at the Holguín institute. The third Institute was at Matanzas and the fourth was established for teenage girls in Las Villas.

During my first administration, this project trained hundreds of young men and women, who were then returned to their homes fully versed in some trade, to replace the deceased head of the household or else they were returned, trained to become good housewives.

Among the many institutions which we created in those days, these polytechnical centers and rural schools were, together with the National Council on Tuberculosis, the projects in which I personally was most deeply interested. As the Civic Military Institutes developed in scope and in their human and social implications, my colleagues and I thought of them increasingly as "universities of life." Naturally, there were some shortcomings and the inevitable criticism. In particular, I was reproached for having provided too much comfort and luxury for the children of poor parents.

Time was not kind to these institutions which combined education with social assistance. When I relinquished office to
_____
[2] Law #707, March 30, 1936.

the newly elected Grau San Martín Administration, the purpose for which they had been created was abandoned and they fell victim to the Auténtico embezzlers.[3] The pupils were chased out of the schools, even though they were orphans protected by special laws, and sent back to their poor homes uneducated. The teachers, who had obtained their posts through competitive examinations and by merit, were summarily dismissed. The services were disrupted; the buildings, gardens and workshops were left untended; the workshops were looted; discipline was destroyed; competent personnel was replaced by political appointees; the funds destined for the institutions were stolen.

This was to be the beginning of the scandals of the so-called "typically Cuban government" of Dr. Grau San Martín. These culminated with the outrages of the "BAGA" (the word was coined from the initial letters of Bloque Alemán and Grau Alsina, referring to Minister of Education José Alemán, a prodigious thief, and the Grau Alsina presidential family). The BAGA was permitted to remove funds from the National Treasury. Incredible as it may seem, the Treasury was placed under the orders of the Ministry of Education for that purpose. *In this fashion, $174,000,000 was embezzled from special funds, pension and retirement funds.*

EIGHT YEARS LATER

By decree #75 of President Grau of January 16, 1946, the Civic Military Institutes were transformed into Polytechnical Teaching Centers. When I took power on March 10, 1952, one of my first acts was to change them back into the "universities of life" of which my associates and I had dreamed.

In 1952, one of my first aims was to restore the teaching and welfare provisions and institutions of my first term of office. All of my attempts to carry education to the far corners of the Republic had been virtually ignored by the two successor regimes of the Auténtico Party and the 1953 Population Census presented a humiliating picture of the state of national education and culture.

My Administration began where it had left off in 1944. One of

[3] The members of the Cuban Revolutionary Party boastfully called themselves the Auténticos, alleging that they were the authentic representatives of Martí's ideals.

our first enactments, Law #45 of May 2, 1952, enlarged the scope of the system which had been initiated by Law #620 of 1936 and established, as a center for the new activities, a responsible organization. This was designed to give peasants' children special training in primary and secondary schools together with Rural Children's Homes. Again, there was the emphasis on better farming and practical skills and trade and, for the girls, on home economics, hygiene and the practical problems of childbirth and child care.

With the reconstruction of the Children's Homes, the rehabilitation job was launched. I saw to it that the original goals were reinstated, that the venture was given adequate financial backing and that inherited debts were promptly paid off. The standard of the Homes was raised to that of the Higher Elementary Schools. Specialization in agriculture and rural industries was the watchword for the inland schools. For coastal people, we added such skills as marine carpentry, commercial fishing techniques and the mechanics of marine motors.

The Teaching Missions had increased from 44 in 1944 to 62 at the start of the 1952 school term. Some 41 rural units with a new subsidiary service of 120 midwives were created for farm mothers. Some 389 rural teachers were reinstated and 40 completely equipped clinical laboratories were put back into service.

The annual students' excursion of the Flower of Martí to the Cuban capital from all isolated points on the Island was reinstated on May 19, 1952 and these trips were awarded as prizes to the outstanding students in the rural schools.

Student museums and laboratories were created for the study of nature, soils and seeds. Savings banks were opened for peasants' children to inculcate habits of thrift. School canteens were organized. We stressed manual training, home economics, vegetable gardens, flower gardens, orchards to be tended by the students and, above all, school libraries. In particular, we developed mobile libraries with a total of 179,738 volumes.

The organization of parent teacher associations was encouraged to develop voluntary initiative in rural education and the campaign against illiteracy. We tried to avoid excessive centralization and encouraged the rural teachers to use those methods they knew best.

In the rural areas, we built a large number of school houses, with workshops and a dwelling for the teacher attached. In the cities where none had previously existed, we started simultaneously and completed 40 secondary schools.

Of the rural schools built in my second administration, 557 were prefabricated of wood with cement-fiber roofs, 553 were brick and 96 were of the "sugar-differential" type. The National Housing Commission also had to rebuild or rehabilitate 54 rural schools destroyed by Hurricane Hilda.

COMMUNIST INFILTRATION

My Government placed a great deal of stress on reviewing the educational system to adapt it to the spirit of the modern school and to be continuously on guard in defense of the patriotic and Christian traditions of the Cuban people. This was particularly the case in the textbook field.

One example is most illuminating. Because of the enormous amount of work attached to the job of the Presidency, I had had to leave most of the responsibilities for guiding our children to my wife. I would make a point of taking a break from my work when they returned from school in the afternoons so I could chat with them, since otherwise I might not have been able to see them at all, for the obligations of my office generally claimed my time until daybreak. These conversations would generally turn to their school grades and I would often leaf through their textbooks.

One afternoon—I will never forget it—I found among their books a text on the geography of Cuba, which they had been given that day. I opened it naturally with a good deal of curiosity. Some of the photographs and some of the passages in the text amazed me.

That day, I went out to sea with a couple of experts on shrimp fishing and I took the geography book along to review it. I showed it to the shrimp specialists in the presence of an industrialist friend. We all agreed that it was unadulterated Communist calumny. The author was, at that time, an unknown and obscure character. Later, he would become notorious for his criminal acts, his relentless cruelty and his numerous trips behind the iron curtain. His name was Antonio Nuñez Jiménez.

This book did not contain a single pleasant or edifying photograph. It was filled with skillful incitements to Communist subversion directed at the Cuban youth and farmers. In tracing the history of the relations between the United States and Cuba, history was crudely falsified and our friendly neighbor was vilified on all occasions.

This libel on our traditions, our aspirations and our history, masquerading as a geography text, had been declared the official text for the entire school system of Cuba by the preceding Auténtico Government of Carlos Prío Socarrás. It was an example of the perfidious manner in which Communist agents had been infiltrating the educational field in order to poison the minds and hearts of our children and also an example of the apathetic attitudes of officials who were supposed to watch over the mental and moral development of Cuban youth.

Needless to say, I immediately had this lying tract withdrawn from the school system, but it was reinstated by the Red tyrant as the official text as soon as he seized power. The outstanding book by Professor Levy Marrero, used during my administration, was burned at an *auto da fé* by the Communist regime of Fidel Castro.

Similarly, under Prío Socarrás, Russian propaganda films were imported from Mexico. My administration banned them and the Communist dictatorship reinstated them.

The physical wellbeing of the Cuban people was of as much concern to my administration as their mental health. We created special children's medical dispensaries at the educational centers with orthodontists for the correction of dental malformations and neuropsychiatrists to aid children with behavior problems. Surveys were made by specialists in tuberculosis, intestinal parasite infections and heart and eye diseases. During the epidemic of Asian flu, doctors visited 607 schools with 114,968 pupils and treated 34,302 children suspected of contamination. As a result, only one death was reported.

To further the expansion of education, 3,028 teachers who had been discharged by the previous administration for reasons or pretexts which had provoked controversy in the courtrooms and in Congress were reinstated and sent where they were most urgently needed.[4]

We formulated a central plan covering kindergarten and school construction, elementary and high school teaching and cafeterias. This plan further developed the start that had been made in my

4 Law #1020 of 1953 and Law #1321 of 1954.

first administration. Some 91 of the educational centers were left in operation, enabling them to contribute still further to the great task of developing culture among the common people. Of these 10 were in Pinar del Rio, 24 in Havana, 24 in Las Villas, 12 in Mantanzas, 12 in Oriente and 9 in Camagüey.

THE SERGEANT-TEACHER

An American writer, who is notorious for his Marxist ideology, while discussing the Cuban situation, had the nerve to say that "during Batista's regime the teachers were fired and for a while the grade schools were placed in the hands of semi-illiterate sergeants." [5] Considering the insignificance of the source and concerned that by refuting Communist propaganda I might unintentionally serve to spread it, I took no notice of this calumny at the time it appeared. At this juncture, however, it may be of interest to compare the assertions of the leftwing writer with the facts. No teachers were fired during my Administration. Far from it, we reinstated thousands who had been dismissed during the Prío regime. Nor were the sergeant-teachers, the pioneers in creating and running the rural schools, uneducated men. On the contrary, the establishment of these schools in the remote corners and mountains of the Island and the self-sacrificing conduct of those Cuban teachers who dedicated themselves to a gallant and victorious fight for rural education are a bright page in the history of my country.

The Rural Education School "José Martí" served as a special academy for final preparation of the rural school teacher, giving him not only the usual educational background, but the special skills needed in the farm areas. This school was suppressed by a Cuban Chief Executive conspicuous for his resentment and apathy at about the time it graduated its first class of teachers.[6] Its magnificent building was then devoted to socially less important purposes.

The Prío Government, which replaced that of Dr. Grau, came with the passage of time to regret this mistake. In view of the crisis which followed in the field of rural education, the Minister of Education in the second Auténtico administration, Aureliano

[5] Carleton Beals, "The Cuban Revolution," *Bohemia*, April 10, 1960.
[6] Executive Decree #276 of President Ramón Grau San Martín, October 16, 1946.

Sánchez Arango, stated at a press conference that, instead of suppressing the Rural Teachers' School, one should have been created in every province of Cuba, as it was the ideal forge for the type of teacher the nation needed. Law #65 of August 1958 finally reinstated the school.

SECONDARY EDUCATION

To improve public school teaching, we undertook a basic reorganization of secondary education. Since Colonial times, the high schools had always been in the capitals of the provinces. After the 1933 Revolution, however, we founded 15 more of them in other urban areas.[7] Between 1937 and 1958, enrollment in the high schools advanced from 12,918 to 49,200, or almost four-fold. In addition, 165 private high schools taught 36,282 additional pupils. The number of high school teachers increased from 509 in 1933 to 1,361 in 1944.

By the beginning of 1958, there were 36 official centers of higher studies in operation. All of these were state institutions and were supported from the National Budget. These included six teacher-training institutions,[8] three schools for kindergarten teachers,[9] eight professional schools,[10] five home economics schools,[11] three schools of journalism and the plastic arts,[12] a school of advertising at Havana, seven of arts and crafts,[13] one of plastic arts in Camagüey and the National School of Fingerprint Technicians established in Havana by Law #233 of June 6, 1952. In addition, there was the School of Aeronautical Techniques at the San Julián air base in Guane, Pinar del Rio, where aviation,

---

[7] In Artemisa in Pinar del Rio Province; in Marianao, Güines, Vedado and La Vibora in Havana Province; in Cárdenas in Matanzas; in Cienfuegos, Remedios, Sagua la Grande and Sancti Spiritus in Las Villas; in Morón and Ciego de Avila in Camagüey and, finally, at Guantánamo, Holguín and Manzanillo in Oriente Province.

[8] At Guanajay, Cienfuegos, Bayamo, Guantánamo, Holguín and Manzanillo.

[9] At Matanzas and Cienfuegos and in Pinar del Rio.

[10] In Artemisa, Marianao, Cárdenas, Colón, Sagua la Grande, Manzanillo, Morón and Victoria de las Tunas.

[11] At Sagua la Grande, Sancti Spiritus, Ciego de Avila, Holguín and Cienfuegos.

[12] At Matanzas, Santa Clara and Santiago de Cuba.

[13] In Pinar del Rio, Artemisa, Sancti Spiritus, Cienfuegos, Cruces, Camagüey and Banes.

ground maintenance and all aspects of repair and overhaul were taught in conjunction with U. S. experts.

Also there was a great deal of construction work. My first administration installed the Havana Normal School in a splendid building in the old Arena Cristal in 1944 and my second term saw completion of its installation and construction of an annex. Four new buildings were erected for the Schools of Commerce. Six of the seven normal schools to train kindergarten teachers were founded when I was in the Presidency.

In 1958, Cuba had 114 higher education institutions below university level, that is to say, institutes, polytechnical schools and professional schools. Of these, 23 had been created prior to the 1933 Revolution; 32 were created during my first eleven years of power; 23 more were set up under the two Auténtico administrations and the last 36 were instituted after the Revolution of the 10th of March 1952. In other words, 68, or more than half of these institutions, were created while I was in power.[14]

In 1957, Cuban institutions of higher education below university level trained 38,428 students. Of these, 13,494 were in business and administration, 7,772 were training to be teachers, 5,639 were concentrating on technology, 3,882 in arts and crafts, 1,841 in home economics, 1,706 in the industrial arts, 1,412 in the plastic arts, 1,088 were studying to be kindergarten teachers, 903 were students of journalism, while the remaining 691 were distributed among advertising (326), aviation (180), physical education (130) and fingerprinting (55).

ELECTRONICS

It was plain to me that Cuba would need a growing corps of young men trained in electronics if she was to take full advantage of the techniques of the age of mechanization, automation and cybernetics. Accordingly, by Law #472 of October 17, 1952, we set up the Technological Juvenile Military Institute for complete education in electronics for 1,000 students of both sexes. The students were confined to children of members of the armed forces

---

[14] In addition, 162 private high schools were incorporated into the official system and the degrees they granted were given official recognition. Registration in the high schools reached an all-time peak. My colleagues and I launched an extensive high school building program and began to introduce modern, functional architecture.

between 14 and 16 years old. The buildings of the military camp that had been erected in Managua in World War II were converted into a great schooling center with large classrooms and facilities particularly adapted to the study of automobile mechanics and radio and television electronics.

SPORTS

In September 1933, the only official sports organization in Cuba was the National Commission on Boxing and Wrestling which had been founded in 1922. We reorganized this in 1934, gave it an arena in the heart of the city (the Arena Cristal) and further encouraged athletics by forming the Olympic Committee in 1937 and working for extensive Cuban participation in the forthcoming Central American sports meet and in international Olympic contests.

Executive Decree #1454 created the National Sports Management in 1938. By the end of my first term, Havana had a beautiful Sports and Convention Palace, which served its purpose until it had to be torn down to make way for a new extension of the Malecón, the ocean boulevard.

I decided to do everything in my power to make Cuba sports conscious, to give Cuban athletes the support they needed to win prestige and glory for themselves and their country in international contests and to try to further the Greek ideal of *mens sana in corpore sano.*

We transformed the Management into a National Commission. When I left Cuban public life, we had a boxing academy and the Civil Aviation and Naval Sports Academy. Hundreds of trophies and medals had been won by young Cubans. Moreover, we had built a splendid sports city with ample space for athletic contests of all sorts in a central location and overlooking an arena that would go down in our annals as one of the greatest achievements of Cuban architecture.

The new Sports Palace had a domed roof without any supporting columns that permitted perfect visibility. Constructed with all imaginable conveniences, even including housing for visiting foreign athletes, it had a seating capacity of 16,000. Olympic swimming pools, baseball diamonds, basketball courts and tracks for athletic meets helped give the Sports City all that was needed for comprehensive athletic programs and contests.

This ambitious building program radiated out to the provinces. Stadiums went up in Pinar del Rio, Consolación del Sur, Cárdenas, Camajuaní, Cienfuegos, Esperanza, Placetas, Sancti Spiritus, Camagüey, Morón, Ciego de Avila, Bayamo, Banes, Manzanillo and other places. For the Naval Sports Academy, we had a building under construction on the eastern bank of the Almendares River. Sports were encouraged by private initiative and we pursued the policy of sending our athletes wherever they could compete. The Cuban sailing team brought glory to Cuba in European waters; our boxers and baseball players ranked with the best; Havana became a center for the great international auto races. Year after year, attendance at sports events continued to increase.

PHYSICAL EDUCATION

The Physical Education Administration was created by Law #283 of August 4, 1952 to bring physical education into all the schools. During my first administration, we built the José Martí athletic center on a great expanse of land close to the sea with an Olympic pool, athletic fields and playgrounds for children. It was returned to us after eight years of Auténtico rule in such a state of disrepair that it had to be entirely rebuilt. A similar, but less ambitious, sporting center was built in the city of Matanzas. In the capital, we began construction of a complex of buildings on the Avenue of Rancho Boyeros to house the headquarters of the National Institute of Physical Education. This splendid construction project was near completion when the Communists took over Cuba. I should add that, in connection with our physical education program, we made sporting and athletic equipment available to students all over the island.

CHILD GUIDANCE

Prior to the 4th of September 1961, what we had in Cuba was, not a reformatory, but a veritable children's prison. Here those children were sent who had deviated from the straight and narrow path. Instead of being morally improved in this place, they were trained to commit greater crimes.

After thoughtful consideration of the problem, my associates and I founded the Child Guidance Center (COI), a veritable school city with well-ventilated classrooms, excellent workshop and vegetable gardens. Here delinquent children were re-educated and trained in the arts and trades.

Returning to power in March 1952, I found that the Center had been sadly neglected as to plant and equipment and that it had also been morally corrupted. We set to work to renovate and reorganize it. Three hundred new beds were installed in a circular dormitory; machinery and tools were replaced in the looted workshops; the hospital was renovated, and new teaching methods were introduced for the guidance of the juvenile delinquents.

SCHOOLS FOR DEAF MUTES

An organization which had been established to educate children suffering from ear, voice and speech difficulties was transformed into the National Institute for Logopedics and Phonics by Law #1380 of May 4, 1954. The teaching staffs of the National Deaf-Mute School and the National Deaf-Mute Asylum were incorporated into the new Institute. Simultaneously, four schools were organized for children suffering from these afflictions in Havana, Matanzas, Santa Clara and Camagüey. All were operational by 1955.

UNIVERSITIES

One of the first acts of the Revolution of the 4th of September 1933 was to grant autonomy to the University of Havana.[15] During my first presidential term, I granted the University the Limones sugar mill with its vast, highly fertile lands. The purpose was not merely to enrich the University, but also to give it an adequate area of experimentation and an incentive to improve the agricultural and industrial sugar production techniques of the nation. The next step was to turn over the Calixto García National Hospital, which was given its own means of support, to the University. This was done by Decree #3610 of December 11, 1943.

My government gave official recognition to the Western University and contributed to the establishment of a university at Camagüey and the University of Northern Oriente at Holguín. By Decree #1575 of April 23, we improved the procedures for state

[15] October 6, 1933.

examination and legal accreditation of graduates of private colleges, universities and centers of higher studies.

Under governmental encouragement, the Pontifical University of St. Thomas of Villanova was expanded; two other Catholic colleges were established, that of Belén and of Saint John the Baptist of La Salle, and also the Protestant Candler College and the lay College at Cienfuegos.

THE FINISHING TOUCH

The National Institute of Culture and Museums was created to raise the standards of Cuban culture. The imposing and beautiful Palace of Fine Arts, inaugurated by my administration on December 15, 1955, was the official headquarters of the Institute.

During the first two years that it was open to the public, its historic, artistic and archaeological exhibits were visited by 297,-670 persons, of whom 61,796 were tourists, mostly from the United States.

On the credit side of the Revolution of the 4th of September 1933 was the erection of a magnificent building for the National Archives. This was opened toward the close of my first Administration. During my second term in the Presidency, we built the National Library, which blended the aesthetic and the functional with outstanding success.[16] Its shelves had space for four times its 270,000 catalogued volumes. Microfilm and photostatic services were installed as well as bookbinding facilities and automatic disinfection.

SOMETHING ABOUT JOURNALISM

Let me add a few words and a few memories concerning journalism. I have always felt devoted to the members of this profession. The establishment of schools and social security funds for newspapermen was always a cause which I supported with enthusiasm. During my first Administration, I contributed to the enact-

[16] Founded by General Leonard Wood in 1901, the National Library had its first quarters in the old Castillo de la Fuerza, to which it was returned after some uncomfortable years in the no longer extant Artillery Workshops. The construction of the new home for the Library was made possible by a modest levy on each bag of sugar produced (Law #20 of May 21, 1941). My decree #1664 of June 12, 1957 turned the Library over to a foundation.

ment of the first retirement law for newspapermen. During my second, this fund was expanded into a full social security system with sound financial backing.

By Decree #1441 of 1942, the Professional School of Journalism "Manuel Márquez Sterling" was created. Its faculty was kind enough to accord me the honor of taking the first examination and to bestow on me its first diploma in journalism. My second administration established schools of Journalism and the Graphic Arts in three provinces and provided funds for their maintenance. Two laws, enacted in 1933, regulated the profession and licensed its members.

Unavoidable duty made me adopt exceptional measures, authorized by the Constitution, during dire emergency, but we never resorted to the measures provided by law against those newspapermen who defamed me and my administration.[17]

The consideration I gave to the press during the most critical moments of Cuba's recent history is attested by facts. Thus, the National Newspapermen's College of Cuba in exile, which is affiliated to the Inter-American Federation of Professional Newspapermen's Organizations, admitted me to full membership in that organization as a qualified newspaperman, by unanimous vote of its Board of Directors at a meeting held in Miami, Florida, on July 27, 1962.

It is sufficient to take a quick glance at what journalism and the press were like in Cuba during the era of the 10th of March Revolution and to see what they have become under the Communist terror. Since the Red regime was installed, the gentlemen of the press have had to go into exile en masse and this necessity applies also to those who were the most ardent and fanatical defenders of Castroism.

---

[17] Suspension of constitutional guarantees is authorized by Article 41 of the 1940 Constitution in cases of "grave disturbance of the social order or public peace" and whenever necessary for "the repression of terrorism or gangsterism." Such suspension was authorized by executive decree subject to ratification by the Congress. Among the guaranties that could be suspended was Article 33 regarding the free expression of thought. The adoption of this measure, as a consequence of events that I did not provoke, was the beginning of the propaganda which sought to depict me as a dictator. Nevertheless, it is a measure enforced in many countries and under much less complicated situations than that which Cuba faced as, for instance, in Venezuela. Despite this, the Venezuelan government of Rómulo Betancourt has been called the "lighthouse of democracy."

One glance at the list of active journalists in Cuba on January 1, 1959 shows how their ranks have since been thinned by imprisonment, cruel torture and death. Completely scornful of the freedom of the press, the Communist despotism has forced the journalists of Cuba to go into exile to save their integrity. The Cuban journalists, and for that matter the foreign correspondents who worked in Cuba, recall with painful nostalgia the time when the Cuban press enjoyed days of freedom, dignity and greatness.

10

The Battle Against Epidemics

As a result of the Revolution of 1933, Cuba became the first country in the world to create a Ministry with Cabinet status to guard the health of its people.

One of the first organizations we created in this sphere was the Technical Institute of Rural Sanitation (ITSR). In short order, we succeeded in eradicating such scourges as framboesia.[1] The Institute was engaged in a frontal assault on epidemics and also concentrated on basic measures for the preservation of health in the countryside. It emphasized what was called "the sanitary tripod of rural improvement": a waterproof cement floor for the Cuban peasant's traditional thatch-roofed hut, a hermetically sealed water well with manual pump and a sanitary latrine, of which tens of thousands were distributed gratis.

The other great organizational achievement of the year 1933 in the public health area was the Malaria Commission, which carried out sanitary works projects in cooperation with the Rockefeller Foundation. In 1934, some 54,232 cases of malaria were reported in Cuba. As the result of a vigorous campaign against the *Anopheles* mosquito, the carrier of this disease, cases of malaria were reduced to 1,105 in 1940. After the second revolution, that of the 10th of March 1952, we launched a new program, sought out the few remaining refuges of the *Anopheles* mosquito in the prov-

[1] "A chronic contagious disease peculiar to the Negro, and characterized by raspberry-like excrecences; the yaws." *The Oxford English Dictionary,* 1961 printing.

inces of Las Villas, Camagüey and Oriente and eradicated these last sources of contamination.

THE YELLOW FEVER MOSQUITO

Humanity is indebted to a Cuban for the discovery of the carrier of yellow fever. Thanks to the genius of Dr. Carlos Finlay, the world was finally rid of this terrible scourge and civilization was able to penetrate inhospitable tropical forests and launch such mammoth enterprises as the Panama Canal.

An international agreement for the eradication of the yellow fever carrier, the *Aedes Aegypti* mosquito, was signed in 1953 between our government and the Pan American Sanitary Bureau in Washington. The immediate problem was to prevent a threatened outward radiation of the *Aedes Aegypti* from its South American foci. We proceeded to increase sanitary supervision of all airports and seaports and to carry the war to the most probable sites of infection.

When work was actually started in March 1954, it was assumed that the infected area would comprise 30,888 square miles (80,-000 km²) of the nation's total area of 44,206 square miles—in other words, two-thirds of the national terrain. A preliminary survey showed that, of 45,912 homes inspected, 9,699, or 21.1%, had deposits of *Aedes*.

This showed, as we had suspected, that Cuba, due to her geographical position and to her great volume of international trade, offered exceptionally favorable conditions for the spread of the mosquito carrier.

In less than two years, we reduced the index of infection to 6.4%. This achievement was all the more remarkable when one considers that the yellow fever virus could be found just a few hours flight from Cuban airports—in Mexico, Guatemala, Panama, Columbia and Venezuela. The Government maintained stocks of anti-yellow fever vaccine at all ports and airfields, to be given to every person leaving Cuba for any of the countries considered dangerous from a yellow fever standpoint.

By September 1958, 1,361,605 houses had been inspected and 24,530,806 deposits and 75,187 breeding areas of *Aedes* discovered. Some 835,550 houses with a total of 19,328,987 deposits were sprayed.

As a result, the national infection coefficient was again reduced —to 5.5%—with the assurance that, in the forthcoming months, there would be still further reduction. These percentages refer only to the breeding grounds of the mosquito. Yellow fever had previously been totally eliminated in Cuba.

THE PROBLEM OF POLIO

In 1944, my Administration completed the construction of a hospital equipped specially for the treatment of polio. Despite evident need, this hospital was not put into service until many years later, when it was named the Institute for Orthopedic Surgery. Meantime, polio remained latent with only occasional outbreaks. When 265 cases were reported in 1955, urgent measures had to be taken. We resorted to preventive measures which resulted in a drop to 56 cases and only three deaths the following year. Dr. Salk's vaccine had already brightened the horizon. We instituted a free vaccination program and sought, as quickly as possible, to immunize the majority of Cuban children.

The large number of aqueducts constructed by my administration made a solid contribution to the eradication of typhoid fever. During the last period of free Cuba, this disease ceased to be a major health hazard. In 1955, 495 cases were reported; two years later, there were only 187.

In 1957, Cuba was stricken with an influenza epidemic, but, of 65,840 cases, only 12 deaths were reported. Hundreds of thousands of people were vaccinated, with special attention given to school children and other students.

We observed international quarantine regulations as scrupulously as possible and this made Cuba the subject of favorable comments throughout the world. *In 1955, only six countries on earth were exempt from quarantine measures of one sort or another. I am proud to say that Cuba was one of them.*

The National Commission for Smallpox Vaccination was created in 1954 in cooperation with the Pan American Sanitary Bureau. Vaccination was carried out systematically with the cooperation of the Cuban people, who were convinced of its efficacy.

By agreement with the World Health Organization, the International Vaccination Certificate became one of our institutions. Moreover, in accordance with the provisions of the International

Covenant on Rabies, we began to produce anti-rabies vaccine for human and veterinary purposes and to make it available at cost to the other countries and territories of the Antilles.

The improvement in sanitary conditions and the great strides forward taken in public health were revealed by the following figures for cases of contagious disease in Cuba, (a country of 6,630,921 inhabitants) for the first six months of 1958:

Tuberculosis	589
Typhoid Fever	187
Diphtheria	85
Malaria	61
Gastroenteritis	57
Chickenpox	46
Leprosy	9
Polio	6
Scarlet Fever	4
Rabies	1

INSTITUTE OF HYGIENE

The National Institute of Hygiene (INH) began operations toward the close of my first Administration. It served as a central laboratory for research and for the manufacture of prophylactic and curative biological products. It soon showed splendid results in diagnosis of rare contagious and infective diseases, in the control of impure foods, drinks and medicines and in the control of the manufacture of medicines and sera.

The powers of this Institute were circumscribed by the Auténtico administration, but, when I returned to power in 1952, I saw that they were restored, particularly in the pure food area. The Institute was encouraged to control standards for insecticides as well as for antibiotics.

Reorganization of the Food Science and Biochemical Departments of the Institute improved the nutrition and public health conditions of the nation. It was in these laboratories that the new anti-smallpox vaccine was developed, in addition to the anti-rabies vaccine, which Cuba had made available to the other nations of this Continent.

The National Center for the Study of Viruses was established as an annex to the Institute for specialized studies of virus diseases.

It was given an excellent laboratory for the production of vaccines.

Between March 1952 and June 1958, the biological laboratories of the National Institute of Hygiene manufactured the following products:

Anti-typhus vaccine	2,819,861
Anti-parasite units (doses)	107,536
Distilled water (liters)	94,132
Anti-whooping cough vaccine	28,942
Diphtheria anti-toxin	22,380
Schick Tests	11,750
Glucose and Physiological Sera (liters)	9,729
BCG Vaccine (tuberculine)	8,200
Antigens for diagnosis of enteritic disease (cc)	4,650

A gratifying result of our conquest of epidemic disease and establishment of modern public health services was that by 1958 the Cuban general death rate was 75 per thousand inhabitants— one of the lowest in the world.

THE THREE "BANKS" OF HEALTH

My administration gave the initiative for the creation of three "banking institutions" for the protection of human health: the Blood Bank, the Blood Vessel Bank and the Bank of Human Organs.

The origin of the blood banks goes back to the first stages of my government. The first one was installed in the Calixto García Hospital. Thereafter, fourteen more were set up in the main hospitals of the nation. Thousands of people owe their lives to blood made available by these institutions, which were always open to those who needed help. In 1952, I provided that the costs of these services be defrayed from funds of the general national budget.

At the Lila Hidalgo Hospital at Rancho Boyeros, the first blood vessel bank in Latin America was organized. Until then, the only other such institution had been in New York City. Staffed by skilled surgeons, our blood vessel bank served to replace defective blood vessels under special conditions and circumstances.

The Bank of Human Organs, established by Law #1595 of August 4, 1954, was designed to obtain and preserve organs or parts of organs of the human body, particularly bones, cartilage and corneas. The Bank was directed by a board on which the forensic medical corps, the Institute of Legal Medicine and the orthopedic surgeons of Cuba were represented. It was located in the new building of the Judicial Morgue in Havana. The law provided that branches of the bank be created in public and private hospitals.

HANSEN'S DISEASE

Cuba's only two institutions for the benefit of victims of leprosy were established as a result of the 4th of September Revolution. These were the Association for the Prophylaxis of Leprosy, Skin Diseases and Syphilis (PLECS) and the San Luis de Jagua Hospital in the province of Oriente.

The Association established ten dispensaries throughout the Island, where victims of Hansen's disease were treated according to the most modern scientific methods and with promising results. Treatment of leprosy also occurred in the Alto Songo and Rincón hospitals. In the last days of my Administration, plastic surgery was applied to remove the scars leprosy left on its victims. We had to acquire special equipment for this type of surgery. In addition, a research department with competent staff was attached to the Association.

THE WHITE PLAGUE

The 4th of September Revolution devoted intense and persevering effort to the protection of the people against the Koch bacillus. The first major step was to create the National Council for Tuberculosis with its hospitals, sanataria, preventive clinics, dispensaries and laboratories for the production of vaccine. The Ambrosio Grillo Hospital in Oriente province and the adjacent Aballí Hospital for children were achievements of my first Administration. By the last years of my second Administration, the battle against tuberculosis among children had been virtually won; the beds in the Aballí Hospital were virtually empty and we decided to convert it into a general hospital for children's diseases.

The great campaign against tuberculosis had been crowned by the construction of five hospitals, 28 dispensaries, two preventive clinics and a fine laboratory. During the last year of my Administration, 145,570 out-patients registered in the dispensaries—most of them for preventive treatment—and 3,228 in-patients were hospitalized. Some 546,275 medical services were provided annually to these tubercular patients and, in addition, 12,450 cases were examined by mobile units in congested city areas.

In 1956, we reorganized the battle against the White Plague, providing new methods and better equipment. A Research Institute was established with a school attached. The Institute was to develop new methods of struggle against tuberculosis and improved diagnostic techniques. The school disseminated public health information. The improvement in diagnostic methods resulted in an apparent increase in the tuberculosis rate in 1957 over that of 1956; this "increase" simply meant that we were finding and correctly diagnosing cases that had been mishandled previously.

Two of the five hospitals—the colossus of Topes de Collantes and Aballí Children's Hospital were made autonomous—for better administration and improved services.[2] These hospitals and the other facilities, such as the dispensaries and the tuberculosis wards in the 17 new hospitals we had built, gave the National Council for Tuberculosis the tools it needed. *They represented an effort to eradicate tuberculosis unprecedented in Latin America.*

THE COLOSSUS OF TOPES DE COLLANTES

In 1944, my administration left the immense building of the Topes de Collantes Sanatorium almost completed. Its situation was ideal for it stood on a mountainous height, which had been made accessible by bulldozing a highway of great scenic beauty over very intractable and rugged terrain. All the equipment, from the power plant to the kitchen utensils, was in the warehouses,

---

[2] My critics sought to discredit the system of foundations and autonomous administrative bodies, which I had introduced into public administration for the rapid and efficient achievement of national and social goals. The Communist government branded the creation of the Autonomous Jurisdiction of Topes de Collantes as illegal, because "it was a service pertaining to the Ministry of Public Health" (Decree #722 of January 22, 1960); nevertheless it did not hesitate to grant the National Agrarian Reform Institute $2,000,000 (Decree #771 of April 21, 1960) to "construct hospitals in Oriente" as if that were not also the function of the Ministry of Health. Decree #722 was used to destroy many fine institutions that had provided vitally needed services to the people of Cuba.

awaiting a few details of minor importance prior to installation and inauguration of the project.

However, the Auténticos were elected in that year and no inauguration occurred. The fine equipment disappeared and was used for illicit purposes and we had to rebuild and re-equip the huge building. The great project was completed during the first years of my last Administration. Finally, on November 11, 1954, the Tuberculosis Sanatorium of Topes de Collantes was formally opened after an unjustified delay of ten years and its 1,000 beds were made available to patients who were able to recuperate in that ideal environment in the midst of pines and eucalyptus trees.

As a matter of convenience and to avoid a repetition of the misappropriation which had just occurred, we placed all national properties in the vicinity of Topes de Collantes under the control of a Board of Trustees with specific administrative authority over the complex. Law #1008 of August 6, 1953 authorized planned development of the zone, including tourism. The historic and architectural attractions of the ancient city of Trinidad contributed to the success of this program. The Autonomous Jurisdiction of Topes de Collantes was a successful experiment in that decentralization of governmental controls which I have always favored.

Subsequently, the Ancón Peninsula, the Civil Hospital and the Aqueduct of Trinidad, the new medical units of the port of Casilda and finally the Luis Ortega Bolaños tuberculosis colony in the province of Havana were all incorporated into the Autonomous Jurisdiction of Topes de Collantes.

From its official opening in 1954 until June 30, 1958, 1,930 patients were admitted into the Sanatorium. Of these, 1,285 were discharged as cured, 30 died and 615 were under treatment on June 30th. Medical services rendered, including those to residents of the district, amounted to 454,953 treatments or consultations, of which 13,785 were of an emergency nature.

As the Sanatorium was in a distant and isolated place, a regular hospital city began to sprout up around it. By the end of 1958, a residence for the director, 20 homes for doctors and two apartment houses, one for nurses and other female employees, the other for men working for the Sanatorium, had been constructed.

The men and women, dedicated to the self-sacrificing profession of caring for the sick, already had their social security fund. To increase their income further, the Government built, near the gigantic new National Hospital under construction, a National

School for Nurses with a clinic adjoining it, that was comparable to the best anywhere in the world. Nursing schools were also added to the new Provincial Hospital of Oriente and to the Camagüey General Hospital. To provide recreational facilities for the nurses of both sexes, I saw to it that the Government officially provided funds to help them establish their club at Vista Hermosa beach to the east of Havana.

11

The Growth of Hospitals

During my first Administration, we were engaged in raising the standard of living of the Cuban workers, establishing better social and economic conditions, improving educational and health standards and in general promoting national progress. In those days, my political enemies focused their criticism on Cuba's military construction which, the "comrades" alleged, was prompted by "warlike" designs. The fact of the matter was that we built new barracks to give the soldiers that minimum of comfort to which they were entitled simply because they were human beings and which had been denied them under a dictatorship which stripped them of human dignity and treated them like animals. If my administration had had "warlike" designs, it would have threatened other countries. The historical record shows that it did not do so.

After my second Administration had gotten under way and at a time when its implacable opposition to communism was clearly apparent for all to see, the "comrades" played a different tune. I was a dictator, a servant of reactionary capital, a President who had no interest in the welfare of the common man. This, of course, was the technique of the big lie, so successfully carried out by Adolf Hitler and so successfully imitated by his Communist totalitarian brothers under the skin.

To demonstrate the untruthfulness of this campaign of calumny, either after the 1933 Revolution or after that of 1952, it would have sufficed for a disinterested observer to have visited any Cu-

ban community and to have asked: Who built this hospital?
Who built this ward? Who was responsible for the courthouse?
Who constructed the school center, the post office building and the
fiscal office? Who built the highway? Or the rural school house?
And the children's homes in the back country? And who provided the teachers of home economics, the doctors, nurses, midwives and the medical supplies for the rural families? Who saw to
it that the workers on the sugar plantations had the right to share
in the profits of the sugar industry? Similar questions might have
been asked concerning civic, religious, welfare and other institutions and similar answers would have been obtained.

Characteristic of these criticisms based on ignorance of the
facts was the charge made in the U. S. State Department's *White
Paper on Cuba* of April 3, 1961 that ". . . the (Batista) regime's
indifference to the needs of the people for education, medical
care, housing, for social justice and economic opportunity—all
these, in Cuba as elsewhere, constituted an open invitation to
revolution." This document was prepared, according to the *New
York Times,* by the socialist historian and presidential advisor,
Arthur M. Schlesinger, Jr., a man profoundly ignorant of Latin
America whose judgment was warped by his ideological prejudices. The *White Paper* was characterized by former Ambassador
to Cuba Spruille Braden, a gentleman distinguished by his love of
truth and justice, as "one of the most indefensible documents
I ever have seen issued by a presumably responsible foreign office." [1]

For my part, I have no desire to argue with Mr. Schlesinger or
with other propagandists. I prefer to state the facts and let them
speak for themselves. In the specific matter of medical care and
hospitalization, it should suffice to state briefly what the facilities
of the Cuban nation were on the eve of the 1933 Revolution and
what they had become when the night of communism fell upon
the island. The record will show that my administrations chalked
up more constructive progress in this field than any other regime
in the history of Cuba.

[1] Spruille Braden, Speech to the Cuban Chamber of Commerce in the United
States, May 17, 1961.

STATE OF HOSPITALS IN 1933

When the Revolution of the 4th of September triumphed, we found that the nation had only 34 state-owned hospitals, together with two municipal hospitals in the city of Havana. These had a total capacity of 6,893 beds. During the first 30 years of Cuba's existence as an independent nation, only ten hospitals had been built with a total of 2,365 beds. The other 26, with a total of 4,529 beds, dated back either to Colonial times or to the days of U.S. military intervention.

By the end of my first Administration, the number of hospitals had been increased by 18 and the number of beds had risen by 6,732, that is to say, they had almost doubled. In addition, 20 new hospital buildings had been erected to replace obsolete installations or to house new institutions.

At the end of my second term in 1958, Cuba had an additional 7,516 hospital beds, raising the total contribution of my two periods of power to 14,248. We had established 15 new hospitals and constructed 53 hospital buildings.

GREAT HOSPITALS

Some of these huge hospitals were not yet in service at the end of December 1958 when I had to leave Cuba, but they were nevertheless fully equipped or, at the very least, their equipment had been purchased and paid for. My Administration had intended to open them formally during the 54 remaining days of its constitutional life.

Fidel Castro did not hesitate to claim these hospitals as his own public improvements. The ignorant and the gullible were supposed to believe that, in just a few months, Castro had created 5,543 hospital beds out of thin air! This was every bit as daring and unscrupulous as the calumny of the 20,000 corpses. In both cases, it was the application of the Hitlerian technique of the big lie!

Despite these fraudulent claims of Castro and his band of murderers, claims which have been uncritically reproduced by some of the more credulous and some of the more unprincipled reporters of the United States press, the hard, stubborn facts remain. We constructed, modernized, extended, equipped and, in short, created the greatest hospital system Cuba has ever known. *My associates and I found 6,893 hospital beds and we left 21,141.*

ORGANIZATIONAL STRUCTURE

With the plan to construct 17 new hospitals and reconstruct others under way, the finishing touch to the public welfare hospitalization program was Law #2077 of January 27, 1955. This statute created a $10,000,000 fund to operate the new chain of hospitals.

In accordance with my policy of administrative decentralization, we set up an autonomous authority called the National Organization for the Administration of Government Hospitals. This entity was charged with coordinating hospital management and the management of other centers of social welfare of a similar nature. It had broad responsibilities for construction, founding and organizing such public centers, for acquiring the equipment needed by the hospitals, etc.

ONAHE, as it was called, survived only the first months of the Communist regime and that after a drastic purge of its personnel. By Decree #145 of March 11, 1959, it was stripped of its autonomy and absorbed by the Ministry of Public Health. On September 15, 1959 (Decree #556), it was dissolved. The Communists had inherited a balance in ONAHE accounts of $5,858,289, net of liabilities. With characteristic disregard for the welfare of the Cuban people, the Reds turned over $1,380,000 of these hospital funds to the Navy. The balance of $4,478,289 was assigned to the unrestricted account of the Minister of Public Health, who squandered it for purposes remote from those originally intended.

FIGHT AGAINST CANCER

Thanks to my wife's untiring efforts and generosity, completely equipped wards were set up, such as the one for children in the Curie Hospital of the League Against Cancer. The Curie and Domínguez Roldán hospitals were dedicated to the investigation and treatment of cancer, were under an efficient and dedicated management and received a fixed stipend for personnel and supplies from the national budget. They also relied on support from the general public.

The Curie Hospital was equipped with a radio-active isotope laboratory, a blood bank and modern X-ray equipment. Support for the Dolores Bonet Clinical Laboratory, constructed in Santa Clara through the philanthrophic initiative of one of that lady's descendants, was incorporated in the national budget.

The new Domínguez Roldán Hospital took the patients who had been under treatment in the old Cancer Institute of the Calixto García Hospital, the cancer ward of which had been set up by President Machado in 1929. In addition, the Government granted about 12,000 square meters of city land for cancer institutions in Havana, Santa Clara and Santiago de Cuba. By Law #1539 of July 27, 1954, a building was erected to house the Juan Bruno Zayas Radium Institute. Its cost, $455,000, was defrayed by the Government. Within this Institute, there was a research laboratory, which received $141,500 from the funds of the National Lottery.

FOR THE BLIND

Private initiative created four organizations to help and educate blind people, all of which had the wholehearted cooperation of my Administrations. Thus, we transferred $165,540 to the League Against Blindness for the construction of a hospital in Marianao. In addition, my wife assigned it $60,000 from National Lottery receipts and $35,000 from other sources. The National Lottery made it possible to give $75,720 to the National Association for the Blind and $165,000 to the Varona Suárez Cultural Foundation for the Blind. My wife was deeply moved by the plight of these people and made large contributions from her private funds.

NATIONAL HOSPITAL

In 1933, the Calixto García Hospital had a capacity of 1,000 beds. As it is located within the University campus, my Administration acted favorably on a request by the School of Medicine and transferred it to the University of Havana as part of the latter's patrimony. After it was completely reconditioned, its capacity was increased to 1,300 beds.

In compliance with a constitutional precept, my Administration began construction of a National Hospital in 1943. However, when the Auténticos took over in 1944, they sidestepped the project. On returning to power in 1952, I had a splendid hospital of 500 beds built with equally important adjacent buildings—one for the Children's Hospital and another for the School of Nurses. All of these were completed; their equipment had been ordered and paid for; their budgets had been presented, and they only awaited formal opening. However, at this point, the Communists took power.

HOSPITALS: MYTH AND REALITY

These figures, and the detailed presentation I have made else-where,[2] give the lie to those who charged my regime with "indifference to . . . medical care." Actually, few other countries had as many hospital beds in relation to population as did Cuba.

Considering only government-operated hospitals and the municipal hospitals of Havana, the total increased from 36 in 1933 to 54 in 1944 and 97 in 1958. The total number of beds rose from 6,893 in 1933 to 13,625 in 1944 and 21,141 in 1958, an increase over the entire period of 207%.

MUTUALIST SOCIETIES

These figures, however, tell only part of the story. Private initiative, which was consistently encouraged by my Governments as a matter of principle, maintained no less than 250 other medical institutions in service—hospital associations, clinics, polyclinics, regional hospitalization centers, institutes, etc., with a combined capacity of 15,000 beds.

A number of regional associations had been born in Cuba during the last decades of the Colonial era. They flourished rapidly under the Republic and were organized on a mutualist basis which permitted the construction of immense sanatoria, that were commonly known as *quintas de salud* (health villas). By September 1933, they achieved such impetus that there was scarcely a nucleus of population of any importance in the nation without one of them. Where a local hospital had not been built, the agents or delegations of these institutions provided their members with the medical assistance and medicines they needed until they could go to a hospital for further or more specialized treatment.

The regional associations of Havana, Santiago de Cuba, Camagüey, Cienfuegos and other cities counted their members in the

2 See my *Piedras y Leyes*, Ediciones Bota, Mexico City, 1961, pp. 128-136.

tens of thousands. No less than 500,000 persons in the Republic counted on these associations for hospitalization and excellent medical service. Some of the associations also provided grade school education and even special training in their own schools for the children of their members. The three palaces of the Galician and the Asturian associations and of the Havana Association of Business Clerks were monuments of democratic mutualism.

Their contribution to the cause of health is unparalleled in the experience of the Americas. Following their example, other and similar medical centers were created with the same sort of regional ramifications. Thus, the health insurance system of the country developed to the point where one could safely say that one of every ten persons throughout the nation participated in the benefits of these institutions at an average cost of only $3.00 per month.

This was the origin of the La Bondad Clinic, the Cuban Beneficial Society, the Surgical-Medical Center of Vedado, the Business Clerks' Medical Association, the Cuban Catholics' Association, the Children's Institute, the Institute for the Aged and many others. Through their offices, these organizations not only provided much needed medical care for their members, but reduced the pressure on the national budget and on the private budgets of the sick.

All of these excellent results from the mutualist hospitalization system were enhanced by the high quality of Cuban physicians. At various international conferences of specialists, they repeatedly offered proof of the excellence of their scientific training. The most famous surgeons from the more advanced countries would not hesitate to turn over their scalpels to their Cuban colleagues. In this field, as well as in others, Cuba ranked second to none.

Unfortunately, there was a great deal of Communist infiltration in the medical profession and this despite the tremendous emphasis my Governments had placed on health and despite the many excellent hospitals and specialized medical institutions it had launched.

HOSPITAL BEDS AND POPULATION

If we combine the number of beds in public and in private hospitals, we reach a total of 35,000 beds in 1958. *With a Cuban population of 6,630,921, the average was one bed for every 190 inhabitants. This exceeds the goal for civilized countries of 200 persons per hospital bed; compares favorably with the United States situation of one bed for every 109 inhabitants in 1960 and places Cuba in the forefront of the world in terms of hospital facilities.*

Five years previously, we had had 235 persons per bed in the Republic as a whole and 100 per bed in the city of Havana. By 1958, Havana had 90 inhabitants per hospital bed.

All that the reader need do is compare this situation with that prevailing in other Latin American, or for that matter, European countries to realize that the charges made in the *White Paper on Cuba* are remote from the truth.

The hospitals of Cuba offered silent, but conclusive, testimony to the interest which I shared with my associates in the health of Cubans in general and in medical assistance to the needy, the aged, the children, the disabled and the underprivileged in particular.

The *White Paper on Cuba* slanders the Cuban people as a whole. Hygiene is a tradition among us, not only public hygiene, but also private hygiene. Ever since the eradication of yellow fever, thanks to the discovery of its carrier by a great fellow citizen, Dr. Carlos Finlay, Cuba has striven for excellence in the field of public health. The squalor of some of our neighbors and the epidemics that lash them could never break through the barriers of our zealous sanitation officers and infect our Island. Until the Communists came, we were not only one of the cleanest, but also one of the healthiest, countries in the world.

12

Institutions of Public Welfare

If it is important to establish public welfare institutions, it is equally important to provide public funds, wherever necessary, to operate and maintain those created by private initiative. Accordingly, the Government, at my recommendation, as chief of the revolutionary program, set up a National Corporation for Public Welfare (CNAP) by Law #708 of March 30, 1936 to maintain privately created welfare institutions which heretofore had barely managed to subsist.

In 1953, we broadened this system by revising the bylaws of CNAP and giving it such additional responsibilities as the elimination of public begging, aid to disaster victims and granting of scholarships.

In my message to Congress of September 2, 1958, I mentioned the fact that no country could ever feel secure as long as the morale of its citizenry was threatened by poverty and ignorance. A constructive nationalism requires the elimination of illiteracy, healing the moral wounds of social inequality and provision for the basic physical and educational needs of underprivileged children and of the aged poor.

By the end of 1958, the National Corporation was completely maintaining 43 institutions and subsidizing 67 others. These benefited 3,377 children and 881 old persons. The classification was as follows:

Institutions	Maintained	Subsidized	Total
Day Nurseries	22	13	35
Nursery Homes	11	2	13
Homes for the Aged	4	—	4
Asylums	1	29	30
Schools	—	14	14
Children's Camps	5	—	5
Miscellaneous	—	9	9
TOTAL	43	67	110

Of these 110 institutions, some are worth special comment. Among them, there was the Carmela Zaldivar Transients' Home, which was opened on February 1, 1954 to provide temporary lodgings for up to 120 children wrested from miserable lives as beggars. The Maria Luisa Dolz Improvement Home was dedicated to the care of mentally retarded children, including their education and treatment in a psychiatric clinic.

The Pilar Pedroso Day Nursery at San José de las Lajas was inaugurated in July 1952. Then there was the Lino Figueredo Summer Camp at Sante Fé Beach (Bauta), which provided surf and ocean bathing for the children in other institutions of the Corporation. There was also a Children's Camp, absorbed by the Corporation in 1956, which provided recreation for the children.

In addition, the Corporation provided milk for children, social welfare for the really destitute, food rations, toys at Christmas and scholarships.

At the end of my first Administration, the CNAP supported 59 institutions. By December 31, 1958, their number had increased to 110. Then the Reds took over and absorbed the CNAP into a new Ministry of Social Welfare (established by Law #181 of March 31, 1959). This completely perverted and denaturalized the charitable institutions we had established. Some were abolished, others curtailed and the rest transformed into Communist indoctrination camps.

To provide propaganda show cases, chiefly for foreign journalists and publicists, the Communist dictatorship changed the names of the philanthropic institutions it had inherited from free Cuba and then claimed them as its own creations. Thus, the Drop of Milk was renamed the Bank of Milk and hailed as an achievement of the Castro Revolution; the Students' Dining Rooms became Students' Feeding Stations, etc. The men of resentment pretended to have created something whereas they had merely stolen what others had built and had failed even to maintain and operate competently that which they had taken.

THE NATIONAL ORPHANAGE

Three charity and maternity homes had been inherited from Spanish rule and these were supported by the Government. The one in Matanzas became the responsibility of CNAP; the institution in Santiago de Cuba was supported from the general budget; the most important of them, located in Havana, received a fertile 337-acre farm from the Government, enabling the young inmates to produce their own vegetables and dairy products. They also received the agricultural machinery they needed from the National Executive Commission of Agricultural and Mining Cooperatives (CENCAM) and $430,620 from the National Lottery.

The historic National Orphanage was run with a truly maternal spirit by the Sisters of Charity under the scrupulously honest management of an austere foundation. It seemed most desirable to move it to a place more secluded from the bustling center of the city and more suitable for education. After consulting at length with lawyers, economists and teachers, my Government transferred the Orphanage to an ideal tract in eastern Havana, which was then booming on the north side of the harbor because of the Tunnel under the bay. The Orphanage was given a financial shot in the arm in the form of $3,080,500, paid for its old site by the Cuban National Bank, which planned to use it for a magnificent new headquarters.

If our plan had materialized, this worthy institution, that boarded, educated and prepared for a dignified and socially useful life over a thousand pupils yearly, would have had a new campus with ample space for playgrounds and athletic facilities and increased capacity for orphans.

We had already temporarily transferred some of the children to the immigration camp at Tiscornia, pending relocation to the new headquarters, when the sad events of January 1, 1959 took place. The great project was destroyed and another institution that promised to add to the richness of Cuban life fell victim to Communist cruelty.

The president of the foundation had been Dr. José Ignacio de la Camara y O'Reilly, member of a distinguished Cuban family of pioneer settlers on the Island. Dr. Julio Cesar Portela was not only the manager; he had been the guiding light of the institution for over twenty years. He was beloved by the children and respected by all who knew him. Because of his irreproachable management of the institution's funds and his loving care of his wards, he had been confirmed in his office by every Administration which had governed Cuba since his original appointment.

However, when Castro and his hordes took power, they arrested him and subjected him to various indignities and false accusations. Dr. Portela was replaced by an incompetent, but "obedient" manager. No sooner had the new Administrator taken over, than he proceeded to expel the Sisters of Charity who had guided their orphan wards ever since their original appointment by Bishop Jerónimo Valdés, the founder of the Orphanage.

FOR THE GLORIOUS VETERANS

The September 1933 Revolution took place in a time of economic crisis and near bankruptcy. In those days, a group of veterans of our War of Independence moved into an abandoned building at the old market, La Purisima, in Havana. This served as their dormitory. Their mess hall was more than two miles distant. When I realized their plight, I arranged to have a temporary Veterans' Home set up at the Rancho Boyeros Exposition Park, where they remained until we built them permanent quarters.

We left three veterans' homes in operation: one named for General Peraza in Havana with a capacity to house 200, the Pedro Vázquez Hidalgo with the same capacity in the city of Holguín in Oriente, and the General Riva, accommodating 50 veterans, in Pinar del Rio.

In September 1933, the men who had fought for Cuba's independence were receiving the miserable pension of $6.00 a month. As the national economy improved, we raised those pensions to $10.66 in April 1935, to $15.00 in August 1935 and to $20.00 in June 1944. In my second Administration, the pensions were set at a minimum of $75.00 (Law #1 of 1957) for all veterans ranking from private to lieutenant.

Some 7,474 veterans were favored by this law: 6,131 privates, 443 corporals, 532 sergeants, 253 second lieutenants and 115 lieutenants. The law gave these pension payments priority and estab-lished an accounting system that ensured that they were paid promptly all over Cuba. Buildings for the veterans' delegations and tombs for the dignified burial of these glorious old men who had won us our national freedom, among them my own father, Sergeant Belisario Batista, were constructed with funds from the National Lottery.

CHILDREN'S DISPENSARIES

Many other social welfare institutions, not attached to the CNAP, were aided or inaugurated, within the limits of the resources available, in the 1933-1944 period. It was in those years that the workers' maternity hospitals were built in Havana and in the provinces. We emphasized children's welfare from the pre-natal stage on and much was done through the inspiration and dedi-cated work of my wife, whose name became synonymous with social welfare in Cuba.

The National Organization of Children's Dispensaries (ONDI) was organized in July 1952 to provide complete hospitalization and medical facilities for children from the cradle to adolescence, with particular emphasis on infancy. The ONDI carried its cam-paign for child health to the most remote areas.

My goal was to have institutions adequate to care for the health of all Cuban children from the moment of birth, deploying the resources of medical science to small hospitals, operating as branches of provincial hospitals, the entire structure to be crowned by a great national hospital. With the cooperation of our best practitioners, pediatricians and other specialists, my wife pushed this great work forward, an activity which expressed her maternal feelings and her deep sympathy for the unfortunate and the downtrodden.

Large financial resources were needed to carry out this vast program, as defined in Law #279 of July 30, 1952. With the ac-quiescence of the management and workers in the breweries, we levied a small tax on beer, amounting to 32 cents on every case of 24 bottles. Of this, 24 cents was allocated to the ONDI and the remaining 8 cents went to the brewery workers' and employees' retirement fund.

On July 2, 1954, we had 20 dispensaries in operation throughout the Republic: 5 of them in Pinar del Rio, 4 in Havana province, 6 in Las Villas, 3 in Matanzas, 5 in Camagüey and 5 in Oriente.

Hospitalization, medication and laboratory tests were given to thousands of children who were attended by highly capable doctors, nurses and technicians. All of the roomy and well-equipped dispensaries had the necessary beds for emergency cases in transit to the nearest hospitals. The well-stocked pharmacies, X-ray services and laboratories and all other departments of the ONDI institutions served the sick without any charge whatsoever.

A General Hospital was built in Havana and three provincial hospitals in Pinar del Rio, las Villas and Oriente. These had a total capacity of 1,500 beds and cradles.

Even before completion of the ONDI program, pediatric treatment had been extended to the remotest parts of the Island. All emergency cases were covered by the system. My wife, who served as Chairman of the Board of Trustees, issued orders that urgent cases be admitted immediately, regardless of the circumstances, by day, by night and during holidays. As long as the condition of a sick child did not improve, he was to remain under the direct care of a physician. When special facilities were needed, they were made available quickly and generously. My wife visited the wards, giving hope and happiness to the sick children. Christmas was always an occasion for Christian cheer and the Three Wise Men invariably arrived with presents.

A survey in 1957 of three municipalities where ONDI dispensaries had been installed demonstrated the benefits to child health. The mortality rate from gastroenteritis, one of the most common infantile diseases, had been 1.63 per thousand cases. After the dispensaries were established, the mortality rate fell to 0.88 per thousand, or a 46% decrease.

From July 1954 to July 1958, the ONDI dispensaries made available 4,223,795 medical services. These included 1,796,056 medical consultations, of which 445,956 were emergency cases; 401,276 injections, 181,991 dental services and 49,791 X-rays and fluoroscopes. There were 2,782 hospitalizations and 2,189 surgical operations.

The Communist regime incorporated the ONDI into the Ministry of Welfare (Law #486 of August 19, 1959) and, instead of increasing its sources of revenue, reduced them (Law #630 of

October 29, 1959) by cutting the tax on beer to 10 cents a case. The sole purpose of this measure was to destroy this philanthropic organization so vital to the health of the Cuban people.

PANADE

In 1952, my government established by Law #124 of June 10 the Foundation for Aid to Children, Old, Destitute and Sick Persons (PANADE) for the following purposes:

To provide social and economic aid to the destitute.

To provide food, clothing, medicines and other direct aid.

To give economic aid to social welfare institutions.

To provide hospitalization, in Cuba and abroad, for poor citizens needing specialized treatment, inclusive of all clinical and surgical charges and travel costs for the patient and his next of kin.

To provide aid to victims of public disasters, such as floods, hurricanes, epidemics, etc.

The funds for these expenditures were obtained from the National Lottery.

My wife had dreamed of this sort of institution for many years and she served as Chairman of its Board of Trustees. She not only personally directed its activities, but went into disaster areas to organize aid. In flood stricken regions, she would go to the areas of maximum damage, wading across swollen rivers to see the situation with her own eyes, evaluate the damage and personally distribute relief supplies.

To enumerate the services rendered by PANADE would require endless pages. They included: food, trousseaus for brides, ambulance and automobile service, land purchases and rentals, scholarships, baby showers, furniture, wheelchairs, orthopedic equipment, special beds, funerals, tools, typewriters, sewing machines, musical instruments of various types, scientific equipment, radios, refrigerators, television sets, blood transfusions, kitchens, oculists' prescriptions, textbooks, medicines, school registration fees, hospitalization, surgery, medical and dental bills, traveling expenses for invalids and their companions, monthly stipends to philanthropic and religious institutions, etc., etc.

REHABILITATION OF INVALIDS

One of the major gaps in our medical and welfare organization was lack of an organization for the treatment, retraining and rehabilitation of invalids, especially those disabled by congenital, pathological or accidental causes that limited their usefulness to society. To make up for this deficiency, we decided to create the National Organization for the Rehabilitation of Invalids (ONRI), financing its needs by modest tax levies.

Employers, workers and private individuals welcomed the new organization enthusiastically, contributing over a million dollars to it in the first year. The ONRI was to become another of the welfare organizations that would lay claim to the First Lady's time.

On June 12, 1954, an orthopedic hospital was opened in Marianao, adjacent to Havana. Here, in less than a year, over 3,500 patients were treated. Nevertheless, this hospital was only a temporary installation while a new one, covering more than 60,000 square meters, was under construction. When this new institution, with a capacity of 170 beds and ultra-modern equipment for rehabilitation of invalids, was formally opened, it earned the approval of the medical profession of the world. In September 1956, when the International Congress of Plastic Surgery opened its sessions in its magnificent amphitheatre, attending delegates expressed their admiration of this fine hospital.

In less than two years (to September 20, 1958), 12,620 patients were cared for here. During the same period, 3,174 major operations were performed and 80,000 physiotherapy treatments administered.

Thus, to complete the work of ONRI, we constructed a hospitalization center to be used exclusively as a home for the physically and mentally unfit. This was created by the initiative of my wife and placed under her direction. We consecrated it to Christ of Limpias.

This institution, the first of its kind in Cuba's history, was opened to the people on April 10, 1957, abundantly equipped with scientific and professional facilities and placed under the care of the Daughters of Charity of St. Vincent de Paul. It started with 250 patients chosen from among the most needy and destitute. This was the pioneer of a series of similar institutions which were completed later throughout the Republic.

ONRI was subjected to its first depredation by the Communist regime when it was incorporated (Law #486 of August 19, 1959) into the Ministry of Public Health. The second blow—Law #728 of February 17, 1960—diverted its funds to other purposes and thus $1,270,000 was taken from it.

STUDENT'S DINING ROOMS

The program to see that all Cuban school children got adequate breakfasts had never been very successful. In fact, it was at a standstill. We decided that it was necessary for the state to assume this obligation.

A preliminary survey showed us that 80% of the school pupils suffered from nutritional deficiencies due to low standards of living, to lack of nutritional knowledge in the homes or to both causes.

Therefore, when the child arrived in school with an empty stomach or an inadequately fed one, it was necessary to supply him, not only with the bread of learning, but with a daily ration. We were expanding this program to cover shoes and uniforms when the Red terror brought our work to a standstill.

Despite the high standard of living attained by the Cuban people, we also had to tackle the problem of inadequate nourishment for the adult poor. Thus, we opened the first People's Dining Room in Havana, to be followed shortly by many others throughout the Island.

Law #1803 of November 18, 1954 gave this operation structure and resulted in the establishment in 1956 of the National Organization of School and People's Dining Rooms. We provided for the maintenance of this organization from National Lottery funds and also used gift contests of the sort employed to advertise certain products. We also levied a tax on race tracks and Jai-Alai frontons and allocated revenue from parking meters.

The first dining room for school children was opened in Guanabacoa in Greater Havana to feed more than 500 children from the public school of that municipality. By the time I left Cuba, there were 88 in operation, 70 more completed and 45 more scheduled to be opened shortly in the six provinces of Cuba.

From the outset, ONCEP began to pay off in such results as increased classroom attendance and more satisfactory student progress as evidenced by grades. ONCEP included a medico-social service for the early diagnosis of illness and simple, inexpensive treatment.

Every aspect of the children's welfare was considered. The school lunches were scientifically prepared to provide the children with two-thirds of their daily nutritional requirements of calories, proteins, calcium, iron and vitamins. Provisioning organizations were set up throughout the country to supply the dining rooms in their zones. These had insulated trucks for meat deliveries.

The school dining rooms were open on week days from 11:00 A.M. to 2:00 P.M. so as to feed the children in both the morning and the afternoon sessions.

The meals were not free. We charged 5 cents for each so that the child would feel he was paying for his meal. This stimulated his sense of dignity and prevented his feeling that he was an object of charity. Of course, the child was never left without his meal because he did not have his nickel. This was foreseen in the budget.

Up to June 30, 1958, ONCEP served 3,147,513 lunches, distributed in school years as follows:

1954-55	38,424
1955-56	364,183
1956-57	888,820
1957-58	1,856,086

This steady increase reflected the fact that the project was being expanded to cover the entire nation.

We left 11 People's Dining Rooms in operation where 1,610,725 lunches were served up to June 30, 1958. There was a nominal charge of 25 cents for each meal. We had been careful not to jeopardize the interests of commercial restaurants in the vicinity and also not to build bad habits in the recipients of this charity. An investigation of the means of every customer was made and the meals were only served to those actually in financial distress. This project contributed to the health of the people and prevented the poor from sinking into a physical state in which they would be unemployable.

On the first day of that tragic month of January of 1959, irresponsible mobs stormed every one of these dining rooms, doing extensive damage. Later, the Rebels used them for their own and their family's meals as they would restaurants. Law #407 of July 19, 1959 incorporated the ONCEP into the newly created Ministry of Public Welfare and its assets of $1,052,000 were then diverted to other purposes more suited to the interests of communism.

THE NATIONAL LOTTERY

The Revolution of the 4th of September 1933 defined the purposes for which funds from the National Lottery were to be expended and the Revolution of the 10th of March 1952 extended these objectives into the field of social welfare. The National Lottery ceased to be merely a means of increasing government revenues and satisfying the urge to gamble; it became a major instrumentality of cooperation with private and autonomous institutions engaged in philanthropic, cultural and social undertakings.

The statistics that follow show the tremendous variety of social purposes which the National Lottery served and the extent to which it stimulated individual and local initiative by providing grants in aid to civic, welfare and religious institutions.

Between March 10, 1952 and September 30, 1958, $60,076,834 of National Lottery revenues were expended on socially necessary projects. About $2,000,000 more was thus expended between that month and the usurpation of power by the Reds on January 1, 1959.

In broad categories, the $60.1 million was spent for the following purposes:[1]

(1) Social welfare: financial aid, clothing, medicine and food for the needy; teaching and culture; aid to invalids and unemployed; Christmas rations and toys; medical aid and treatment all through PANADE...................... $10.2 millions

(2) Support of students' and peoples' dining rooms through ONCEP .... $ 9.0 millions

(3) Road and street construction and repair and local aid in urban and rural areas through CENPLUC .... $ 7.7 millions

(4) Project financing through National Bank of Cuba .... $ 5.5 millions

[1] For a complete breakdown, see *Piedras y Leyes, op. cit.*, pp. 154-159.

(5) Construction of National Lottery Bldg... $ 3.5 millions

(6) Social security funds for government employees and servicemen...................... $ 3.7 millions

(7) Asylums and day nurseries, homes for children and for the aged through the National Corporation of Public Assistance.............. $ 2.6 millions

(8) Assistance to literary societies and other associations .... $ 2.2 millions

(9) All other............................ $16.7 millions

13

Fiscal Policy and Taxes

When I took power in March 1952, Cuba faced a severe fiscal crisis. There were many reasons for this. The previous Auténtico Administrations had plundered the Treasury to the tune of tens of millions of dollars for purposes of personal enrichment. The 1952 sugar crop was excessively large and downward adjustment of plantings in the two succeeding years were necessary. Revenues from various tax sources had been diverted and there had been lavish and suspicious resort to tariff and fiscal exemptions.

Accordingly, it became necessary to resort to deficit spending as a stopgap. In succeeding years, the budgets were balanced by resorting to corrective fiscal measures and finding new sources of revenue. In this situation, we issued Treasury notes to cover obligations that, because of the cyclical components in the economy, could not be met immediately from current revenues.

Within two years, we were able to end the critical situation we had inherited. The medicine was curbing wasteful government expenditures, while at the same time expanding Cuba's social and economic development plan. This fiscal policy resulted in the steady growth of real national income, which reached an all-time high in the last years of my administration.

HIGH BUDGETS

We maintained high budgets at all times with the conviction that government spending stimulated currency circulation and national wealth. In the 1957-1958 fiscal year, budgetary revenues reached the highest level in Cuba's history, $397,040,930, as compared with an estimated $309,459,260 during fiscal 1952-53, the first year of the revolutionary regime.

CUBAN GOVERNMENT REVENUES
(in millions of dollars)

Fiscal Year	Direct Taxation	Indirect Taxation	Other	Total
1955-56	78.1	254.3	13.2	345.6
1956-57	89.3	280.6	13.3	383.2
1957-57	106.6	275.7	14.8	397.1

Averaging this period, revenues came from the following sources:

Source of Revenue	Average Amount 1956-58 (in $ millions)	Percent of Total
Income Tax	70.5	18.5
Property taxes	30.7	8.1
Production & Consumption taxes	151.0	39.7
Taxes on foreign trade	108.8	28.7
Miscellaneous	17.9	5.0
Totals	378.9	100.0

A NEW FISCAL POLICY

My Government discarded the traditional motto of "everything that the government wants, whether rightly or wrongly" and substituted a fiscal policy of full conformity to law which, without resort to extraordinary measures, collected the revenues that were needed. This eliminated the misgivings of certain investors, who had been appalled at the multiplicity of taxes and the complexity of the Cuban tax system. Ambiguous legal opinions had created continuous controversies concerning the reach of the tax on dividends, which affected both domestic and foreign investors. To avoid further retroactive interpretations of fiscal regulations, we enacted Decree #1111 of April 22, 1955, which revised and eliminated many claims of the tax authorities in this area.

PERSONAL INCOME TAX

My first Administration had created this source of government revenue in addition to taxes on capital and corporate and real estate income.

To improve collection of revenue from these sources, we completely reformed the tax administration system by Law #318 of August 6, 1952, setting up mechanisms which would keep the Government correctly informed concerning income and capital and thus ending the widespread evasion of payment of these taxes. Organizations which specialized in economic matters assisted my Administration in this area. By Law #439 of October 4, 1952 and subsequent measures, we created a more flexible and efficient system and extended it to other agricultural, commercial and financial activities.

REAL ESTATE TAX

Here again, the problems of control, evasion of tax payment and irregular and erratic inspections created a chaotic situation. Law #1943 of January 22, 1955 modernized the legal basis, regulations and procedures, some of them dating back to 1892, of the tax on Real Estate and Transfers of Property. Tax evasion was reduced by listening to the suggestions of the taxpayers and treating them as partners of the Government.

TAX ON SUGAR

The sugar industry had been burdened with a variety of taxes,[1] the collection of which required a great deal of effort and expense by both Government and the industry. It had repeatedly

[1] These taxes were 10 cents levied by a 1917 law, 9 cents by a 1936 law, 6 cents by a 1940 law and 5 cents by a 1941 law. Molasses was taxed a quarter of a cent per gallon.

been proposed that these various taxes be consolidated into one. After a careful study of the matter, we did this by Law #1362 of April 10, 1954 and changed the basic assessment established in 1941. A single tax per 325 lbs. of sugar was established with the proviso that this amount would be retained when the capacity of the bags was reduced to 250 lbs. The same consolidation was applied to blackstrap molasses, which had previously been encumbered with five separate tax laws.

THE GREAT TARIFF REFORM

The tariff law which had been in effect since October 19, 1927 impeded the economic growth of the country. Accordingly, my government directed the National Economic Council to study the matter and propose reforms. A cabinet-level committee began to study the report of the Council on August 15, 1956.

The previous year, major changes had been instituted in nomenclature and definition of dutiable items. In accordance with our rule of consulting public opinion in a democratic fashion, public hearings were held in which all interested parties could express their views.

That part of the national output which was to be protected or simulated by tariffs was subjected to duty revision first, all changes being in strict accordance with our economic treaties and agreements.

One can gain a conception of the magnitude of the task when it is considered that there were 1,095 items and 5,505 sub-items, based on the Brussels nomenclature as adapted to the realities of our own economy, or a total of 6,600 items which had to be reviewed. This compared with the 1,075 items comprising the 1927 tariff.

CUSTOMS PROCEDURES

Cuba's first customs regulations were laid down in Military Order #173 of June 22, 1901. As these were quite inadequate for an administrative system, we ordered their complete reorganization on June 12, 1953. Laws #1337 of March 30, 1954 and #1952 of January 25, 1955 established an efficient and flexible system for customs clearance at the various ports of Cuba. Customs revenues had always been a major source of revenue for Cuba and, at the time of our emancipation from Spain, they were the preponderant source of government revenue.

PORT IMPROVEMENTS

By a law of July 24, 1917, a "port improvement tax" was collected at every Cuban port. This tax was later increased by 25% and revenue from this source during 1944-1952 amounted to $17,303,-400. The law provided that all port improvements were to be paid from these tax proceeds and that $500,000 was to be set aside yearly for general expenditures of the Republic.

During my first Administration, we completed a major dredging operation in the port of Cárdenas and built the largest wharf ever seen in Cuba, recompensing the contractor with certificates of completed work, bearing 5% interest, which were completely redeemed from the port improvement tax revenues when collected.

The success of this project was a stimulus to productive use of these tax revenues as, during the previous 20 years, the only thing that had been done in this area was dredging at the port of Isabela de Sagua with inadequate equipment, a project that never approached completion. Inadequate dredging operations at Cochinos Bay had been financed in part by loan funds.

We brought in technicians and specialists to consider the broad problem. They advised the use of powerful, modern equipment —suction dredges, which were very costly to purchase and operate. For efficient use, these dredges had to be kept in operation at maximum capacity. Unfortunately, we did not have the funds for the execution of this plan.

Accordingly, my second Administration, by Law #352 of August 21, 1952, covered project costs by pledging future revenues from the port improvement tax, paying the contractors deferred payment certificates of work done.

Once this financial device had been made operational, we were able to dredge the port of Isabela at the mouth of the Sagua la Grande river, to drain and improve the Paso Malo lagoon in Varadero and to do various other dredging jobs in Oriente, Camagüey, Pinar del Rio and Havana provinces. We were also able to clean the harbor of Havana by dredging the Marimelena inlet. This was indispensable to the maritime traffic of the Belot Oil Refinery and the new Shell refinery then under construction. The oil companies needed deep channels so that their large ocean-going tankers would have direct access.

NATIONAL ECONOMIC COUNCIL

We created the Economy Board by Decree #1437 of April 1, 1943 and later, by Law #2069 of January 27, 1955, transformed it into the National Economic Council (CNE) and gave it technical responsibility for making plans for the regulation and coordination of the Cuban economy to achieve high levels of employment, output and government income.

During the Auténtico era of 1944-1952, our economic policies were interrupted or discarded, a circumstance that aroused public opinion, especially in financial and business circles, and created a strong demand for tariff and fiscal reform.

Ever since national independence, the Cuban economy had been essentially an export economy. As long as policies were pursued which undermined the incentive to invest, industrial development was stagnant and a large portion of the Cuban people suffered from unemployment between sugar harvests. This condition was made worse by the mechanization of the sugar industry and by technological progress.

It was absolutely essential, therefore, to discover, stimulate and develop new sources of production. It would be no easy matter to find foreign markets for new Cuban products since this meant breaking down the tariff barriers against our goods.

The excessive dependence of our exports on sugar is illustrated by 1955-1958 figures. Sugar and its derivatives accounted for $563.3 millions of exports; minerals and metals for $47.2 millions; tobacco for $46.1 millions; food products for $24.6 millions; forest products for $7.8 millions and miscellaneous for $6.5 millions. Sugar thus accounted for 80% of the total.

STIMULATING INDUSTRY

This problem inspired the enactment of Law #1038 of August 15, 1953, governing guidance, regulation and protection of industrial development and reorganization of all existing rules and regulations in the interest of increasing employment levels. Three years after the enactment of Law #1038, Cuba had acquired

39 new industries under its protection. These had a permanent labor force of 6,858 workers and employees and had contributed additional production worth $48,850,071.

IMPROVING TRADE BALANCE

Thus, my Administration sponsored an economic development program that required: (a) purchase of machinery from abroad in considerable quantities, (b) imports of metals and other essential raw materials, and (c) increased fuel consumption.

While we still imported food products that could be grown at home, there was a strenuous effort to diversify agriculture, one that called for research, time and deployment of resources. With rising population and income, we could foresee substantial increases in grain consumption—particularly rice and wheat, which we imported to the extent of $59,500,000 in 1955 and $62,900,000 in 1958. We also had to import fats, certain fruits, vegetables and various preserves. Yet we were moving toward greater self-sufficiency in food production. Cuba's imports of U.S. farm products declined from $146,800,000 in 1957 to $132,300,000 in 1958. Nevertheless, Cuba remained the number one market for U.S. agricultural products, considerably larger than Mexico with $106 million and Venezuela with $84 million of agricultural imports in 1957.

MACHINERY AND FOREIGN EXCHANGE

If we wanted more industries, we had to import machinery and this required foreign exchange. In the four-year period 1955-58, we imported $439,900,000 worth of machinery. At the end of my administration, Cuba's dollar reserves were somewhat depleted. Yet in return, we had numerous flourishing industries, most of them entirely new to us, as a result of our efforts to stimulate industrial development. Many of these new plants could be readily seen, as they were adjacent to the Central Highway.

To achieve this great expansion in production, we did not knock at the doors of the International Bank for Reconstruction and Development or of the other international banks. We proved Cuba's ability to stand on her own feet and we carried out in practice the principle I had stated at the Panama Conference of 1955, namely, that "the raising of the standard of living of our peoples and the mobilization of our sources of wealth is the individual concern of each nation." I had added that, while international cooperation through negotiations, agreements and accords, was convenient, "we should not expect our principal aid to come from abroad."

14

The Public Debt

On March 10, 1952, we inherited three outstanding loans. The first was a credit of $11,200,000 which had been authorized by a law of August 29, 1905. The second was an $85,000,000 loan, authorized by a law of February 14, 1938, to fund obligations contracted by President Gerardo Machado in carrying out the Public Works Plan that gave Cuba the Central Highway, the National Capitol, the second Aguada del Cura aqueduct of Havana and other benefits. There were $48,218,800 bonds of this issue outstanding in December 1958. Third, there was a $25,000,000 issue, authorized in July 1948, to pay back pensions to veterans of the War of Independence. By Law #15 of November 22, 1949, another $120,000,000 had been borrowed for this purpose. Of these two Auténtico loans, $99,480,000 was still outstanding in 1958.

The Government of the 10th of March, therefore, assumed loans with a face value of $241,200,000, of which $86,983,900 had been amortized. The consolidated balance outstanding was slightly in excess of $155,000,000. In addition, we had to float loans of our own to promote the welfare of the nation.

NEW LOAN FLOTATIONS

From the outset, Cuban investors showed their confidence in our Administration. A $120,000,000 loan was floated to save the sugar industry from the collapse it faced as a result of the Auténtico blunder of permitting the mammoth sugar harvest of 1952.

Thereafter, three major long-term bond issues were floated for a total of $595,000,000. Moreover, medium and short-term Treasury obligations, amounting to $126,000,000, were floated. Thus, the aggregate of these obligations was $721,000,000, which was reduced by December 31, 1958 to $610,922,435 by full and prompt payment of interest and principle.

On taking power on March 10, 1952, we found that the national finances were in a state of chaos. One reason was the irresponsible authorization of the huge sugar crop of 1952 by the Prío government—a purely political measure. Another was that the reserves of private retirement funds had been embezzled in a scandalous manner. Moreover, high Auténtico officials had pretended to burn, and thus withdraw from circulation, tens of millions of dollars worth of bank notes, which were in reality simply stolen.

These felonies had disrupted public finances and undermined public confidence. Before launching our plans for social and economic development, we considered it essential to clean up this sordid mess and accordingly Law #925 "for the reform of the National Treasury" was passed on June 30, 1953.

Audits, completed by the Court of Accounts on December 31, 1951, had revealed a cash shortage in the Treasury of over $100,000,000. Most of this was due to the misuse of funds, collected by the Government as trustee for private institutions. The state had had the moral and legal duty to protect these funds, but, under Auténtico rule, it had done the opposite. The withdrawals were chiefly due to an internal loan, which had been floated without legal authority and without the consent of the creditors or depositors of the funds whose assets had been borrowed. Such consent was a *conditio sine qua non* in matters of this nature. To make the situation even worse, paper and worthless credit accounts from banks and firms that either no longer existed or had become totally insolvent were included in the balance sheet as Treasury assets.

The Law for the Reform of the National Treasury, together with other rulings and measures in the same area, took care of the cash shortage by authorizing the issuance of "credits on the Treasury" which were to be converted into Government bonds in the 1960 and 1961 fiscal years. After verification by the Court of Accounts, this issue was set at $100,000,000 and it covered all the claims of the social security funds and other groups defrauded by the Treasury under the previous Administration.

VETERANS, THE COURTS AND NEW PROJECTS

Law #1232 of December 28, 1953 authorized flotation of a $145,000,000 loan to consolidate five separate debts of the State.

No additional taxes were levied to service this consolidated issue. Funds from current taxes were used together with proceeds from the sale of stamps of the Building of the Tribunals and the Palace of Communications and two yearly grants: one of $1,200,000 from the National Lottery and another of $720,000 from the proceeds of the Public Works Tax Plan (Law #613 of 1952).

Holders of bonds of the five old issues were offered $74,000,000 in the new bonds in exchange. All but holders of $1,000,000 worth of the old bonds accepted, a remarkable testament to the financial solidity of the 10th of March administration. The $1,000,-000 in old bonds was redeemed with cash.

The proceeds from the new bond issue enabled us to provide the working capital of the Cuban Foreign Trade Bank and the equipment for the Cuban Institute of Technological Research—two organizations created by our Administration.

THE SOCIAL AND ECONOMIC DEVELOPMENT PLAN

To carry out the vast plan adumbrated by Law #1589 of August 4, 1954, it was necessary to attract domestic and foreign capital through a government bond issue. The funds thus obtained would be used for public improvements, profitable enterprises and social welfare services. Accordingly, a Fund for Social and Economic Development was instituted and the Chief Executive was authorized to issue bonds at 4%, payable in 30 years, up to a maximum of $350,000,000.

To make the public believe that the borrowing was much greater than it actually was, the Communists circulated a rumor to the effect that other debts, over and above the $350,000,000 issue, had been incurred by the Bank of Economic and Social Development (BANDES) to the extent of $235,000,000. This was the approximate amount of the financing done by BANDES with these funds, but it represented an asset, rather than a liability, since those who had borrowed it owed BANDES the money. In other words, the investors in the loan were creditors of the Government; the Government was a creditor of BANDES and BANDES was a creditor of those to whom it had lent the money. Since profitable projects were involved, these loans were liquidated without encumbering the taxpayer and while benefitting the national economy.

OBLIGATIONS OF THE STATE

The Cuban practice had been to consider that the various outlays in the budget should be met from the corresponding revenues. This created the anomaly that the State, which is always and juridically the same person, took a different attitude toward its various debts, depending on when they were created and what sources of revenue they laid claim upon.

It was detrimental to the nation that surpluses in preceding budgets should be allocated to "special credits," while legitimate debts of the nation remained unpaid because the specific budget income sources upon which they were to draw were inadequate.

The only moral attitude was to pay off the legitimate creditors of the State promptly. When these payments could not be made in cash and when due, because of lagging governmental collections, then the creditors were at least entitled to get negotiable instruments drawn on the Treasury and acceptable in payment of taxes. Of course, these debts would appear in subsequent budgets either as debit items or as a deduction from receipts in the year that they fell due.

This situation prompted the promulgation of Law #1225 of December 15, 1953, providing that all legitimate obligations of the State were to be paid from the nation's revenues. This law also provided for the issuance of promissory notes in payment of current government obligations. These notes could be transferred by bank endorsement and thus were bearer instruments.

Until then, unpaid obligations of the state had constituted what was known as "the floating debt," that is, the eternal deferment of payment, since there was no provision for their inclusion in subsequent budgets.

Our promissory notes matured within a year, bore no interest and could not be issued in a total amount greater than 20% of average annual government revenue during the preceding five years.

We used this instrumentality whenever it was desirable as

we did the Treasury notes. Both were normal administrative devices, almost routine in the public finances of democratic countries. They brought about eminently satisfactory economic results.

THE PUBLIC DEBT UNDER CASTRO

Many ignorant, naïve and gullible people swallowed the Communist propaganda which sought to discredit the fiscal policies of my Administration as spendthrift or unsound. The same people who spread the lie of the "20,000 corpses" and the fantasy of a public debt of $1,400,000,000 went into an orgy of inflationary public spending as soon as their turn arrived.

The total addition to the Cuban national debt, as of December 30, 1960, was $644,795,000. More recent figures are provided by *Un Estudio sobre Cuba,* which has already been cited. According to this, the public debt of Cuba, *without including obligations of the State in private hands,* amounted on April 26, 1961 to $1,119,664,065, of which $45,485,000 represented foreign debt.[1] By now, the Communist regime has no doubt created a much greater public debt than the $1,400,000,000 its lying propagandists charged my government with having incurred.

[1] Álvarez Díaz, *op. cit.,* p. 1,373.

15

Banking, Currency and National Income

The Revolution of September 4th occurred at a time of economic and financial collapse. Cuban exports had fallen from $272,440,-000 in 1929 to $84,391,000 in 1933, or by more than two-thirds. This was almost entirely due to the decline in sugar exports from $216,590,000 to $61,255,000. There was an even greater reduction in Cuban imports, which fell from $216,215,000 in 1929 to $42,-362,000 in 1933 or by three-fourths.

Government revenues shrank to a fraction of normal. Currency in circulation declined from $72,186,000 to $46,816,000, while demand deposits shrank from $119,046,000 to $56,273,000. Payment media per capita had plummeted from $54.25 in 1929 to $26.03 in 1933, a decline of over 50%. Moreover, bank loans dropped by 58% from $241,700,000 to $101,725,000. The banks still held in their portfolios millions of dollars worth of dubious loans which had been contracted before the 1920 sugar crash. In fact, bank loans contracted subsequently to 1921 were almost entirely related to sugar production. For instance in 1933, bank acceptances totaled only $2,295,000. In addition, there were $33,700,000 of obligations contracted abroad with collateral of $19,333,000, consisting of cash deposits and short-term assets.

The Revolution began under these inauspicious economic conditions. One of the Government's primary tasks was to restore faith and hope in the hearts of the people.

CURRENCY

In those days, our money consisted of paper bills, silver, nickel and bronze coins from the United States and $12,693,700 in Cuban silver and nickel coins, the value of which had been maintained at par with the dollar, even under the most adverse conditions, ever since they had been minted by the law of October 29, 1914 under the administration of President Menocal.

The issuance of paper currency, or silver certificates, was an achievement of the Revolution. After several attempts, the first of which occurred toward the very end of President Machado's tenure of office,[1] the first issue of $10,000,000 was authorized by Law #670 of November 9, 1937.

Successive mintings of silver coinage became necessary to stimulate our economy. This induced speculators to engage in agiotage and soon the value of our currency depreciated. When $10,000,000 worth was minted in 1935, the peso was at first quoted at a small discount from the dollar. This continued after the minting of another $20,000,000 worth as authorized on June 22, 1936. When another $20,000,000 was coined (Law of June 23, 1938), the discount widened because of the expectation of further mintings. This discount reached its maximum 12 27/32% in December 1938.

Drastic measures, adopted through Decree #1358 of June 10, 1939 brought these dangerous developments to an end. Banks were required to keep reserves in the proportions established by law. The Monetary Stabilization Fund was created to service the foreign debt and maintain the international value of the peso. Exporters of sugar and molasses were required to exchange 20% of their dollar earnings for pesos at par. This was later increased to 30% of the total value of exports. Eventually, we were able to make both American and Cuban currencies legal tender and provide for their exchange at par by Act of Congress.

As a result of these measures, the discount declined steadily, reaching an all-time low of 1/16th of 1% in December 1942. *In the following month, the Cuban peso was quoted at a premium over the dollar and throughout 1943 the peso was in so much demand that more than 70% of government revenue was col-*

[1] Law of May 16, 1933. Machado resigned on August 12, 1933.

lected in pesos. Thus, within a short period of time, the Cuban peso had become one of the strongest currencies in the New World.

THE GOLD RESERVE

I recommended that Congress approve a law which would back the silver certificates with a reserve of gold bullion and dollar exchange. This was enacted on May 5, 1942. The Government then proceeded to exchange silver certificates for United States currency and to use the latter to buy gold bullion, which we deposited in the vaults of the Federal Reserve Bank of New York. This gold purchase program began on May 3, 1943 with an authorized purchase of $15,000,000 worth. When I left office in October 1944, Cuba had a gold reserve of $99,999,138.

THE FIRST STEPS

There were four major financial obstacles to economic development of the country: inadequate internal credit, the dual currency system, lack of a national banking system and lack of bullion reserves.

I determined to create the necessary economic and financial instruments for the solution of these problems as I had promised during the 1940 electoral campaign. We obtained the advice of a United States technical mission, comprising agricultural credit experts and specialists from the Treasury and the Board of Governors, Fedeal Reserve System. After several weeks of intensive work, the commission turned in a valuable report, which recommended the creation of a Cuban central bank and the reorganization of the Monetary Stabilization Fund.

Considerably before this, in fact in 1936, we had established the Technical Committee on Banking and Currency Legislation. Its recommendations had served as the basis for the laws which ended speculation in our silver currency. For six months (June to December 1937), the Technical Committee had stayed in Washington, where it drafted plans for the creation of a Supreme Banking Council, a Bank of the Republic and an Agricultural Credit Bank. It also proposed reforms in our currency system and a law regulating banking.

The report of the Technical Committee was widely circulated among individuals and corporations interested in banking. Later, it was submitted to the Senate (a body which had been apprehensive about such measures in 1921 and 1922), which opened public hearings on these projects at which the leading banking, economic and financial spokesmen testified.

While these public hearings were still in progress, the Technical Committee presented two reports on legislative projects and banking legislation which provided the foundations for our national bank.

This was not a favorable moment for enactment of the needed legislation. The project was interrupted by political opposition and intense concentration on electoral matters. Yet these plans resulted—six years later—in the creation of the National Bank of Cuba (BNC) and its associated institution, the National Bank of Agricultural and Industrial Development (BANFAIC).

THE NATIONAL BANK OF CUBA

The creation of the National Bank of Cuba marked a turning point toward vigorous development of our resources. I decided to extend its activities into fields which, if they had been foreseen by law, had not been defined there.

A policy of freedom of exchange made me dictate measures repealing various wartime financial controls and give the Monetary Stabilization Fund additional powers connected with exchange controls, compliance with payment agreements, movement of foreign exchange and regulation of the gold standard (Law #569 of December 1, 1952).

Law #384 of September 9, 1952 provided the National Bank of Cuba with a broader and more solid structure. It regulated three essential activities of the Bank: deposit insurance, procedure in cases of payment suspension or liquidation of private banks and rules for certain specialized banking institutions.

DEPOSIT INSURANCE

The purpose of deposit insurance was to encourage saving and create an atmosphere of security, eliminating the lack of public confidence in banks caused by the bank failures of 1920 and other periods. These failures had left the country in crisis and desolation. We decided to follow the procedures of countries with a vigorous economy, which tend to insure all forms of wealth, including deposits.

This insurance covered depositors of member banks of the National Bank up to $10,000. It guaranteed payment, in the event of failure of the depository bank, to the depositors through the Depositors' Insurance Fund. This Fund was supervised by a committee comprising the Minister of Finance, the President of the National Bank and a representative of the stockholders. It operated with a capital of $10,000,000.

By extending the same deposit insurance system which prevailed in the United States banking system, the Depositors' Insurance Fund destroyed the incentive to place savings deposits in the United States rather than in Cuba.

The Fund was authorized to issue obligations, if necessary, at an interest rate not higher than the lowest rediscount rate of the National Bank, to be purchased by retirement and pension funds and social security institutions created by law.

The powers of the National Bank to intervene to protect the insured depositors and the other creditors of associated banks were carefully defined. If the situation of the bank subject to intervention was such that suspension of operations became advisable, the Depositors' Insurance Fund was specifically authorized to take over administration as trustee for the depositors and to adopt all necessary measures to protect the rights of the parties affected.

SAVINGS AND LOAN ASSOCIATIONS

Law #384 defined the requirements which savings and loan associations must meet and provided for their regulation and for cases of liquidation. Thus, even though they were not covered by the Depositors' Insurance Fund, the depositors in these banks were given maximum security.

The flourishing condition of these institutions under our Administration is shown by the table. Figures are in millions of dollars.

Year	Capital	Assets	Subscriptions	Reserve
1953	2.9	32.5	28.3	26.8
1954	3.0	35.8	31.5	30.0
1955	3.2	38.4	34.2	32.6
1956	3.6	40.8	35.6	33.7
1957	3.6	42.3	36.8	34.8
1958	3.8	43.2	37.2	35.1

BANKING OPERATIONS

As a result of our policy of regulating banks to increase their security, they flourished. The figures which follow cover the consolidated operations of the 15 banks associated with the National Bank of Cuba. Again, figures are in millions of dollars:

Year	Capitalization	Savings Deposits	Total Deposits	Loans
1951	37.1	113.6	667.7	394.7
1952	41.7	141.2	656.0	461.1
1953	40.8	159.6	629.0	427.8
1954	45.4	178.6	635.0	466.1
1955	49.3	212.2	704.0	532.5
1956	67.0	293.5	948.0	666.1
1957	74.2	395.8	1,089.9	784.5
1958	77.3	443.7	1,076.7	836.3

The above data, taken from the Annual Reports of the National Bank of Cuba, cover calendar years and reveal the impact of our economic policies after 1954 and the uninterrupted growth to new record highs of banking capital, savings, total deposits and loans. In 1957 and 1958, bank deposits exceeded one billion dollars. As for loans, the flow of private capital to business and industry also reached levels that have never been equalled.

To increase the resources of the banking system, we required all private retirement funds to deposit with any of ten banks approved by the National Bank for funds of official institutions. This placed at least $100,000,000 a year into the circulation of the banking system.

The operations of the new Cuban Clearing Chamber, which replaced the old Havana Clearing House, reflect the financial progress made during my Administration:

Year	Bank Clearings (millions of dollars)	Index
1951	4,130	100.0
1952	4,738	114.5
1953	4,237	102.5
1954	4,411	107.6
1955	5,045	122.1
1956	5,792	140.2
1957	6,746	163.2
1958	6,909	167.2

CURRENCY IN CIRCULATION

When banknotes of the National Bank of Cuba were substituted for the old silver certificates, further minting of silver coins ceased except for those needed in the normal course of business and except for a few patriotic and commemorative mintings, such as that celebrating the Golden Jubilee of the Republic in 1952 and the Centennial of José Martí in 1953. The last also served the purpose of introducing the new 50-cent and 25-cent pieces to replace the old 40-cent and 20-cent coins.

When I left office at the end of my first Administration in 1944, $234,125,212 of silver certificates were in circulation. These were backed by a reserve of $79,850,000 in silver and $151,240,982 in gold. This reserve ratio of 98.09% was the highest in our history.

When I again took power in 1952, National Bank of Cuba bills to the value of $393,624,894 were in circulation. In 1958 at the end of my Administration, $488,500,000 were out. This was backed by 55.4% more reserves than the 25% coverage prescribed by law.

After the tragic seizure of power in January 1959, a grim story of financial wrecking slowly began to unfold. In 1960, the gold reserves began to vanish while the printing presses were kept busy making additional paper money. This destruction of the monetary reserve and of the peso as a store and standard of value would have been incomprehensible had it not constituted an integral part of the Communist plan to expropriate the thrifty and to wreck the Cuban economy.

NATIONAL INCOME AND GNP

In 1957, the gross national product of Cuba was $2,803,300,000, an all-time high. The following tabulation shows the movement of Cuban national income from 1902 to the end of 1958 by Administration. The figures were compiled by the National Bank of Cuba and are in millions of dollars.

Administrations	*Average National Income* (in millions of dollars)
Tomás Estrada Palma (1902-06)	232
Charles E. Magoon (1906-09) (U.S. military intervention)	244
José Miguel Gómez (restoration of the Republic)	335
Mario G. Menocal (1913-21) (World War I boom)	676
Alfredo Zayas (1921-25) (Period of postwar readjustment)	708
Gerardo Machado (1925-33) (Great Depression)	563
Provisional Governments (1933-36) (Period of transition)	364
Miguel M. Gómez (1936) (Period of transition)	510
Federico Laredo Brú (1936-40) (Period of readjustment)	500
Fulgencio Batista (1940-44) (World War II)	883
Ramón Grau San Martín (1944-48) (Inflation)	1,400
Carlos Prío Socarrás (1948-52) (Korean War and Marshall Plan)	1,773
Fulgencio Batista (1952-58) (Social and economic development)	2,053

Of this Gross National Product, which rose during my first six years of office from 2.1 to 2.8 billion dollars, the proportion taken by government expenditure fluctuated between 12.4% and 13.2%.

This is very modest in comparison with the United States and Western Europe.

Prior to 1956, the increase in national income was due to the effect of loan-financed public works, to private investment and to a higher value for exports, in that order. These factors changed in quantity and position in 1957 in favor of private enterprise. This was primarily due to a larger sugar crop than that of 1956 sold at more advantageous prices. This accounted for 73% of the $343,-100,000 increase.

This bonanza situation was reflected in the growth of the National Bank of Cuba, the assets of which rose from $650 million in 1952 to $891 million by mid-1958. Its capital of $5.7 million in 1952 almost tripled in the ensuing six years. In a 1956 report, the U. S. Department of Commerce concluded: "Cuban national income has reached levels which give the Cuban people one of the highest standards of living in Latin America." [2]

[2] U. S. Department of Commerce, *Investment in Cuba,* Government Printing Office, Washington, D. C., 1956, p. 184.

16

Financing Production, Foreign Trade and Fishing

As we saw it, the National Bank should not be limited to the conventional activities of a central bank of issue and rediscount. It was to become the nucleus of a congeries of financial organizations which, through long-term investments, would make available the capital resources required for the nation's economic development.

To achieve this, it was not necessary to change the National Bank's fundamental charter, but merely to complement it with other institutions. The creation in 1952 of the deposit insurance system and later, in 1958, of the National Institute of Reinsurance, put the nation on the road to continued economic and financial progress, even beyond the heights attained in 1957. Only the victory of international communism prevented these prospects from being realized.[1]

The nationalist solution to the problem of sugar overproduction in 1952 showed that private enterprise was prepared to assume risks and bear responsibilities in the realization of a master plan for economic development. We were able to attract savings and stimulate a high level of investment in Cuban development. The National Bank contributed to this dynamic forward movement of the economy.

[1] Testifying before the Senate Internal Security Subcommittee on August 30, 1960, former U. S. Ambassador to Cuba Earl E. T. Smith said: "Nineteen hundred and fifty-seven was one of the best years in the economic history of Cuba." *Communist Threat to the United States Through the Caribbean, Hearings,* Part 9, p. 694.

AGRICULTURAL AND INDUSTRIAL DEVELOPMENT

The Agricultural and Industrial Development Bank of Cuba (BANFAIC) was created with a capital of $25,000,000. Its first operations were highly successful and by December 31, 1958, it had extended $103,005,700 of agricultural and $43,215,570 of industrial loans. Of these, only $430,000 had been advanced prior to the Revolution of the 10th of March 1952. No less than 148 borrowers, most of them new industries, obtained loans from the Industrial Branch of BANFAIC. The Bank's loan contribution to Cuban economic development totaled $146,221,270.

NATIONAL FINANCE CORPORATION

Article 49 of the Organic Law of the National Bank of Cuba banned loans or advances to provinces, municipalities, autonomous corporations of government or private individuals. Nevertheless, such loans were necessary and accordingly the National Finance Corporation (*Financiera Nacional de Cuba*) was created by Law #1015 of August 1, 1953. In doing so, we were exercising the power deriving from Article 264 of the Constitution "to regulate the development of national wealth by carrying out public improvement projects to be paid, wholly or in part, by those who benefit from them."

The *Financiera Nacional* was organized as an autonomous entity, representing both government and private interests. Insurance companies and private banks were equally represented with the State in subscribing its initial capital of $4,000,000. By June 30, 1958, its capitalization had increased to $6,326,955.

The goals of the new organization were to finance income-producing public projects to the extent that they were self-liquidating, to stimulate public savings and to issue securities, backed by the income-in-escrow of specific projects being financed.

The achievements of the National Finance Corporation were enormous. These included: the tunnel built under Havana Harbor; five aqueducts, among them South Bend (*Cuenca Sur*), which solved the water problem of the nation's capital and of Marianao; the expansion of the Standard Oil Refinery on the Havana waterfront; two maritime terminals; three supermarkets; the Windward Tourist Center (*Centro Turístico de Barlevento*) near the capital and the completion of the Municipal Palace of Marianao. In addition, there was the first hydroelectric power plant of Cuba (PRICHEC), the completion of which on schedule was made impossible by the spread of 26th of July terrorism.

The National Finance Corporation also contributed $36,000,000 to the building and expansion program of the Cuban Power Company. Launched in 1954, this $135,000,000 project involved the issue of bonds, which were promptly bought up by Cuban investors. When common stock of the Cuban Telephone Company was offered the public a short time thereafter, the response was equally favorable.

SOCIAL AND ECONOMIC DEVELOPMENT

Back in the old days after the 1933 Revolution, we had worked very hard to put across a modest three-year plan. Since the Cuban economy was still under the influence of depression, the task had been difficult.

In the 1950s, the situation was entirely different. In the course of a few weeks, we floated two large loans: one of $120,000,000 to finance the sugar surplus and another of $145,000,000 for public improvements and consolidation of previous bond issues. Cuban investors, who had welcomed the 10th of March Revolution with sighs of relief, promptly absorbed these bonds.

Our plans for development were based on some of the views I had expressed at the Inter-American Summit Conference at Panama in 1955. There I had said that the development of their national resources by the Latin American Republics individually was essential, particularly for those nations which had not yet reached a high level of economic and social evolution.

It was imperative that Cuba cease to be a monoculture, dependent for its economic health on the hazards of the sugar crop and of the world sugar market. We would have to diversify our production and, through progressive industrialization of the nation, free ourselves from dependency on foreigners.

Accordingly, the Bank of Social and Economic Development (BANDES) was created with a capital of $15,000,000 by Law #1947 of January 22, 1955. BANDES was to complement the activities of the National Bank, which, by virtue of its role as a bank of issue and central bank, was not allowed to use its assets for long-term loans or the purchase of long-term obligations, with the exception of regulated open-market transactions in government securities.

BANDES was a special bank to provide resources and make advance payments to autonomous credit institutions and banks, enabling them to finance development projects comprised in the master plan for social and economic development. In these transactions, the securities which the borrower might issue or advance would be discounted or else medium- or long-term loans would be made with them as collateral.

Every loan application was closely scrutinized. When accepted, the issue was backed by a first preferential mortgage on the private company and the BANDES subsidiary. This system created a new market for capital, encouraged and protected domestic savings and attracted foreign capital to Cuba.

Finally, the minimum capitalization of Cuban banks was established at $500,000 with an additional $25,000 for each branch in order to offer greater protection to the banking system and to depositors. The banks were authorized to hold government securities up to 40% of their reserves and to subscribe to and float government issues, in certain types of banking operations, up to 10% of their deposits.

FRUITFUL RESULTS

The operations of BANDES were highly successful as contributions to our effort to secure the economic independence of Cuba. The following tabulation shows the breakdown of BANDES loans and investments:

BANDES LOANS AND INVESTMENTS
(in millions of dollars)

Category	Amount	
(A) Transportation:		
Aviation	20.5	
Railways	69.7	
Maritime	0.1	
Motor	21.9	
SUBTOTAL	——	112.2

(B) Industrial:

Chemical	26.5	
Stone, Cement & Ceramics	4.0	
Metals & Metallurgical	21.3	
Packing	1.1	
Foodstuffs	1.2	
Textile	1.2	
Industrial City	16.0	
SUBTOTAL	——	71.3

(C) Miscellaneous:

Government Departments	14.2	
Banking Institutions	7.7	
Toll Highways	40.0	
Tourist Centers and Hotels	55.3	
Maritime Projects	55.4	
Labor Unions (loans)	1.1	
Private and Public Construction	36.7	
Sugar Industry	29.8	
Electric Power Output	20.0	
Communications and Mapping	14.0	
SUBTOTAL	——	274.2
GRAND TOTAL		457.7

FOREIGN TRADE EXPANSION

With a capital of $3,500,000, the Cuban Bank of Foreign Trade (BCCE) was created by Law #1425 of May 12, 1954 to finance the development and promotion of foreign trade, assisting private enterprise where necessary.

The BCCE was highly successful in winning new markets. The stimulus it gave Burley tobacco producers was a decisive factor in getting this variety of tobacco into world markets. It financed the purchase of 13 merchant ships with a total tonnage of 39,277 tons. It cooperated in improving the coffee crop, initiating new export policies and arranging through its channels for shipment of $15,000,000 worth of coffee overseas. Results would have been even more impressive had it not been for the ravages of Castro and his outlaws in the coffee-producing zones, particularly those of Oriente. Sugar sales through this organization to countries which had not been regular customers of Cuba totaled $120,000,000. The BCCE arranged for the display of Cuban agricultural and industrial products at several international fairs, thus opening new and promising markets for them. The Bank filled another function of vital importance by closing transactions in non-convertible currencies.

Under the Communists, the Bank was transformed into the Bank for Cuba's Foreign Trade (Law #793 of April 25, 1960). As such, it became an instrument of the State monopoly over foreign trade. It seized control over foreign exchange and became the totalitarian agency for a variety of barter and compensation deals.

NEW HORIZONS FOR FISHING

The reorganization of the fishing industry and its modernization to provide a better living for the fishermen and a more varied, abundant and inexpensive diet of seafoods became a high priority objective of my second Administration. A parallel development of the canning industry was necessary to preserve the products of the fisheries and increase demand for them.

Thirteen thousand persons depended directly and another 10,-000 indirectly on fishing from the sea for their livelihood. This was one vital dimension to the problem. Another was the need for a larger output of seafood to supply proteins during the dry season, which is a period of meat shortage.

In my 1952 campaign, I had pledged myself to get special legislation on fisheries enacted so that the industry would be coordinated and guided by appropriate organizations under the direction of men with great experience in the field. The first step was to ease the requirements for fishing licenses (Law #47 of May 5, 1952). The second step was to create the National Association of Owners of Fishing Vessels for the protection of the interests of the industry (Law #1670 of August 28, 1954). A Center of Fishing Research, which was already in existence, was attached to BANFAIC as was the Felipe Poey Fishermen's Credit Association, comprising the owners of the Havana fishing fleet.

In February 1953, we purchased a refrigerator ship with 500,-000 pounds capacity. A wharf at Tallapiedra docks in Havana was transferred to BANFAIC for research. The Research Center came up with very valuable findings concerning oysters, groupers, bonitos and shrimp. It designed low-cost, highly versatile fishing vessels capable of sailing both over shallow waters and the smaller weedbeds and over the open ocean with complete seaworthiness.

One of the results of the research program was the discovery of a large shrimp bank in the waters to the south of Cuba. This was important enough to warrant the purchase of a large shrimp trawler, the Don Carlos de la Torre. This was the first step toward providing the nation with an oceanographic institute, equipped with high frequency detectors, circular nets and special fluorescent lights used in fishing for shrimp and sardines.

After carefully considering all angles of the problem and after a series of tests, soundings and trips to the shrimp beds (which I joined when my brief Presidential weekends permitted), the Minister of Agriculture and his staff of technicians and fishermen came up with practical proposals. These were embodied in Law #1891 of March 11, 1955. This created the National Institute of Fishing (INP) with full responsibility for taking the initiative in exploiting the resources of the sea. Other activities, also of importance, such as sport fishing, were also represented in the Institute. Flexible closed seasons were proclaimed to conserve fish and crustaceans which were approaching depletion or extinction. Regulations were issued on the use of trawler nets and purse seines to protect young species.

During the first year of the National Fishing Institute's operations, the production of seafood totalled $5,451,225 as against $2,474,100 in 1951. Despite her great marine wealth, Cuba had been importing about $6,000,000 worth of codfish, sardines, herring and other species, chiefly from Canada and Norway.

Government initiative and the expansion of the fishing industry gave a vigorous stimulus to the canning industry. In 1957, there were ten factories in Cuba which canned 2,400,000 pounds of bonito and 200,000 pounds of lobster. Thus, most of the difficulties, caused by inadequate fishing vessels, obsolete equipment and antiquated methods, had been overcome.

The supply of fish and other seafoods tends to fluctuate wildly. Many species roam over vast expanses of ocean. Others migrate to distant places. It is not unusual to find what appears to be a great bank in the midst of a productive fishing area vanish almost completely in the course of a few days.

To initiate the Cuban fisherman in the modern practice of his vocation by direct training in large, up-to-date vessels, the INP contracted for the use of the Japanese ship, *Sumiyosi Maru*, enrolling native fishermen for training on board her. In the first five trips through Cuban waters, which served to explore the coastal shelf and deep waters as well, 3,209,350 pounds of fish were caught.

The continuous and powerful northers of the winter of 1957 damaged many boats. To make the necessary repairs and keep the crews active, the smaller shipowners had to apply to the State for loans. A government-endorsed credit of $102,170 was extended through BANDES to 40 small shipowners.

On January 28, 1958, we laid the cornerstone of a great fishing terminal in the port of Havana, equipped to handle 60,000 pounds of seafood every eight hours, with cold storage capacity for a million pounds of seafood, warehouses able to handle another 100,000 pounds and with all the space and equipment needed for processing, packing, canning, deepfreezing and waste conversion. Once the fishing terminal was finished, the ships would no longer have to wait for days at sea before they could berth and unload their catches. We believed that, with the terminal in operation, the fishing industry would become more profitable and the shipowners would overcome their reluctance to give their crews a more generous share of the catch and their aversion to testing new techniques and methods for developing the riches of the ocean.[2]

[2] The Communist regime has taken credit for the Fishing Terminal as it has for other projects it inherited. An example of its propaganda is in the February 26, 1961 issue of *Bohemia*, which states: "The fishing terminal represents an investment of $15,000,000; it has cold storage capacity for one million pounds of fish, with a freezing and processing plant . . . The cornerstone of the Fishing Terminal was laid during the tyranny of Batista, but nothing was done to go ahead with the project. The purpose of the Terminal was to control, through this wharf, which is more than 100 feet long, the complete supply of seafood arriving in Havana, thus killing the other fifty fishing ports throughout the Island."

17

Land Reform and Rural Credit

Land reform was needed in Cuba and, during my two Administrations, we proceeded with a variety of reform measures in the interests of the peasants and designed to increase and diversify crop production. We would have gone further, in a responsible and constitutional manner, if we had had the time. At no time did we consider the revolutionary seizure of private holdings of individuals without compensation, judicial process or recognition of property rights. The Communist version of land reform inevitably destroys the foundations of justice and freedom.

The true agrarian reform began in Cuba when my Administration introduced measures which assured coffee growers fair returns and gave the workers a minimum wage and a pay scale which fluctuated with the market price of unhusked beans. A resurgence of a prosperous coffee agriculture, which had almost vanished between the last Wars of Independence and the 1933 Revolution, became visible in the mountainous regions of three of our provinces. The next step was to grant land from the national domain to the peasants and then to recognize the right of tenants and squatters to remain on the lands of the sugar plantations under the conditions or contracts in effect.

That was the first phase of a genuine, practical and nationalist agrarian revolution. The second, the Law of Sugar Coordination established equilibrium among the three key factors in the industry without disturbing the free play of competition. Small growers—those producing less than 750,000 pounds of cane[1]—were given special protection, which was later extended to all subtenants and other elements with modest economic power in sugar cultivation. We also eased the payment of debt, regulated the rentals on coffee fincas and provided a flexible wage scale for cutting, hoisting and hauling sugar cane, which varied with the price of sugar, but which could not fall below established minima.

THE AGRARIAN PROGRAM

The 1953 Population Census revealed that 43% of the people of Cuba lived in the countryside. Yet the nation was importing $150,000,000 of foodstuffs which could have been grown at home. Major reforms in agriculture were obviously necessary and it was equally essential that they be coordinated in a general plan. Starting with the premise that the peasant's tenure of his land must be considered fundamental, we formulated an eight-point agrarian program based on recognition of the right of private ownership:

(1) Promotion of agricultural production, especially of foodstuffs.

(2) Establishment of centers of agricultural information, technical, economic and marketing assistance.

(3) Teaching the peasant families to reorganize and improve their methods of tillage.

(4) Development of agricultural cooperatives on a nationwide scale.

(5) Reorganization of rural education to provide more practical teaching and to inculcate the advantages and techniques of cooperatives.

(6) Construction of a network of paved highways and gravel roads to improve access of farm produce to distribution centers and consumer markets.

(7) Reconstruction and rehabilitation of farm housing.

(8) Development of rural credit institutions to free the farmer from usury and ensure that he be the master of the land and never its slave.

This program was launched with the full cooperation of the

[1] There were 13,641 of them who produced a total of 4,284,593,750 pounds of cane.

creative forces of private enterprise and within the democratic framework of a free country with free institutions. The results, in most cases, surpassed our expectations.

THE PEASANT AND THE LAND

We enacted Law #247 of July 17, 1952 to benefit the small tenant farmers who lacked title to the land and to increase governmental guidance to agriculture. This statute protected the tenure of all farmers who had been in possession of farms of 167 acres or less on March 10, 1952. These peasants and farmers were given immediate peaceful and guaranteed possession "to be followed by complete and definitive ownership of the land and by the organization of producers' cooperatives . . ."

Law #247 protected the poor peasants who had always lived under conditions of insecurity on land owned by others. They were unable to secure their tenure at law because they could not afford the complicated litigation involved. The new law set up simple and inexpensive procedures for validating legitimate tenure within the framework of private property. Law #288 of August 1, 1952 gave further protection to peasants and farmers with less than 167 acres.

As a temporary, emergency measure before promulgation of Law #247, we proclaimed on June 3, 1952 a moratorium on landlord proceedings to evict tenants from farm land. The existing laws on landlord-tenant relationships gave inadequate protection to the parties concerned. As a result, there were minor disorders which had an adverse effect on production and food supply. The stay of eviction proceedings was designed to insure uninterrupted production on those lands which were subject to litigation until the disputes could be finally and expeditiously settled under the new agrarian law.

COMMUNAL FARMS

There had been constant clamor from the possessors of holdings, known in our country as communal farms, for the legal establishment of their permanent right of possession of the land they had tilled for years. This matter was complicated by the heated controversies of opposing interests, which had sought since the beginning of the Republic to have these lands divided. They had been unsuccessful. For our part, we intended to try to do it. We promulgated Law #297 of August 5, 1952, which terminated all litigations concerning boundaries under Military Order #62 of 1902. This law also terminated all other proceedings and established the right of peasants, who had been in possession of lands within the communal farms for more than one year, to record their titles.

Numerous legal actions were brought under this statute, but, in the case of the San Felipe Ranch at Holguín, the Supreme Court ruled that four articles of Law #297 were unconstitutional. Our Administration naturally obeyed the ruling of the Court. New legislation was enacted, in accordance with the Supreme Court majority decision.

LAND MONOPOLIES

We were desirous of limiting excessively large land holdings without destroying efficient agricultural production. We protected the interests of the peasants in this area without adopting collectivism.

By contrast, the Castro regime completely disregarded the principle of eminent domain with just compensation, one universally recognized by civilized society. Land was expropriated without reference even to the Communist Law of Agrarian Reform, whereupon the victims were offered so-called compensation in the form of "bonds," which the Government did not even bother to print!

When expropriated farmers dared to take their case to the Supreme Court, they were threatened and intimidated. The label of "counterrevolutionary" was pinned on those who opposed these arbitrary procedures. This constitutes a felony under the laws of the dictatorship and subjects the "guilty" party to long prison sentences or execution by firing squad.

The cattle industry, a shining example of Cuban hard work and initiative, was almost totally destroyed by the Communist regime. On December 31, 1958, there were 5,385,000 head of cattle in the pastures of Cuba. The typical Cuban cattleman worked hard to keep his pastures in good shape, sought to improve his herds by careful breeding with top-quality animals and struggled without rest to increase his herds and put more fat on his animals. He was driven from his land by the so-called agrarian reform. The result was that a prosperous industry, which had done a great deal to improve the diet of the Cuban people, was destroyed by neglect and incompetence. Castro and his Communist henchmen cared so little for their country that they shipped even breeding cattle to Russia, allowing Cuba to go hungry. The poultry industry was wrecked in similar fashion with the result that chickens and eggs are scarcely obtainable in Communist Cuba.

MECHANIZATION OF AGRICULTURE

To increase farm output, we had to mechanize agriculture. The team of oxen had to be replaced by the tractor, the rumbling oxcart by the pneumatic tire. Since a large part of the farm population was too poor to purchase the new equipment, the Government provided (Law #506 of November 1, 1952) the necessary funds and established agricultural committees in each municipality to assist the poorer farmers in tilling their fields, providing them with the use of whatever mechanical equipment they needed.

The first purchase comprised 980 pieces of equipment, including 162 tractors. The following year, tractor-plowed acreage ran into the millions and hundreds of irrigation wells had been drilled.

AGRICULTURAL AND MINING COOPERATIVES

The Executive Committee of Agricultural and Mining Cooperatives (CENCAM) was created by Law #1642 of August 14, 1954 to accomplish the following objectives on a nationwide scale:

(1) Build irrigation and pumping stations.

(2) Provide silos and other grain-storage facilities.

(3) Set up ore concentration plants.

(4) Pursue economic measures to increase agricultural and mining output through use of modern equipment, providing the farmers and miners with technical education as to its use.

(6) Diversify farm production.

The first project of CENCAM was in the rich, extensive rice zone of Consolación del Sur in Pinar del Rio. CENCAM provided the farmers of the zone with tractors, plows, grading equipment, planters, fumigators, harvest combines, huskers and grain wagons. Irrigation systems were set up for the rice acreage, produce farms and tobacco fields of the community. Pumps and drilling equipment were made available for deep wells. Better use of surface water was obtained.

In the basin of Sagua la Grande and Sagua la Chica Rivers, comprising five municipalities in the province of Las Villas, the most important of which was Calabazar de Sagua, there was a large expanse of dry rice acreage owned by small farmers. They lacked technical assistance, could not afford mechanization and were too poor to withstand the fluctuations of farm prices. To avoid losing everything, they were forced to sell their crops at any price.

The CENCAM stepped in and provided dryers, silos, warehouses and other facilities, conveniently located for all the farms in the zone. Later, it brought in tractors, plows and graders, launching a program of agricultural production that was an outstanding success by the end of 1958. In that year, the number of participating growers was close to 500 with 13,200 acres under rice, yielding 20,000 lbs. per acre. When the Communists took over, this community program was absorbed by the centralized, bureaucratic monstrosity, INRA.

In Caujerí, Guantánamo (Oriente Province), primitive sowing and harvesting methods were in use and there were no storage facilities. Moreover, the area was handicapped by having only a single outlet, the Abra Pass, which had been chiseled by nature between two mountains. In the rainy season, it became a river. This was a fertile valley, where corn was grown by a large number of small farmers who had no capital and were continuously exploited by middlemen and gouged by money lenders.

Here we put into effect a program similar to the one at Calabazar de Sagua. The CENCAM doubled production, bringing it up to 60,000,000 pounds, improved the quality of the corn and built silos and warehouses. When the small grower could store his crop, he could afford to wait for fairer prices.

With the aid of the National Executive Committee of Local, Urban and Rural Foundations (CENPLUC), another autonomous organization, created to crisscross the nation with graded roads, a 14-kilometer road was built through the mountain pass. This not only protected the peasants from the torrents of the rainy season, but linked their farms with the Blue Highway, making low-cost transportation of corn to markets in Guantánamo and Caimanera and to the seaports of Boquerón and Baitiquirí possible.

The cost of hauling corn was reduced from 25 cents to 10 cents per hundred pounds and the two-hour trip from the valley was cut down to ten minutes to the Blue Highway. Thus, we achieved the economic liberation of the community and raised the living standards of the 1,200 families who lived there.

Three more agricultural centers were created by CENCAM: one in Florida in Camagüey for rice; another in Potrerillo in Las Villas for agricultural and mining operations and the third in Colón (Matanzas) for rice crops, produce and citrus. Each of these communities had a large concentration of small farmers in need of machinery, credit and technical education. When these advantages, which previously had been the exclusive possessions of the great landlords, were distributed among the small cultivators, the latter were able to look forward confidently to a better life.

RURAL CREDIT

We guided BANFAIC into agrarian credit as the commercial banks avoided loans to small cultivators. After conscientious joint studies with officials and technical advisors of BANFAIC and with the new Agricultural Census in sight, we created a system of Rural Credit Associations, which were to supervise the operations of farm cooperatives throughout Cuba, including planting and harvesting, storage, transportation and processing of the crops.

Thirteen of these associations were created with 11,013 members, representing 116,111 farms with a total area of 87,070 square kilometers. Capitalization of $1,650,000, of which $650,000 was contributed by BANFAIC, gave them financial solidity.

The Rural Credit Associations always insisted on equitable prices for their members and in sale to retail outlets through a minimum of intermediaries. In February 1954, the Associations created a Cooperative Agency of Distribution and Supply (ADASCA). This group started its activities at La Trocha and engaged in the sale of its agricultural products, especially oranges, on a large scale. ADASCA proved its usefulness when the market price of potatoes fell and it was able to export 12,500,000 pounds of this crop to the United States, Canada and Puerto Rico at a profit.

LOANS ON CROP COLLATERAL

When BANFAIC created this type of credit in August 1953 to provide for the needs of small farmers, a $2,000 ceiling was established and a maximum maturity of 12 months for all loans. Growing crops were the collateral and no liens or certificates of title were required. In the four-year period 1953/54 to 1956/57, 16,308 loans were made, totalling $8,819,641. Thus, the average loan was for $540.50.

With the Rural Credit Associations in operation and ADASCA functioning as their sales agency, the cooperatives proceeded toward group purchase of their farm implements, seeds, fertilizers, household articles and contracts to use agricultural machinery, storage facilities and crop insurance. This rapidly expanding system of democratic cooperation permitted, among other things, the purchase of fertilizers at $20 below prevailing retail prices. Similar reductions were obtained in insecticides, fungicides and high-grade seeds. Large-scale seedbeds were cultivated which, in the one year 1955/56, yielded 35,000,000 plants.

But credit alone could not solve the most pressing problems of the small farmer. Living far from urban centers, he was supplied by middlemen who usually charged exorbitant prices. We set up warehouse and distribution centers, which supplied the small farmers with food, clothing, hardware and other items at fair prices.

Small depots of agricultural machinery were set up with the cooperation of the Bank to aid cooperators with the use of mechanical equipment for the cultivation of their land. Crop storage space was rented them as a normal component of loan contracts with crops as collateral. The perpetual problem of the small farmer—the need to dump his crops when harvested regardless of market prices—was at last overcome. Finally, group insurance, chiefly against fire, was underwritten to the extent of about $3,-000,000. This expanding coperative program was in full swing in the latter part of 1958 and, had there been a democratic succession in Cuba, it would have been expanded and improved. As it was, the Communists eradicated it totally.

AGRICULTURAL FINANCING

Between March 1952 and June 1958, the Agricultural Division of BANFAIC alone lent a total of $103,005,700 against $142,086,000 of crop and produce collateral. These loans were distributed as follows (figures in millions of dollars):

Crop or Product	Loan	Value of Collateral
Rice	38.5	48.0
Coffee and Corn	22.5	32.1
Tobacco	11.7	20.5
Coffee	9.0	11.2
Cattle	8.0	10.4
Potatoes	0.8	1.5
Corn	0.8	1.3
Beans	0.3	0.5
All Other	11.6	16.5

VENTA DE CASANOVA

Under the Agricultural Development Plan, my administration bought the huge Venta de Casanova estate in Oriente Province and proceeded to evaluate the land in terms of its agricultural possibilities. My plan was to settle the peasant families there who had previously tilled the soil as tenants or laborers. We concluded that this land by itself was not enough to achieve our goal of transforming these penniless cultivators into prosperous farmers who could contribute to the economy of the nation. Accordingly, 33½ acres of the estate's total of 16,214 acres, situated in the municipalities of Palma Soriano and Jiguaní, was set aside to become the nucleus of our entire training and production program. It had a warehouse which could hold 1,500,000 lbs. of rice, a husking machine able to handle 15,000 lbs. an hour, ample drying equipment and several buildings to house the technicians, agronomists and other personnel.

My second Administration proceeded to distribute several state-owned farms that had been expropriated and paid for in full with over 55,000 acres. Among the estates awaiting distribution when the Communists took power were Caujerí, Ubitas and Realengo in Camaguey.

REFORESTATION

In 1957, we created the Executive Committee on Forest and Agro-Pecuarian Restoration (CEREFA) to intensify afforestation, poultry production and cultivation of oilseeds. Trainees received special courses in Provincial Agricultural Schools. Nurseries, cultivating the most desirable types of trees, were encouraged. Technical aid was given to the Organization of Public Forests in the various localities and to the National Forestry Society. In 1957 alone, some 650,000 saplings were distributed among 500 applicants.

18

Aiding Crop and Livestock Production

All plans to develop agricultural resources or, for that matter, economic resources in general must be based on a thorough knowledge of what is possible. Which cultivations can be substantially improved? What sort of herds can best be increased? How can the potential riches of the subsoil and of the sea be developed? How can ground water best be utilized? Increasing output, expanding internal and foreign markets and assuring fair returns for the workers and adequate incentives for the investor are also important factors.

These and similar considerations inspired our agricultural program and channeled it into practical areas.

EXPERIMENTAL PLANTINGS

The September Revolution found an experimental station operating in Santiago de las Vegas. Highly successful and productive research was conducted in its laboratories and fields.

During our first administration, we created the Tobacco Experiment Station in San Juan y Martínez—the heart of Cuba's tobacco zone—and later a substation in Cabaiguan, Las Villas, to serve that central province.

While working to rehabilitate our coffee plantings, we established a Coffee and Cocoa Experiment Station in Oriente province. This was followed by three sub-stations in different parts of that province (Alto Songo, Bayamo and Yateras) and later two others in Las Villas (Trinidad) and Pinar del Rio (Cabañas).

When we granted the Limones sugar central, with a mill which was working at full capacity, to the Autonomous University of Havana, my associates and I had hoped to see experimental sugar cane fields sprout up under the guidance of the University's professors of agronomy. However, rather than use the mill and its fertile land for research and study, the University leased them to private enterprise as a source of additional income. When we saw what was going on, we established an experiment station in Jovellanos, Matanzas, comprising two plantations that produced 25,000,000 pounds of sugar cane. Interesting experiments were carried on there in the field of plant disease control and in the creation of a hybrid cane of high yield and viability.

By Decree #583 of May 2, 1958, we set up an Experimental Station for Pastures—later the Cattle Raising Experiment Station of Cuba—on 40 hectares in Camagüey. Here 150 varieties of forage plants were cultivated and many foreign types were introduced. These would be tried out on various farms and fed to the cattle in cooperation with those ranch men who were interested in improving methods. We reached positive conclusions concerning the best pastures and forages to fatten steers on the basis of high protein yield and drought-resistant herds.

Space limitations make it impossible to discuss all the agricultural products which were studied—both those cultivated in Cuba and those capable of being cultivated there.

We began with cotton, which had been grown over large areas under Colonial rule, at which time Cuba exported the staple. My Administration carried out experiments on 335 acres at Ciego de Avila in Camagüey and in Dayaniguas in Pinar del Rio. The positive results achieved in control of cultivation and production costs in the last years of my second Administration were later proclaimed as its own achievement by the Communist dictatorship.

Geographical conditions favored olive cultivation and we imported 160,000 plant stocks from Portugal and planted them in different zones.

A hundred acres of soybeans were planted in Ciego de Avila to determine the ideal conditions for producing this food, which provides, not only high quality oil for human consumption, but also an excellent high-protein meal for animals.

Another 167 acres were planted to sesame with a view toward developing an oil industry. These seeds yield a high grade oil of considerable nutritional value for humans. In Mexico, for instance, sesame oil is in great demand by housewives.

In 1958, the last year of Cuban freedom, our agricultural production, measured in terms of value, broke down as follows:

Sugar cane	56.7%
Rice	6.6%
Coffee	5.4%
Tobacco	2.5%
All Other	28.8%
TOTAL	100.0%

BRIGHT-LEAF TOBACCOS

My administration had four main goals in the field of tobacco cultivation:

(1) Assure profitable prices for growers.

(2) Maintain the high quality and reputation which has made Cuban tobacco internationally famous.

(3) Develop new varieties of bright-leaf tobacco with the same desirable qualities as our traditional black leaf tobacco.

(4) Win new markets and expand old ones.

We maintained minimum farm prices for leaf tobacco, enforced them rigorously and thus ensured that the cultivator's hard toil was fairly recompensed. We encouraged fair labor agreements between workers and farmers to provide more employment opportunities at better wages. In some cases, auction warehouses were rebuilt and in others constructed from scratch with funds supplied by Government.

As a result of these untiring efforts, the quality of Cuban Burley and flue-cured tobacco leaf began to gain international recognition. With the assistance of the Cuban Bank of Foreign Trade, the European market absorbed the first 670,000 lbs. placed on the market. In the following year, 1958, we were able to sell 4,000,000 lbs. abroad.

We installed the first drying plant in Cuba on the highway between La Salud and Gabriel. It covered an area of 7,500 square meters. Utilization of drying processes in this plant improved the quality of our cigarettes, which were a blend of light and dark tobaccos, and increased their market value.

In all trade agreements opening up new foreign markets, we insisted on clauses which favored the Cuban tobacco industry. In 1954, our tobacco sales abroad exceeded the $41,000,000 level which my Administration had inherited and there were steady increases thereafter until exports reached $52,000,000 in 1958.

COFFEE CULTIVATION

As we have seen, the 4th of September Revolution reinvigorated the coffee industry. The first major step, taken by Law #486 of September 14, 1934, created the Cuban Coffee Stabilization Institute (ICECAFE). After that, a series of measures became law, ranging all the way from seed selection to revamping of bean harvesters' wages, which heretofore had been miserable and a disgrace. In time, we stimulated coffee crop increases enough to meet domestic needs and even make it possible for Cuba to receive an export quota.

When I returned to power in 1952, the coffee industry was again on the verge of disaster. A crop of 62.5 million pounds was being harvested at a time when a 40 million pound surplus from the previous crop hung over the market. The anarchy within the industry (a consequence of the do-nothing policy of the previous Administration) paralleled a similar situation in sugar and tobacco. The exports which we had won and which had gained Cuba a quota in the world coffee market had virtually disappeared under Auténtico rule. In 1951 and 1952, Cuban exports of coffee were worth merely $4,000 a year.

The economic recovery of Cuban coffee agriculture was initiated by allocating the entire 1952-53 crop to the domestic market (Law #435 of October 1, 1952). The reason for this decision was that domestic demand was well above estimates and that by this allocation we hoped to prevent rising costs to the Cuban housewife. At the right moment, minimum prices were fixed for coffee beans, both green and roasted, and BANFAIC was authorized to loan on the crop as collateral.

The 1952-53 crop yielded 68,721,200 lbs. and there was little hope of a larger harvest the following year. As a trend toward lower prices became evident, we insisted on maintaining the minimum prices guaranteed to the growers to enable them to meet production costs and develop efficient cultivation methods. Law #1091 of September 22, 1953, based on the earlier statutes I have already mentioned, authorized BANFAIC to continue to extend loans against crop collateral and to buy harvests, as trustee, from the farmers whose crop it held as security for loans. The experience of those two years demonstrated the need of continued loan aid to the coffee industry. The dual purpose of this was to ensure better prices for growers and reasonable prices to consumers. Accordingly, Law #1555 of August 4, 1954 created the Coffee Purchase and Sale Administration (ACVCAFE) with a fund of $800,000 with which to start operations.

In short order, the results of these measures became apparent. The 1954-55 coffee crop totalled 83.8 million pounds, exceeding that of the previous year by 3.8 million pounds. The 1955-56 crop soared to 121,226,700 lbs., representing an increase of 37.5 million pounds over the previous year. The 1956-57 harvest was down to 79.6 million pounds, but in 1957-58, despite the terror unleashed in the countryside by the bandits of the 26th of July movement, output climbed to 94.8 million lbs. Beginning in 1956, Cuba regained her position as a coffee exporter. In that year, our sales abroad reached $20,828,000.

Production in 1958-59 fell to a mere 67.5 million pounds. The reason for this decline was the tragic developments that led to Red conquest of the island on New Year's Day of 1959. Of 334,-162 acres planted in bearing coffee trees, only 212,295 acres were actually harvested.

As a member of the Coffee-Growers' Federation of Central America, Mexico and the Caribbean, Cuba subscribed to the agreement for the stabilization of world coffee markets—and particularly the United States market—which was approved by fifteen Latin countries in Washington, D. C., on September 27, 1957. In 1957, Cuba sold $8,269,383 worth of coffee to the United States. This fell to $5,424,498 the following year because of the marauding activities of Castro and his Comintern agents.

Cocoa, which had played an important role in Cuban agriculture in the past, began its comeback after the March 1952 Revolution. High grade strains were imported and, after careful selection of seed varieties, new plantations were started. In 1958, my Administration left 22,445 acres under cultivation with a total production of 4,800,000 pounds.

CORN

In March 1952, the Cuban corn economy was in wretched shape. A controlled price of $4 per quintal had been set on the farm, but nobody paid over $2. The BANFAIC, which had just been organized, did not have warehouses, husking machines or even manpower. Nevertheless, we set up a loan fund for growers and advanced money on corn at 70% of the legal price. By June 30th of 1952, these loans totalled $572,870.

A surplus of 30 million pounds loomed over the coming crop. To solve the surplus problem quickly, we decided to stimulate an infant fodder industry. Moreover, to encourage greater domestic consumption of corn, we obligated the Armed Forces to feed it to their livestock. In one year, 50,000 quintals were consumed in this way. Exports to Caribbean countries were also stimulated.

Law #1092 of September 22, 1953 helped meet the grower's demand for stabilized prices. It authorized BANFAIC to buy shelled corn over the next two years for 3½ cents a pound and sell it on the open market when propitious. Law #1554 of August 4, 1954 created the Corn Stabilization Administration (AEM), under BANFAIC supervision, to provide credit aid to growers.

The minimum price was again reduced. AEM moved cautiously at first while the market held firm at $3. Eventually, businessmen decided to export corn to Spain and Puerto Rico and the balance between production and consumption was slowly restored.

In 1958, 418,750 acres were planted, producing 322 million pounds of corn that brought $9,660,000 to growers. The stimulus given production under the Plan of Social and Economic Development had finally put an end to the unstable corn situation that my Administration had inherited in 1952.[1]

---

[1] The very same week that Castro promulgated Law #851, confiscating U.S. properties and corporations in retaliation for United States withdrawal from the Cuban sugar market, he was compelled to turn to the U.S. to buy corn! Despite promises that the agrarian reform would enable Cuba to produce her total domestic requirements, INRA farmers suddenly found that they had poultry feed for only ten days. After convincing themselves that Argentina was in no position to make quick deliveries and that the Czechoslovak corn had been offered them at prohibitive prices, they placed an order for 150,000 bags in the U.S., followed by another order for 100,000 bags a few days later.

RICE

When I turned over the Presidency to my successor in October 1944, I left him completed studies of various projects, which combined development of rich hydroelectric potential with irrigation of rice lands. Whether because he was badly informed or in accordance with his practice of never continuing projects initiated by another Government, Dr. Grau San Martín abandoned these projects so useful to the national economy.

We completed the first of them in our 1952 Administration. After the organization of the Irrigation Community of Buey River, thousands of acres were planted to rice, a basic staple of both rich and poor in Cuba. Our success with rice research and cultivation prompted many farmers, especially in the provinces of Oriente, Camagüey and Pinar del Rio, to extend their sowing program to cover rice.[2]

In November 1952, rice farmers had $957,600 in crop credits. This credit program stimulated a vigorous market reaction and it became necessary to provide warehouses in Manzanillo, Caibarién and Havana.[3] On June 30, 1954, loans outstanding amounted to $2,839,312.

As time passed, all the components of the rice industry, from tillage and the husking mills to ultimate marketing of the product, were coordinated by Government. This eliminated wild swings of prices, windfall gains and losses and malign political influences which, if left to their own course, would have jeopardized healthy development.

Rice planting on a large scale was progressing under the protection of an international agreement that fixed a yearly import quota of 325,000,000 lbs., subject to increase as necessary, to meet any deficiencies in domestic production or any rise in domestic consumption. At the time this agreement became effective, Cuba

[2] Law #1525 of July 9, 1954 gave a concession for a hydroelectric dam on the Toa River in Oriente that would have enormously improved the productive capacity of a vast farming zone. The bloody developments in Oriente, however, snagged the project. By Resolution #98 of February 23, 1959, the Communist regime transferred the concession to the National Development Commission. But it was never completed.

[3] Soon after this, three more warehouses were built in Manzanillo; a fourth in Caibarién, two more at Veguitas (Bayamo), another at Artemisa and still another in Consolación del Sur in the province of Pinar del Rio.

was not producing enough rice to meet domestic requirements over and above the import quota. This made the quota arrangement advantageous for us.

Law #2026 of January 27, 1955 created the Rice Stabilization Administration (AEA) which levied 10 cents a hundred pounds on husked rice, whether of domestic or foreign origin. The new organization received $1,500,000 from BANDES as initial operating capital.

One of the AEA's first steps was to set basic prices—taking as a basis the prices in the United States for the different varieties of rice and adding shipping costs, insurance and customs duties. Purchasing centers were opened in Manzanillo and Caibarién for the benefit of growers with less than 837 acres under cultivation.

THE WHITE STREAK

An epidemic of unknown origin devastated the rice plantations and spread discouragement among the farmers. From the very first, Cuban technicians suspected that it was a virus infection. We decided to secure the services of Japanese specialists as they had had long experience in fighting plagues in the Japanese rice plantations and were reported to be the finest in the field. These experts confirmed the diagnosis of the Cubans and reported that this type of disease was not known in their country. Many of our rice farmers were ready to give up.

Soon after the discovery of the white streak, as we called this plague, we found the means of suppressing it. Yields that in some zones were 40,000 lbs. per 33-acre section or even less were soon increased to 80,000 and even 100,000 pounds. Cuban technicians had conquered the plague and the battle for rice had been won.

The most immediate consequence of the Red takeover in 1959 was the discontinuance of rice imports from the United States in line with the Sino-Soviet "anti-imperialist" policy. There was also a drastic fall in domestic production. The Reds endeavored to offset the decline by imports from Ecuador, Egypt and Red China. These countries never supplied the balance of Cuban consumption needs. Moreover, the rice obtained was very inferior to the premium quality rice with which Cubans were familiar.

Trouble increased due to the chaos caused by confiscation of the rice plantations. Ignorance and greed were in the saddle. The

Communist Administration pledged to produce "all the rice needed for domestic consumption in 1961." Yet by that year, output was below the figures attained in my Administration (and population had increased considerably in the meantime). Cuba remained dependent on imports for over 50% of its supply. "An irrefutable proof of the collapse of rice production," Álvarez Díaz and associates write in the authoritative work I have already cited, "is the ration established in March 1962 of 6 pounds per person monthly. Normal consumption before 1959 was 10 pounds monthly per person." [4]

CATTLE

In the last years of the War of Independence, our cattle industry was almost annihilated. Yet, within a few years of Republican life, the great enterprising spirit of the Cuban people brought it back on its feet. The 376,650 head of cattle reported in the cattle census of 1899 increased to 2,579,500 in 1906 and four years later a minimum herd of 4,000,000 was constantly maintained.

In 1952, Cuba suffered from a terrible drought and the rain gauges showed an average rainfall of 1.07 inches, an all-time low. These drought conditions persisted throughout the following year and got even worse in 1956-57. Since our Cuban dry season coincides with the period of greatest economic activity, November to April, the loss of cattle weight of up to 25% created a major imbalance between supply and demand for beef. This deficit would become even more acute in April and May of the arid years and sometimes the supply of meat would be interrupted.

Faced by one of these cyclical crises, we had to act quickly to ensure a continued supply of beef to the people. As a first step, I ordered a cattle census (Law #138 of June 12, 1952) so we would know the actual facts and have a more realistic insight into the situation. We could then plan the strengthening and expansion of the industry.

The job of taking the census was given to the National Army, which had done such a brilliant job in taking a cattle census in my previous Administration. This work was assigned to the Rural Guard Corps and the Veterinary Department. The Census showed 4,032,684 head of capital, 80,000 head less than the 1946 count. We obtained these figures from the Army for the insignifi-

[4] *op. cit.,* p. 1,598.

cant cost of $60,000. Five years later, our herds were estimated at 4,500,000 head, including 9,000 dairy cows. *Cuban beef production in 1957 was 488,000,000 pounds. Thus, per capita beef consumption was 73 pounds per year as compared with 80.5 pounds in the United States in the same year.*

When the Communists took over, nationalization by INRA resulted in widespread destruction of herds. The mismanagement, stupidity and incompetence of the untrained Red interventors created further havoc. In this situation, the Cuban people began to suffer for the first time in years from a stringent meat shortage. While the regime naturally suppresses basic statistics, since they would show the magnitude of its failures, we know that the ration system as early as 1960 provided for only ¾ of a pound of beef *and pork* per person per week. This worked out to 39 pounds of both meats per annum as against the 73 pounds per annum of beef alone under my Administration. Moreover, supplies were by no means sufficient to honor the ration stamps.

THE MEAT PROBLEM

The apostles of "agrarian reform" proclaimed that the Cuban cattle industry had been the preserve of great landlords. A cursory look at the statistics shows, however, that of 120,000 ranches 38,-000 had less than 10 steers, 37,000 had from 10 to 50 and 7,500 had from 50 to 100.

Moreover, cattle ranching, because of its demands for water and rainfall, is most efficient when conducted on very large acreages. The large ranches never hesitated to spend huge sums of money to import the finest breeding stock and to develop the types of meat and dairy products best adapted to the Cuban climate and environment. It was largely due to their efforts that the Cuban cattle industry ranked as one of the finest in the world.

Whenever economic studies showed that prices needed revision, they were revised. The increase in per capita income under the Plan of Social and Economic Development was reflected in steadily increasing meat consumption by the Cuban people. Meat was always available in abundance except on meatless Fridays when other products replaced it.

Having overcome our production difficulties, we were soon able to export and Law #1042 of August 27, 1953 authorized the export of Brahma and Brown Swiss cattle.

Simultaneously, the dairy industry was encouraged. The pork industry was growing and output of bacon, ham and pork was expanding. The Government encouraged the efforts of the Cuban Hog Growers Association to bring stability and progress into this field. Moreover, civic and industry groups, organized to promote new cattle fair grounds and exhibitions of agro-industrial products in such different parts of the Island as Pinar del Rio, Cienfuegos and Santiago de Cuba, all received government encouragement and aid.

THE POULTRY INDUSTRY

After the 10th of March 1952, the Cuban poultry industry began to take enormous strides forward. In 1952, Cuba imported 8,708,-852 dozen fresh eggs. By 1958, these imports were down to 337,-910 dozen. Domestic production of eggs rose from 11.3 million dozen in 1956 to 26 million in 1958. Further rapid increases were projected for future years.

Our domestic egg consumption of 316.1 million units (1957), which did not include household production, gave Cuba a per capita consumption of 47 eggs yearly as against 67 in the United States.

In 1958, there were 20 million chickens in Cuba. Of these, 18 million were butchered annually, yielding 36 million pounds of meat. In addition, 975,300 dozen eggs in incubators were imported and incubator farms were encouraged. These had not existed in Cuba before 1952.

New businesses and industries were constantly developing for the better utilization of these dairy and meat products.

THE WRECKERS

The flourishing condition in which we left the Cuban poultry industry proved particularly attractive to the Communists. INRA charged poultry farmers with deliberately decreasing production after the Red seizure of power and this was used as a pretext for expropriating 30 of the finest poultry farms in Cuba (Resolution #198 of August 4, 1960) and turning them over to the management of the comrades, people who were ignorant, incompetent and corrupt. As a result of this criminal stupidity, the poultry industry was wrecked and chicken and eggs became almost unobtainable in Cuban households.

The full extent of the havoc caused in poultry and hog production was revealed in a statement by the Cuban Veterinarians' Association in Exile and carried by the Associated Press on May 27, 1963.

The Association predicted that within eight months Cuba's once flourishing poultry industry would be destroyed by disease and lack of breeding stock. It added that cholera and other epidemics were raging unchecked among the hog population.

"There is 100% incidence of either infectious bronchitis or Newcastle disease in poultry farms," the report, which was released by Dr. Cristobal González Mayo, President of the Association, stated.

"Pullorum disease and typhus also are present on all poultry farms on the Island. In hatcheries, there is no sanitation control of any kind. All breeding stock is infected.

"Further there has been no foundation stock for a long time and breeding reaches the fourth generation."

Dr. González Mayo added that the quality of fowl had degenerated to such an extent that they averaged less than two pounds and that broiler production was down to 300,000 units per month. (This compared with 1,500,000 broilers butchered monthly in 1958.)

Because of the lack of vaccines, medicines, hygiene and technical personnel, hog deaths "have reached astronomical proportions to the point where some farms lost all their animals," the report added. Among the stricken areas were Sagua La Grande, San Cristobal and Bahía Honda. Erysipelas, which caused 30% hog losses in the last region, was spreading all over Cuba.

Thus, the "agrarian reformers" turned out to be the wreckers of agriculture and animal husbandry. The anthem of world communism, *The Internationale*, begins with the words, "Arise ye prisoners of starvation!" Yet it turns out that "the prisoners of starvation" are primarily those unfortunate human beings who live under the hammer and sickle.

19

The Sugar Industry: From Chaos to Stability

The history of the sugar industry in Cuba has been characterized by massive and violent fluctuations. In 1895, at the beginning of our final military struggle for independence, production reached 1,000,000 long tons. When peace returned, there were not enough standing cane fields or enough sugar mills left to produce a quarter of that amount. But the Cuban people, in cooperation with North American capital, set to work to reconstruct the industry vigorously and swiftly: 300,000 tons in 1900, 636,000 in 1901 and 850,000 in 1902, the first year of the Republic. In the following year, 1903, we again passed the milestone of a million tons.

The harvest just before World War 1, that of 1913, climbed to 2,442,000 tons and, when the Armistice was signed in November 1918, Cuba was placing 3,000,000 tons of sugar yearly at the disposal of her Allies at sacrifice prices as her contribution to the triumph of the great cause.

THE DANCE OF THE MILLIONS

During the last years of the War, the Cuban harvest had remained around 3,000,000 tons. In 1919, the first postwar year, it exceeded 4,000,000 tons at a price of 5.06 cents per pound. In the following year, there was unprecedented speculation and a crop of 3,742,323 tons was sold at an average price of 11.95 cents, which yielded $1,022,300,000. Yet, even before the end of that year, prices had begun their abrupt descent and the 1921 crop fetched an average of 3.10 cents. The spread of 8.85 cents between one year's crop and the next dealt a tremendous blow to the stability of the Cuban economy.

It took many years before the nation recovered from the blow. The nickname which the public gave to the astronomically priced 1920 crop was "the dance of the millions." All attempts to improve the sugar situation were in vain. During the years following 1924, crops of between four and five million tons were put on the world market and in 1929, the year which marked the onset of the Great Depression, Cuba harvested 5,156,279 tons. This was the highwater mark up to that time. The average price was 3.82 cents. Meanwhile, in the United States, an economic disaster gained momentum which would shrink the nation's income by 50 billion dollars.

FACING ADVERSITY

Cane cultivation was expanded and huge mills were built in the provinces of Camagüey and Oriente to process the cane into raw sugar. These great enterprises seemed to have been born under evil stars. After the 1929 crop came that of 1930—4,671,000 tons sold at an average price of 1.23 cents. In 1931, the crop declined to 3,121,000 tons, but the price fell further—to 1.11 cents. In 1932, 2,604,292 tons were produced, only half of the 1929 figure, but the price was the infinitesimal figure of 0.71 cents. Then in 1933, we had the smallest harvest since 1912, only 1,994,238 tons, selling for 0.97 cents per pound.

Thus, in twelve years, the price of sugar had fallen from 11.95 cents to less than three-quarters of a cent and volume had fallen by over two and a half million tons. The value of the mainstay of the Cuban economy had shrunk by 94% in price and by about 96% in foreign exchange value. This brought the Cuban economy to a desperate plight.

From September 4, 1933 on, Cuba waged the hard and difficult battle to save her sugar industry. The highly protective Hawley-Smoot Tariff, adopted on June 18, 1930 had immeasurably increased our difficulties by imposing a tariff of two cents a pound on our sugar shipments to the United States. In September 1934, the new Reciprocity Treaty with the United States reduced this duty to nine-tenths of a cent. Moreover, Cuba received a quota equivalent to 28.6% of United States sugar consumption. These arrangements were a signal economic triumph for the government of the Revolution of the 4th of September. Thus, we moved out of economic adversity and the sugar industry slowly regained a degree of prosperity.

THE SUGAR COORDINATION LAW

This statute gave field workers and tenant farmers a share in the profits of the industry. In 1944, the last year of my first Administration, the crop was the largest since 1930—4,171,200 tons. Although we could have obtained better prices, we sold the crop for 2.45 cents in accordance with our wartime international commitments to our Allies. We assured the United States abundant supplies of sugar and, by holding the price down, made a substantial economic contribution to the Allied forces abroad fighting Nazism and fascism.

THE MARSHALL PLAN

To meet the shortages caused by the ravages of war in other countries, we maintained sugar production at high levels in the immediate postwar years. The Marshall Plan, launched by the United States in 1947 to assist economic reconstruction and halt the spread of communism, provided Free Europe with the fantastic sum of 12 billion dollars in foreign aid over three and a half years. This made it easy for Cuba to dispose of her three subsequent sugar crops at an average price of 4.35 cents per pound.

The termination of the Marshall Plan in 1950 coincided with the outbreak of hostilities in Korea. The Auténtico Administration reacted by stepping up sugar output to 5,589,000 tons in 1951, which was sold at 5.08 cents a pound. Surpluses began to accumulate the following year, which should have rung an alarm bell. Instead, free (non-quota) production was authorized, although no new markets were in sight, which brought output to an all-time high of 7,011,637 tons.

This blow dealt to the economic future of the nation and to the interests of workers and producers was not primarily due to economic miscalculation. The Presidential campaign of 1952 was in full swing and President Carlos Prío decided to make the sugar crop a major campaign issue. Planters were allowed to grind all their cane; workers were promised more hours of work and better bonus payments; sugar mill owners were promised tax advantages, provided, of course, they made generous contributions to the campaign fund of the Auténticos. The country was supposed to re-elect the Administration because of a general economic euphoria. The deluge and the inevitable reckoning were postponed until after the elections.

Consequently, the sugar crisis was the first serious problem which the Government of the 10th of March Revolution had to face. It was not a simple one. We could not cut production because the cultivation cycle had about reached its halfway point. Something had to be done efficiently and decisively to relieve the pressure on world prices caused by the enormous surplus from the previous year and the huge crop under cultivation. It had to be done fast, without hurting the mills, without ruining the cane planters and without creating falls in wages and salaries. We had to avoid a price slump, which would mean an expanding spiral of deflationary stagnation radiating throughout the economy.

Right at the outset of the new regime, we faced decisions of extreme gravity. We asked for a vote of confidence from the three sections of the sugar industry most directly affected and from the nation's banking system. It was absolutely necessary to withdraw 1,750,000 long tons from the market, placing them in a stabilization reserve to be sold in full as soon as possible at reasonable prices and by 1956 at the very latest. In other words, the surplus had to be taken off the market and dumped gradually. The organizations charged with this delicate task accomplished it fully in the course of four years.

At the end of the sugar production season, we enacted Law #224 of July 8, 1952 which spelled out the procedure to be followed. Sugar mills, cane planters and workers patriotically supported the government plan. Cuban banks contributed the necessary $120,000,000, without asking for outside help, and taking the surplus sugar as loan collateral. This colossal operation we proudly carried out with our own resources as a nation. Some 350,000 tons were taken from the stabilization reserve and set aside for United States consumption within the quota provided for by the Sugar Act. This amount was to be deducted from our yearly export quotas to the United States market over the next five years.

What was particularly attractive about this procedure was that we sold the 350,000 tons at an agreed-upon price which was double the world price.

CROP CURTAILMENT

It was also necessary to reduce 1953 sugar production to sensible levels. However, I was reluctant to take that step without consulting the sugar industry. Law #6252 of May 12, 1952 created a special commission to hear the views of interested parties.

Total output for 1953 was set at 5,000,000 tons (actually it reached 5,007,060 tons) and each mill was assigned a quota based on its 1947-52 operations. In line with my general policy of protecting small enterprise, I increased the base quota of the smaller mills up to 100,000 bags and set 2½% of the total quota aside, that is to say, 125,000 tons, for the protection of the small planters and a similar amount for the protection of those mills, generally the small ones, which faced major economic difficulties. These restrictive measures were kept in force until the 1956 crop of 4,500,000 tons was sold at an average price of 3.81 cents. By then, the entire 1952 surplus had been sold at normal prices and the $120,000,000 loan had been totally repaid.

The 1957 crop of 5,506,000 tons was sold at 5.05 cents per pound, one of the highest prices since the dance of the millions. Terrorist activities were designed to burn and destroy the 1958 cane crop. Nevertheless, we managed to meet our quota and to increase it to cover unforeseen improvements in demand in some places and decreased production by other producers, notably Hawaii and Puerto Rico. This put another 100,000 tons into production. Accordingly, total output for 1958 exceeded that of the previous year, reaching 5,613,000 tons of sugar and 253,265,000 gallons of high-test molasses. The production of green sugar for cattle feed was also very important that year. All told, the national income from sugar amounted to $660,000,000 in 1958.[1]

---

[1] Law #1335 of March 30, 1954 authorized sugar mills to continue grinding cane that would otherwise have been left uncut in the fields. Its purpose was to produce high-test molasses after filling the sugar quota. This benefitted workers, planters and mill owners. The same law authorized the Cuban Sugar Stabilization Institute (ICEA) to buy the molasses crop for export. Proceeds of these sales went into a special fund for producers. In 1955, 13.1 billion pounds of cane produced 220 million gallons of high-test molasses.

WORLD SUGAR AGREEMENT

Having solved the problem of the mammoth 1952 sugar crop with the approval of the people, we decided to tackle reorganization of the sugar industry in accordance with the Sugar Coordination Law. That meant striving for international agreement to balance world supply with world demand, to assure stable prices for our producers and to find markets outside the United States.

With the agreement of a large number of countries, and particularly the United States, an International Sugar Conference was held in London. On October 21, 1953, an international agreement, regulating and stabilizing the production, consumption and prices of sugar and supplanting the 1937 sugar covenant, emerged from the London meeting.[2] Among its salient provisions, were the following:

(1) The basis for export quotas was raised. Cuba's quota tonnage was increased by 165,000 metric tons to total 2,415,000 tons.

(2) There was a slight reduction in both maximum and minimum prices and in their range of permissible variation.

(3) A more flexible mechanism for the quota system, which was advantageous to exporting member nations and disadvantageous to non-member exporters, was adopted. This advantage was to be maintained regardless of price rises within the agreed-upon range.

(4) Closer regulation of declared export shortages to allow them to be covered from surpluses without affecting the market, as in the case of the 1952 Cuban surplus was instituted.

(5) The Sugar Council was authorized to regulate, at its own discretion, the use of sugar not destined for human consumption.

GREEN SUGAR

This 1953 agreement was particularly beneficial to a part of the industry which had already been considered as a major expan-

2 The seemingly permanent crisis in sugar had moved Congress to approve the Chadbourne Plan (Law of October 15, 1930), which was supposed to stabilize the world price of sugar. This law was in force until 1937, but its success was dubious. In May 1937, the London International Agreement was signed to regulate production and sales. This covenant was technically in operation until it was replaced in 1953 by the new London International Agreement.

sion possibility in our Social and Economic Development Plan, namely, green sugar (low quality raw sugar and third-grade lumps, together with high-test or inverted molasses for animal feed). This had great possibilities for our internal market and also a real potential in world markets as ingredients in feeds for livestock and poultry. The manufacture of green sugar was first authorized in Cuba by Decree #1249 of April 19, 1956. Shortly thereafter, 180,374 one hundred pound bags were being produced by the Rio Cauto, Tánamo, Santa Martha and Cunagua sugar mills.

NEW SUGAR BAGS

During the last years of World War II in Europe (1942-44) we tried to meet a just demand of the labor unions that the sugar bag be reduced from its standard 325-pound size as a means of cutting down muscular strain and physical toil. We were not able to do this at the time because of the opposition of various interests, production difficulties and the shortage of shipping space during wartime.[3]

During my second Administration, the military-logistic problem no longer existed and I gave immediate attention to the matter. Law #581 of December 9, 1952 reduced the standard sugar bag from 325 to 250 pounds. My Government also gave the workers their other major demand: representation on the Cuban Sugar Stabilization Institute on equal terms with the mill owners and planters.

SUGAR CANE PLANTERS

In addition to the basic law of the industry, the Sugar Coordination Law, we instituted special legislation to protect the small planters. Law #664 of January 29, 1953 extended this protection to all planters producing less than a million pounds of cane. These small farmers had become twice as numerous by 1953 as they had been in 1937, when the Sugar Coordination Law was enacted.

The common law was too slow and cumbersome to settle the

[3] The jute had to be imported from India and obviously the larger the bag the less jute required, since the surface of bagging increases with the square of any dimension and the volume of sugar carried with its cube.

numerous disputes between planters and mills concerning the liquidation of cane, belonging to the planters, by the mills that ground it. Great hardship to planters and workers resulted. Law #805 of April 17, 1953, as amended and improved by Law #2048 of January 27, 1955, sped up the procedure and protected the injured parties.

Eventually, the relationship between the sub-planters (small tenants who tilled their land personally) and the mills was regulated by special legislation—Law #11 of July 30, 1956.

We protected the independent cane planter in his right to retain his quota. We prevented the elimination of the railroads as cane carriers. Every year, at their general conventions, the tenant cane planters expressed their gratitude to me and to my Administration.

Unhappily, all these constructive efforts, extended over so many years, to regulate the sugar industry on the basis of social justice and free enterprise and in a manner consonant with Cuban institutions were swept aside as soon as INRA made its appearance.

NATIONAL OWNERSHIP OF MILLS

In 1939, there were 174 working sugar mills in Cuba. The number fell to 161 and remained at that level from 1954 through 1958. In 1939, only 56 sugar mills were Cuban-owned and they produced only 22.4% of the sugar output of the nation. In 1954, there were 116 Cuban mills and in 1958, 121 Cuban mills produced 62.1% of our sugar.

PRODUCTION OF SUGAR BY NATIONALITY

	Cuban Mills		American Mills		Other Nations	
Year	No.	Pct. of Output	No.	Pct. of Output	No.	Pct. of Output
1939	56	22.4	66	55.1	52	22.5
1954	116	57.8	41	40.0	4	1.2
1958	121	62.1	36	36.7	4	0.3

The nationalization of the sugar industry was effected naturally, without any violence whatsoever. Cubans not only bought out these foreign investments, but they extended their purchases of land and sugar mills to Florida, Mexico and Venezuela.

COMMUNISM AND THE SUGAR INDUSTRY

The first step of the Castro government was to seize all sugar plantations owned by persons connected with my Administration. Thereafter, on various pretexts, all sugar mills on the Island were nationalized, regardless of the owner's nationality or politics. Sugar "cooperatives" were set up under INRA on over 2,680,000 acres of expropriated land. Five-man "Soviets," comprising delegates of the INRA, members of the Rebel Army and representatives of the agricultural and industrial unions (which the dictatorship was in the process of turning over to the Communist Party), were constituted in each sugar mill.

People's Stores were then set up in the mills and plantations. These were given a monopoly status and, since the workers were paid in scrip, valid only in these stores, they were compelled to buy there. The ICEA was turned over to a triumvirate of Communist officials, on the pretext that it had failed to do its job, and was in effect abolished.

THE NATURAL MARKET

Geography, climate, history and economic law make the United States the natural market for Cuba. Ever since independence was won from Spain, it was clear that Cuba's destiny as a free nation would be linked with the Colossus of the North. A great market a short distance from us was a stimulus for the vast and intensive development of our tropical export agriculture, particularly our sugar industry. In return, we enjoyed undeniable and large advantages. Among these was the fact that the United States supplied most of our imports and provided investment capital for our economic development, industrialization and diversification.

The breaking of these deep-rooted traditions and close economic and political ties, the ending of commercial relations with a great neighbor capable of supplying all our wants cheaply, was justified by the Communists as "liberating us from our slave masters." The alternative chosen was to tie Cuba completely to an alien system, repugnant to our institutions and to our heritage of freedom, economically rather primitive and involving an impossible economic relationship because of the thousands of miles of ocean and land separating us from the Soviet Union and from Red China. This decision, dictated by Communist international political aims, was a crime against the people of Cuba and treason to the Cuban State. Had the interests of the Cuban people been considered at all, it would also have been an act of incredible stupidity.

The rulers of Cuba have cut the nation off from the American sugar market. The longer Castro and his Communists rule the Island, the more probable it is that this loss will be permanent. In return, they have negotiated barter deals with the U.S.S.R. However, this Soviet market for Cuban sugar exists merely as a political expedient; it has no economic rationale and will probably disappear in the course of a few years, leaving Cuba a blighted nation.

Even according to official INRA figures, Cuban sugar cane production has suffered a disastrous decline, dropping from 48.0 million metric tons in 1958 to an estimated 37.4 million metric tons in 1963. The fall in sugar production is proportionately much greater than that in cane since a large part of the latter is left to rot in the fields by the incompetent INRA bureaucracy and its discontented hordes of dragooned "volunteer" workers.

Writing in the *New York Times* for April 8, 1963, Ruby Hart Phillips observed:

"Four years of Fidel Castro's Communist rule have brought virtual economic ruin to the once relatively prosperous island of Cuba. And the prospects for this year are even bleaker for the Cuban people." Mrs. Phillips pointed out that five of Cuba's 161 sugar mills had been dismantled and cannibalized to provide spare parts for the others.

The catastrophic decline in raw sugar production from over 5.5 million tons in Cuba's last year of freedom (1958) to about 3 million tons in 1963 contributed to a worldwide inflation of sugar prices. With spot sugar selling at 15¢ a pound on international exchanges, the beneficiaries from this windfall were not the hard-pressed people of Cuba, but rather their Russian masters who had bought most of the crop at low agreed-upon prices.

20

The Mining and Smelting Industries

To the country's four traditional mineral exports—copper, manganese, iron and chrome—we added a fifth mineral during my first Administration that was destined eventually to be the most important and promising of all. That mineral was nickel.

The discovery of rich nickel ore deposits in the northern part of the province of Oriente was of vital importance to the democratic world in its conduct of global war and gave Cuba the opportunity to develop a new and most important industry at Lengua de Pajaro on the Bay of Levisa. With the full backing of my Administration and financial resources furnished by the Government of President Franklin D. Roosevelt, a large-capacity modern plant was built at Lengua de Pajaro. This brought life and vigor to this small community which was soon to become an important production center.

NICARO

Construction of the Nicaro plant began in 1942. The plant initially cost $30,000,000, but expansion and improvement of facilities brought this figure up to $110,000,000. After the end of World War II, the U. S. Government suspended production.

It was obviously important to Cuba that this major industry, which was then controlled by the Cuban Nickel Company, should be reactivated. Law #509 of November 4, 1952 authorized the company to make geological exploration of certain mining claims located within the National Park in the Sierra Cristal at Mayarí, Oriente, to determine their nickel and cobalt reserves with a view to possible industrialization. Cuban reserves of these minerals would be valuable for those projects for hemispheric defense with which I consistently cooperated.

On the first year of my second Administration, the old Nicaro plant resumed operations, exporting 8,234 tons, worth $5,993,377, of a product that had not moved in international trade at all between 1948 and 1951.

The Nicaro plant provided jobs for 2,800 Cubans and represented a contribution of at least $4,000,000 to the national economy in wages and goods. Between 1944 and 1947, it had produced 82.5 million pounds of nickel oxide with a value of $17,000,-000. Between 1952, when operations were resumed, and 1957, we exported 224,621,700 pounds of nickel oxide worth $84,887,310.

COBALT AND MOA BAY

In 1953, Mr. Langbourne N. Williams, President of Freeport Sulphur Company, wrote me that their investigaions had confirmed the presence of more than 40 million tons of nickel ore, together with considerable quantities of cobalt ore, in the Moa Bay area. They estimated a concentration of 29 pounds of nickel and 5 to 6 pounds of cobalt per ton of ore.

After testing the efficiency of a new method of ore separation at its Louisiana pilot plant, Freeport Sulphur organized the Moa Bay Mining Company as an operating subsidiary under the facilities granted by our Law of Industrial Stabilization. A $75,000,000 plant to extract and concentrate nickel and cobalt was built at Moa Bay in northern Oriente.

The completion of this plant made Cuba the second largest nickel producer in the world and the world's leading cobalt producer.

In 1957, our nickel production reached the record high of almost 50 million pounds despite the intense waves of sabotage and terrorism launched by the so-called rebels of the 26th of July.

One of the chief purposes of Castro and his Communist masters was to prevent the Free World from receiving these supplies of vital strategic metals and of diverting them to the Soviet bloc. Accordingly, Castro enacted Law #617 of October 27, 1959, which levied a punitive 25% ad valorem tax on mineral exports. The

Moa Bay Mining Company complained that this tax made continued operation of the plant impossible, but the Government ignored it. As a result, the plant was shut down in March 1960, throwing 2,800 Cubans out of work. Later, in August of that year, it was confiscated.

The following month, an announcement was made in the United States that Nicaro had also shut down. The Communist regime offered to buy the plant for $5,386,000. It had cost $110,-000,000. In October, it was seized by Castro's militia. Soviet technicians under the direction of one Ivan Stigurin appeared almost immediately. They boldly announced that the Soviet Union would ship in all the ammonia and spare parts needed to put the plant back into production.

Confiscatory taxes and nationalization had achieved their purpose—to deprive the Free World of two minerals vital to its defense and to turn these strategic materials over to the Soviets. The following table shows the rise of Cuban mineral exports under freedom and its decline when Castro took power:

Year	Nickel Exports	Total Mineral Exports
	(in millions of dollars)	
1952	6.0	23.6
1954	12.8	29.9
1956	14.8	34.8
1958	19.5	44.2
1959 (Castro)	9.0	15.9

STEEL INDUSTRY

Despite the handicap of lack of suitable fuel, we started a steel industry in Cuba. We attempted to overcome the seemingly insurmountable barrier of absence of coking coal by using bagasse from the cane crop.

Our first step was to produce pig iron and set up concentration plants that would enable us to export metal rather than ore. Simultaneously, we stopped the export of scrap steel, which had run to millions of tons yearly.

BANDES financed the Antilles Steel Company to build a steel mill to produce an estimated 112,000 tons of sheets annually. Republic Steel Corporation contributed $2,000,000 to this venture.

We also cooperated in the establishment of a metal and alloys plant, Metals and Alloys Corporation of Cuba, and in the construction of another plant to produce ingots from scrap metal. This installation was to produce 24,000 tons of centrifugal tubing —for aqueducts—using an exclusive Belgian foundry process. Its corporate name was National Basic Metallurgical Corporation.

ATOMIC ENERGY

A 10,000 kilowatt atomic reactor was installed in Pinar del Rio, a region known for its cupriferous deposits of almost unlimited potential. At the same time, we proceeded to build a nuclear research laboratory based on enriched uranium.

In 1956, Cuba displaced New Caledonia for the first time as the world's second producer of nickel. With her five cobalt fields, she attained first place in the world in production of this key atomic-age metal. In the same year, Cuba joined the world's great manganese exporters—Russia, India, South Africa, China and Brazil. In 1957, she became the world's eighth largest producer of chrome ore.

CEMENT AND OTHER INDUSTRIES

Until 1952, there was only one plant for Portland cement production in Cuba. This had been built at Mariel by the International Cement Corporation during the administration of President Zayas. By 1958, two more were in operation: one in Santiago de Cuba and the other in Artemisa in Pinar del Rio. Their *raison d'être* was to meet the enormous demand created both by the public improvement projects of our Administration and by the private building boom.

As this tremendous construction boom gathered momentum, other industries sprang up to serve it, such as cement mixing companies with large fleets of mixer trucks, stone quarries, cement block factories and numerous other enterprises, which thrived largely due to the financial cooperation extended by the economic organizations created under my Administration.

A $6,000,000 glass container plant was built by Owens Illinois Glass Company. The ceramics industry showed promising growth and Cuba was soon self-sufficient in bathroom tiles and various fixtures.

Through CENCAM and BANFAIC, we gave preferential attention to the financing problems of small mining enterprises, particularly in the metallurgical zones of Las Villas and Oriente provinces. In Santa Lucia, Pinar del Rio province, we aided in the establishment of a sulphuric acid plant and recovery of lead, gold and silver, using iron pyrites as a raw material. Of equal importance was the contribution of the State to the development of nitrogen, glycerin, acetate, plastics and aluminum products plants. The bottled gas industry for home consumption expanded beyond expectations. By the end of 1958, there were no less than 20 producers of bottled gas in Havana alone, among them the Shell Oil Company.

BLACK GOLD

In May 1954, an oil well was drilled at Jatibonico, Camagüey, which turned out to be such a big producer that it aroused a great deal of interest on the part of Cuban capital in petroleum exploration and production.

Measures adopted by our Administration stimulated investors and technicians. Costly drilling equipment was acquired and turned over to the National Development Commission for deep drilling operations. Applicants for this equipment had to wait in line.

Attracted by the results at Jatibonico, several companies announced their intention to drill. By Law #1526 of August 8, 1954, my Administration regulated the terms of cooperation with oil prospectors. This Law to Stimulate Oil Drilling and Production of Other Hydrocarbons facilitated the making of geological surveys and the drilling of test wells. This policy was extended to cover such other producing oil fields as Motembo, Jarahueca and Bacuranao. It resulted in increasing the number of exploration companies, in the course of three months, from 10 to 42.

OIL REFINING

On November 2 of the same year, we promulgated Law #1758 which granted special 20-year privileges for oil refineries, both for those already in existence and for new ones.

The law was enthusiastically received. Esso, which had been established in 1883 and was the oldest refinery in Cuba, invested $30,000,000 in expanding and modernizing its Belot refinery in the Havana harbor, increasing capacity to 35,000 barrels a day. Two new refineries were built. The Royal Dutch Shell refinery, erected at a cost of $28,000,000 in Havana harbor, had a capacity of 28,000 barrels per day. Texaco invested $35,000,000 in construction of a refinery in Santiago de Cuba with capacity of 20,000 barrels daily. Thus, two great oil companies, that previously had shipped refined products into the Cuban market, now became refiners and helped increase Cuban capacity from 20,000 to 83,000 barrels per day. This, of course, substantially increased industrial employment and made a significant contribution to our national income, industrial output and capital investment.

We also aided in the installation of a small refinery near the Jarahueca oil field, providing the enterprise with its building and following procedures similar to those we had resorted to in Jatibonico, where we built the Petroleum Research Laboratory and saw to it that the heavy drilling equipment which the Government had purchased was kept in constant operation.

This too was destroyed by the Communists. By early 1960, the Castro regime owed vast sums to the oil companies.

In February, the Red regime signed an agreement with the Soviet Union whereby Cuba was to receive 10,000,000 tons of crude oil in return for 5,000,000 tons of Cuban sugar. Previously, most Cuban oil had been imported from Venezuela.

Communist pressure was exerted on the Texaco refinery to make it take Russian oil. However, due to the company's contractual obligations, because of the Government's mounting debt to it and because of the inferior quality of Soviet crude and the damage it did to modern U.S. refining equipment, Texaco refused. When the same proposition was made to Esso and Shell, 47 Soviet technicians were already in Havana. On receipt of a negative reply, the refineries were summarily confiscated and turned over to the Russians.

21

Beaches, Hotels and Tourism

Just as autonomous administrative entities were created for public improvement projects and to create, develop and maintain philanthropic institutions and recreational and other community projects, so decentralization was carried into other sectors of Government. By freeing these operations from red tape and enlisting the cooperation of the private groups concerned, we achieved promising results. These autonomous entities were never allowed to disrupt the unity of the State and certainly not to become states within the State like the University of Havana or the monstrous INRA of Castro.

TECHNOLOGICAL RESEARCH

Although a research laboratory had been created with BAN-FAIC, primarily for investigations of minerals and other raw materials, and another one at the National Development Commission, we organized the Cuban Institute of Technological Research (ICIT) under the jurisdiction of the Ministry of Agriculture. Its chief purpose was to do research in connection with natural resources development.

In June 1952, in accordance with the proposals of the Truslow Mission of the International Bank for Reconstruction and Development, we set up the National Economic Council which drew up the organization plan for the entity that would later be known as the ICIT.

On December 28, 1953, we decided to earmark part of the proceeds from the bond issue for veterans' benefits, courts and other projects to pay for the equipment of the autonomous Institute. A year later, by Law #2117 of January 27, 1955, the Cuban Institute was actually launched. At this time, the sugar situation was such that it became imperative that we develop new sources of national income and hence of employment.

The Institute was assigned an operating capital of $500,000. Agriculture and industry were represented on its board, especially the sugar industry, which, despite its importance, had never had any laboratories other than those at the mills. The laboratory of the Ministry of Agriculture, together with its new building, was transferred to the Cuban Institute.

NATIONAL PLANNING BOARD

This organization was created by Law #2018 of January 27, 1955 as a "technical, consultant organization of the Executive Department and to provide a scientific foundation for national economic development and for the appraisal of land." It was to draw up national and regional regulatory plans[1] and also to study improvement of communications and greater efficiency and economy in the use of land and the exploitation of natural resources.

Upon my recommendation, it began operations with a national plan and then proceeded with a plan for Greater Havana and plans for the three tourist areas of greatest potential: Varadero, Trinidad and the Isle of Pines.

A precondition for the elaboration of these plans was an extremely accurate map of the territory and adjacent keys in addition to full demographic, economic and other data. This project was very costly. The first task was to separate the mapping and cadastral survey from the planning projects. To this end, we created the Cuban Institute of Cartography and Cadastral Survey (ICCC) by Law #2049 of February 5, 1955.

While the survey and cartographic work was in progress, the National Planning Board completed the first Pilot Plan of the Island of Cuba, containing physical, geographic, social and economic data basic to the activities of the nation. Using the topographical map of Greater Havana as its starting point, the Board

---

[1] These regulatory plans defined the norms which economic development should meet and the conditions it should comply with.

proceeded with its regulatory plan. The area affected included the neighboring towns of Marianao, Santiago de las Vegas, Regla, Guanabacoa and Santa Maria del Rosario.

The Isle of Pines had great potential sources of wealth and, due to its natural beauty, unexcelled medicinal waters, historically close connections with the United States and proximity to the nation's capital, major possibilities as a tourist center. I was determined to have the Isle included in the plans for regional progress. Accordingly, I requested the Board to prepare a pilot plan for this area that would coordinate all the projects of my Administration affecting the Isle of Pines, such as road systems, residential parks, hotel zones, tourist facilities, etc.

A project of no less importance comprised the Trinidad zone in the province of Las Villas and was centered at the Topes de Collantes Sanatorium. By the end of 1958, work was progressing on the pilot plans for Santa Clara, Cienfuegos and Santiago de Cuba.

THE GREAT MAP

I was determined to have Cuba mapped in a scientific fashion. The Organic Law of Cartography and Cadastral Survey provided, in accordance with the Constitution, for the exact measurement of the nation's territory and other topographic studies.

Use of most advanced geodetic and topographic procedures and tridimensional aerial photographs, which showed precise, reliable details, contributed promptness and economy to the task. However, since the aerial photos available to the ICCC had all been taken prior to 1953, we made an agreement with the U. S. Army Map Service—through the Interamerican Geodetic Service —to take new photos. At the same time, we contracted (on November 27th, 1956) with the Aero-Service Corporation of America for the completion of new topographic maps of Cuba within a period of two years, to be printed in full color, with level curves every ten meters on a 1:50,000 scale.

This entire gigantic project was completed on schedule. No less than 324 sheets of the Great Map were made and sent to Philadelphia for printing. For control purposes, a total of 2,345 stereoscopic models of the 115 flight lines of the air photos had to be made, covering the entire territory and taken with photogrametric equipment.

This map, which was being printed in December 1958, provided exact data on the geographic, topographic and other important features of the Island. The map presents the data necessary for the sound development of our national resources, for regional development projects and for equitable cadastral planning.

OTHER CARTOGRAPHIC WORKS

In addition to the Great Map, the ICCC mapped Greater Havana in six colors on a 1:2000 scale. Numerous offset copies were made on the Institute's press. Thus, 9,000 copies of the Marianao section were run off and used to number and name its streets. Road maps were made of each province and of the Isle of Pines. Hundreds of requests for aerial photos were made by both public entities and private enterprise, especially by groups interested in petroleum discovery. Moreover, maps were printed for each locality in connection with the Census of Population. After completing the topographic map, the ICCC started work in late 1958 on a geological map of the country.

TOURISM

By Law #137 of June 12, 1952, we reorganized the National Tourism Corporation and transformed it into the Cuban Institute of Tourism. The main objective was to assist and stimulate private enterprise and to eliminate red tape.

Without adequate facilities and access, the best tourist attractions are worthless. We found that even in the capital, hotel facilities were inadequate. In Havana, seven old hotels had been torn down; four were being turned into boarding houses and, of the few that remained, eleven had closed down their restaurants. Outside of Havana, only three provinces had first class hotels. In the main cities, the best hotels closed their restaurant facilities to the general public, making them available to regular guests only.

To make Cuba a tourist center ranking with the best in the Americas was a titanic job. Nevertheless, the country possessed exceptional possibilities: one hour flying time from Miami and four from New York and Mexico, natural beauty, a favorable climate, lush tropical beaches, romantic colonial cities, year-around sunshine, health spas, unexcelled hunting and fishing, the striking beauty of our women and the traditional hospitality of our people.

We began by reviewing the regulations governing ticket agencies and the work of guides and interpreters. Customs red tape was minimized and travel barriers to tourists and transients from the Americas were eliminated. Tourists from all American countries were allowed to visit Cuba for 29 days without a consular visa (Law #1832 of December 10th, 1934). Red tape was eliminated to allow them to bring their cars and drive them throughout the Island. This was also done for private boats and aircraft. Another law promoted the construction of inns and motels along the highways and waterways, requiring a minimum area of 8,000 square meters at a distance of not less than 30 meters from the highways (Law #813 of April 18, 1953). We enacted the Hotel Law (#2074) granting tax exemptions to all new hotels, motels and similar establishments providing tourist accommodations.

The results soon became apparent. A great flow of native and foreign capital was directed into the tourist industry and this was matched with government funds. Thirteen absolutely modern hotels were built on first class locations to provide 2,258 rooms. Some, like the Havana Hilton and the Havana Riviera, were given direct financial assistance by Government. Between 1953 and 1958, the following hotels were built in Havana:

Hotel	*Number of Rooms*
Havana Hilton	630
Havana Riviera	400
Capri	252
Copacabana	132
Havana Deauville	120
Vedado	120
St. John's	108
Commodore	100
Colina	80
Lido	68
Rosita	58
Caribbean	50
Siboney	40

By the end of 1958, Havana had 42 hotels with a total of 5,438 rooms as against 29 hotels with 3,180 rooms in 1952. Furthermore, construction was about to begin on two others, one of them with 1,000 rooms at the waterfront in Vedado.

Hotels were also built in other Cuban cities. In Cienfuegos, the Jagua Hotel-Motel; at Ciego de Avila, the Ciego de Avila Hotel; and on the Isle of Pines, the Mineral Springs, the Green River on the bank of the Las Casas River and the Annex and the Santa Fé. The boom in the hotel and tourist industry provided employment for every member of the Cuban Gastronomic Federation and Hotel and Restaurant Employees' Union at top wages. All this was destroyed at one sweep when Castro took power, confiscated the hotels and turned them over to Communist agents and Soviet military personnel.

During the five years immediately prior to the Revolution of 1952, Cuban tourists abroad spent $57.8 million more than foreign tourists spent in Cuba. During the last five years of my Administration, this balance changed to $39.0 million in our favor. The reversal occurred, not by impeding foreign travel by Cubans, but by the positive step of almost tripling tourist expenditures in Cuba. During 1958, 218,000 of the 308,000 tourists who came to Cuba arrived from the United States.

BARLOVENTO

The Barlovento (Windward) Tourist Center, the only one of its class in Cuba, was created not far from the capital, between the neighboring Jaimanitas river and La Puntilla. It covered an area of 600,000 square meters comprising a series of islets and peninsulas linked by bridges and separated from each other by canals 30 meters wide; a residential section with only one entrance and with every lot directly on the navigable canals; some 596,000 square meters of land were reclaimed from coastal wastelands by means of a huge dredging and refilling project in a swampy area. The value of this was appraised at $8,100,000.

PANORAMIC HIGHWAYS

The construction of panoramic highways of great tourist attraction, linking Cuban towns, otherwise practically isolated from each other, by means of coastal roads linked to the Central Highway, offered great possibilities for the development of new industries. My Administration was not satisfied with the revamping, in the western portion of the Island, of the Northern Circuit Highway from Mariel to Pinar del Rio. Thus, a super highway was constructed from Havana to the port of Mariel, beginning at Santa Fé.

Cuba's inter-American commitment to the Pan-American Highway, linking the Continent, had been completed with the new highway from Pinar del Rio to the cove of La Fé, on the western end of the Island. From there, the route would proceed by ferry to the port of Juárez, in the Yucatán peninsula, where it would merge with the Mexican section of the Pan-American Highway.

The three tunnels, two under the Almendares River and the third under the harbor of Havana, relieved motor vehicle congestion and ever-present traffic snarls and also contributed greatly to the expansion of new urban areas tourism. The Pinar del Rio North Circuit Highway, in addition to being the only overland means of communication for four sugar mills, is also the route leading to the Valley of Viñales, an area of incomparable beauty located near the famous San Vicente mineral springs of sulphuric waters. It is also adjacent to Stone Age mounds that intrigue archaeologists. The entire region contains so much of interest that we had intended to turn it into a National Park.

In the same Province of Pinar del Rio there are other medicinal baths of a thermal or sulphuric nature which have attained world fame. We restored them, put in modern facilities, embellished the surroundings and improved access. Twenty-five buildings were constructed at the entrance to the town in order to house families who had been evicted by eminent domain because of the project. The medicinal baths of San Diego de los Baños soon became one of Cuba's great attractions.

We built the Tourist Center of the Western Mountains in another part of Pinar del Rio. Among its many natural attractions were the internationally famous orchids growing wild at Soroa. This region was linked to the Central Highway with a first-class road. The project included construction of a 227-room hotel and a number of attractive cabañas.

ISLE OF PINES

Many projects were completed on the Isle of Pines. Named "Island of the Evangelist" by Columbus and "Treasure Island" by Cuban tradition, it lacked access and we had to build several splendid highways. The almost impassible road that linked Santa Fé with Nueva Gerona had to be completely rebuilt. Private enterprise backed the Government in these projects and created numerous new sources of employment.

Law #2071 of January 27, 1955 declared the Island and its adjacent keys to be a tourist zone up to a distance of 15 nautical miles to seaward. Since the Isle is famous for its abundance of wild life, we installed the facilities necessary for hunting and fishing. To stimulate its agricultural and industrial development, the Isle of Pines was turned into a free port zone. A foundation was created for its afforestation.

THE WHITE WAY

Prior to March 1952, construction had begun on a superhighway, chiefly for tourism, to be known as the White Way and to extend from the nation's capital to the numerous beach resorts on the north coast east of Havana as far as Guanabo. My Government extended this highway all the way to Matanzas, passing through picturesque Boca de Jaruco. We had to overcome great engineering obstacles until the road reached Dos Rios via La Cumbre. The highway provides a colorful view of the ocean throughout and skirts the lush valley of Yumurí. This scenic highway of more than 70 miles considerably reduced the distance between Havana and Varadero Beach.

THE BLUE BEACH

Due to its location, its extent, its fine, white sand and the blue transparency of its waters, Varadero is one of the most beautiful beaches in the world. Since it had tremendous potentialities for tourism, we created the Planning Commission of the Varadero Tourist Center by Law #2082 of January 27, 1955 to promote the beach center and create the Varadero Tourist Center Authority. These organizations were vested with the powers necessary for the full development and urban improvement of Cuba's Blue Beach.

The Varadero Airport was promoted to international status and its landing strips extended to 2,000 meters. Varadero was provided with an aqueduct and a canal 150 feet wide was dredged to connect the Paso Malo Lagoon with the ocean on the north side. Another canal was dredged on the south side, to the estuary of Cueva del Muerto in the Bay of Cárdenas. The peninsula of Hicacos, was turned into another island by the dredged canals.

The problems that this project created for maritime and land traffic were overcome by constructing a drawbridge with sufficient central clearance—six meters above sea level—to allow passage to 95% of all pleasure craft without raising the bridge. When the dredging was completed, the Lagoon became a yacht basin and marina for hundreds of yachts. It had a spacious building to house immigration and customs officials in addition to other installations for yachtsmen and boat owners.

In December, 1958, an expressway from the drawbridge to the tip of the Hicacos peninsula was nearing completion. All along the route, there were protected mooring facilities for all types of pleasure craft. The Chapellín channels and its estuary were linked by another canal 8,537 meters in length. The estuary itself was continuously sprayed to destroy insects and larvae.

The effects of this program were soon visible. Varadero became the realization of the dreams of the Cuban people and private investors showed increasing enthusiasm for its famous *Playa Azul* (Blue Beach). Thus, private investment in Varadero increased from $245,000 in 1951 to $2,589,000 in 1956—a tenfold advance.

22

The Highway Construction Program

In 1941, during my first Administration, we obtained a loan of
$25,000,000 from the Export-Import Bank to repair the Central
Highway and undertake other projects in the public interest. The
National Development Commission (Comisión de Fomento Nacional—CFN) was created to carry out these tasks and serve
other vital national needs.

The highway repair program was started with modern labor-
saving equipment. Simultaneously, we commenced building a network of feeder and service roads. In 1944, when my term of office
expired, we left 1,086 kilometers of roads under construction or
under contract and 798 kilometers of completed roads. The aqueducts of Santiago de Cuba, Camagüey and Holguín were also
under construction as was the Agabama River project, which was
designed to solve and did eventually solve the water problem of
the city of Santa Clara, capital of Las Villas. Six cold storage warehouses for farm produce had also been completed and were in
operation.

When I took power again in March 1952, I decided to proceed
with all the unfinished projects of the previous Auténtico Administration. Many were of doubtful utility. However, since large
sums had already been invested, their completion seemed war-
ranted. We finished them all, including particularly the tunnel
under the Almendares River, upgrading standards and quality in
accordance with the importance of each project.

We decided to give priority to public improvements most urgently needed to stimulate agriculture, such as a network of intersecting roads crisscrossing the entire country. We would also stress projects necessary to community renewal and business enterprise. Highways and service roads, silos and wharves, dredging projects, bridges and dams were among the wide variety of tasks assigned to the CFN.

CENTRAL HIGHWAY

When the Central Highway was first completed in May 1929, the first signs of the Great Depression were being felt throughout the country. Hard times were in store for us. Truck competition was about to deal a staggering blow to the railroads which heretofore had been the dominant medium for transportation between provinces. During the crisis, the enormous potential of the Highway became evident. Because of the burden of the sugar crisis, accentuated by the Hawley-Smoot Tariff, however, this was more prospect than reality.

The 1933 Revolution ushered in an era of economic recovery, slow at first, but persistent and sure. The country was growing rapidly in population. As the number, weight and speed of motor vehicles were increasing even more rapidly, the Central Highway soon proved inadequate for its purpose. Moreover, it was being rapidly destroyed and by 1952 deterioration was so extensive that some of its sections were almost impassable.

We did a thorough reconstruction job, replacing huge stretches of roadbed and concrete and surface compound, rebuilding culverts and shoulders. We had to eliminate surface cracks, cave-ins and other damage. Almost total reconstruction of the sections from Punta Brava to Pinar del Rio, from San Francisco de Paula to Matanzas and from Santa Clara to Santa Rita in Oriente were necessary as these had become hazardous to traffic.

Reconstruction of the Central Highway used 1,913,000 lbs. of steel bars, 117,150 square meters of reinforcement mesh, 79,600 cubic meters of fill, almost 5 million square meters of bituminous concrete surfacing, over a million meters of shoulders and embankment that had to be cleaned or repaired and many similar items.

We also tackled the problem of highway intersections. We introduced the cloverleaf access system, first at the White Way, later on the Varadero Tourist Highway and finally on the Central Highway itself.

THE HIGHWAY ACHIEVEMENT

Connecting highways had been constructed which branched out from the center of the Island to the ports. However, the ports and the other towns on both coasts remained isolated from each other. To solve this difficulty, we proceeded to carry out a grandiose project conceived in 1952—the construction of the North Circuit and South Circuit Highways.[1] These operations were almost complete when the Reds took over at the beginning of 1959.

The total length of the Central Highway is 1,180 km. The highways built under my second Administration totalled 2,186 km. In addition, we built or rebuilt another 1,148 kilometers either wholly or in part.

These figures do not include routine highway maintenance and repair of thousand of additional miles of roads, many of them asphalt surfaced. When rebuilt roads are added, the total mileage is 19,172 km. This work involved a vast amount of detailed engineering operations: bridges had to be built to span rivers; metallic superstructures were replaced by concrete ones; highways were reinforced to meet the stresses of heavier and faster vehicles and ever-increasing traffic loads. The cave-ins that are such a general problem on Latin America highways were practically eradicated from the Cuban road system.

REVITALIZING COMMUNITY INITIATIVE

The lethargy of community life in Cuba was the result of economic factors and of excessive centralization. Practically all the services that the municipalities should have rendered had been left to the National Government. In view of the fact that such essential local services as education, health and social welfare were seriously deficient, we reverted to a procedure that had proved most successful in my earlier Administration.

The municipalities of Cuba could hardly maintain a first-aid station, build an aqueduct or improve the one they had, to say nothing of undertaking such local improvements as setting up

[1] See *Piedras y Leyes, op. cit.*, pp. 280-4, for details.

parks or paving their streets. Hygiene, police and schools also came under the jurisdiction of the Central Government.

Everything needed to be done, but the State could not do it all with its ordinary resources and alone. Under the circumstances, the system of foundations seemed the best answer. The Government would do its part if the citizens of each community put their shoulders to the wheel.

This approach, which had been very successful under my first Administration,[2] was discarded by the Auténticos. We restored, revised and amplified it in 1952. This expansion meant that local public improvements became the responsibility of the citizens of the localities, aided technically and financially by the National Government.

We first created simple Foundations for Service Roads (Law #477 of October 24, 1952). The provincial committees came next. These coordinated local projects and strove to gear public works activity in with employment need. After that, we created Local Foundations for Urban Projects to carry out "municipal projects, especially self-supporting enterprises in the interests of the communities." Both systems were under the general supervision of the National Executive Committee of Local, Urban and Rural Foundations (Comisión Ejecutiva Nacional de Patronatos Locales, Urbanos y Campesinos—CENPLUC).

We agreed to extend Government aid for local service road projects provided the roads did not exceed 10 km. in length or cost over $1,000 per kilometer and provided the local foundations put up 30% of the cost. These private contributions were acceptable up to 50% in labor, building materials and use of equipment. We defined local service roads as those connecting agrarian, maritime or mining centers or rural crop centers within the same municipality to main highways.

If construction costs exceeded $1,000 per km., private contributions would have to be 20% more in cash. If the road was built by the municipality, the State's contribution would be 40% of project cost. Funds were obtained by the State from budget appropriations and from the National Lottery.

[2] As evidenced by the foundations of Pinar del Río and Matanzas.

REALIZED HOPES

Did the CENPLUC foundations live up to our expectations? Yes, indeed, they were successful from the start. The countryside was rapidly covered by a mesh of roads and the cities witnessed a tremendous growth in their community projects, transforming their appearance and improving the living conditions of their inhabitants. The following figures speak for themselves:

—3,849 foundations were created, of which 2,642 were for service roads and 1,207 for local urban projects. They carried out $48.7 millions of projects.

—Some 15,594 km. of roads were built at a cost of $22.2 millions, of which the foundations contributed $8.5 millions and the Government $13,8 millions.

—We built 4,411 city blocks of new streets, most of them with culverts, sidewalks and drainage. This was the equivalent of 1,764,400 square meters and cost $26.5 millions, of which the foundations contributed $16.9 millions.

—Ten towns were supplied with electric light and power.

—City halls were built in two towns; two seawalls, 26 public parks, not to mention other public buildings and memorial landmarks, were constructed.

The CENPLUC was unquestionably an institution worthy of support and deserving even wider scope. It was one of our most democratic institutions as it was deeply rooted in the people from the outset. The people governed and directed it with complete autonomy. It was an organization which relied on its own resources and initiative (backed by Government contributions and technical aid) and which had a proud record of accomplishment for the benefit of many communities and a large backlog of work in process. This institution, which was such a proud example for the peoples of the Americas, was abolished as soon as the vandals of the Sierra Maestra took power.

Instead, the Communists created the INRA, a bureacratic monster, totalitarian and centrally directed. As early as January 26, 1959, less than one month after taking power, the Reds liquidated CENPLUC on the grounds that it "duplicated the functions of a department of the Ministry of Public Works."

PARKS AND GREEN AREAS

The National Parks and Green Areas Administration (ONPAV) was born on April 2, 1955. It proceeded to provide our cities with new parks and playgrounds, to build new promenades, to repair and improve existing recreation areas and to concentrate on improving recreational facilities for the children. ONPAV organized 94 foundations for the conservation and embellishment of local parks.

At the National Park of Sierra del Cristal, more than 100,000 trees were planted and measures were taken to prevent indiscriminate felling of the pines. A census of commemorative monuments and historic landmarks was made to aid in their preservation. More than thirty children's playgrounds were set up through the country and equipped with recreational equipment. Some 34 municipal parks were either built or completely rebuilt.

23

Maritime, Rail and Air Transport

In 1933, the condition of our transport system was chaotic. The oldest component, maritime transportation, was at a standstill. Crushed by truck and air competition and burdened by unwise regulations, the railroads were chronically in the red and on the verge of bankruptcy. The airlines, with a brilliant future, were the prey of privileged gangs of grafters. Aviation was particularly in need of government regulation and government financial aid.

REGULATORY ORGANIZATIONS

In March 1952, we incorporated two key commissions into the Ministry of Communications, placing them under a new Undersecretary. Thus, a special department had been created to handle transportation problems.

Later, in July 1953, we organized the National Transport Corporation, the head of which was a member of the Cabinet without portfolio. The duties and powers of the two commissions were transferred to the new Corporation. The National Transport Corporation was advised by a Technical Commission, representing the public carriers and the trade unions.

Our first attempt to reorganize the transportation industry was by Law #1486 of June 10, 1954. Through this act, we hoped to curb the extensive illegal traffic and unlawful competition which jeopardized the nation's carriers and the State's investment in them. The industry suffered from cut-rate pricing and cut-throat competition.

Law #1486 was a painstaking approach to the task of comprehensive regulation of transportation. It set up uniform accounting systems, controlled rate differentials, established rules designed to protect human life and conserve the highways and laid the foundations for complete reorganization of the carriers, especially the trucking companies. Law #1553 took further strides in these directions.

MARITIME TRAFFIC

In Colonial days, there was a prosperous coastal shipping trade between the main ports of Cuba due to the lack of rail communications between Las Villas and Oriente provinces. National independence, however, brought with it an expansion of the railroad network. Coastal shipping consequently declined, while ocean shipping thrived because of the sugar boom and the growth of foreign trade.

Our geographical situation and our numerous excellent natural harbors gave us splendid prospects for the development of a merchant marine, provided an adequate credit and financial system was devised. One of the best instruments to attract capital was the ship's mortgage. This device, established by Law #1420 of March 12, 1954, made the vessel collateral for loans. Since the old Code of Commerce, adopted in Spain in 1885 and extended to Cuba, did not cover this type of loan, we had to devise our own rules and regulations in this area. The problem that we faced and solved was to devise a system which would enable shipowners to get credit on ship collateral and to enable creditors to attach that collateral readily in case of loan default.[1]

Due to the expansion of our trade, continuous improvement in wharves, warehouses and port facilities was necessary. Assigning the two wharves at the Paula docks to the national merchant marine laid the foundations for this improvement. Construction

---

[1] Orders for seizure or attachment of ships, issued by Cuban courts, had proved difficult to obtain, cumbersome and a severe handicap to the business of the owners. Law #1585 of August 4, 1954 changed the procedural rules, created adequate methods of protection and custody and allowed the vessels to continue in service while remaining under the jurisdiction of Cuban courts.

of a marine terminal in Havana harbor with all necessary facilities was another major step in this direction. The old terminals of Tallapiedra, Hacendados and Atarés dated back to Colonial times, while at Regla the obsolete buildings of the Bank of Commerce (also built in Colonial days) were still in use.

In addition to the Maritime Terminal of Havana, built at a cost of $30 million, similar facilities were erected at Bahía Honda and at Mariel, an excellent auxiliary port for Havana. Others were constructed at the Bay of Matanzas and the port of Guayabal on the south coast of the province of Camagüey to service important sugar mills.

During my previous Administration, we had constructed the gigantic Cárdenas and Dubrocq wharves for the free port of Matanzas, created by Law #490 of September 14, 1934.[2]

THE DRYDOCK

Drydocks were not new to Havana. Years ago, there had been a small, floating drydock operated early in the Republican era by the Krajewski Pessant Corporation. When it disappeared (for reasons best known to that firm), all repairs and shipyard work were done at the shops of Viuda Ruiz de Gámiz. Later, this became the Havana Marine Railways, Inc. My first Administration bought these facilities to effect urgent repairs for the Cuban Navy. This was the cornerstone of the future Cuban Navy Shipyard.

These drydock facilities had been sorely needed for a long time as the port of Havana had almost the heaviest marine traffic in the world. The project began to materialize with the technical advice of naval engineers from the United States and from our own Cuban Navy. Approved on January 27, 1956 at a cost of $10,000,000, the drydock was designed to handle repairs of at least 75% of the vessels calling at the port of Havana—namely, those not over 475 feet long. The utility of the drydock from an

[2] Other important harbor projects were completed by Texaco in Santiago de Cuba, by Esso in the Marimelena Estuary of Havana Bay, by Freeport Sulphur Company in Moa Bay and by the Cuban Nickel Company in the Bay of Levisa. All were important marine terminals capable of handling deep-draft merchant ships with docks, wharves and, in many cases, seawalls. In January 1957, we granted a concession for the construction of a causeway over the ocean between Caibarién and its neighboring port, Cayo Francés, on the northern coast of the province of Las Villas, to meet the needs of that large and growing region.

economic point of view was shown by the fact that the Cuban Navy had been spending over a million dollars yearly for major ship repairs in U.S. yards.

Work was due to begin in 1959 on a shipyard at the port of Mariel. This was to cost $86,000,000. The project had been studied exhaustively. On October 30, 1958, the Mariel Shipyard Company was launched for the construction and repair of ships and for other work related to the shipping industry. Anglo-Cuban investors were interested in the project which was to start with $20,000,000 of operating capital, of which $15,000,000 would have been provided by government financing agencies and $5,000,000 by the British investors.

Cuban contractors were to handle the work with the technical assistance of British firms. The yard was to have had a shipbuilding capacity of 125,000 tons, a capacity to build ships up to 14,000 tons and an initial output schedule of 25 vessels of 5,000 tons each. This shipyard project was complementary to the drydock and both would have been geared into the development of a Cuban heavy metals industry based on our abundant ore resources.

RAILROADS

Cuba has the honor of being the first country in the Americas, with the exception of the United States, to have built and operated a railroad. That memorable day in 1834 when the first Cuban train pulled out of Havana bound for the town of Bejucal, hauling passengers and cargo, is one of the highlights of our economic history. Railroads were laid throughout the sugar and coffee regions, linking mills and plantations with the nearest seaports. Nevertheless, at the end of the Colonial era in 1898, Cuba's railroad reached eastward only as far as Santa Clara and westward only to Consolación del Sur.

During the period of transition from Colony to Republic, the railroad system, which had been created by British capital, was consolidated. U.S. and Canadian capital financed a railroad system linking Havana with Santiago de Cuba. This was intended to stimulate agriculture and business throughout the eastern part of the Island.[3]

[3] The United Railways of Havana, comprising the Havana Railway, the Matanzas Railway and the Júcaro and Cárdenas Railway in the early days of

In March 1952, Cuba had two railway systems. The United Railways of Havana and Regla Warehouses, Ltd., and the Consolidated Railroads of Cuba. The first ran from Guane to Santa Clara, the second from Santa Clara to Guantánamo.

When I returned to power in 1952, I found railroad transportation on the brink of chaos, especially the United Railways, which had suffered an appalling shrinkage in passenger and freight revenues. The company was practically bankrupt. We came to its aid and began giving it funds on a temporary basis while trying to work out a permanent solution. It was clear that the choice was between government takeover and disappearance of the line.

Law #980 of July 24, 1953 solved this problem by State purchase of the United Railways of Havana, together with the Havana Terminal Railroad, Havana's Central Station, the Marianao and Havana Railroads, the Central Railway of Matanzas and the Cuban and International Express Company, for $20,000,000.

When the transaction was consummated, a joint enterprise was created—the first of its kind in Cuba—under the corporate name of Cuban Western Railroads with a capital of $30,000,000 for reorganization and operations.

The road ahead was hard. Obstacles had to be overcome, sacrifices borne and setbacks suffered. But we made progress. In less than three years, the personnel cutbacks were eliminated. Workers, laid off, but held as a reserve manpower pool by agreement between the union and Government, were called back on the job. Wage cuts were repealed and, in the end, the nation again had a thriving railroad system. Reorganization costs had been held down to a bare minimum. The assets bought for $20,-000,000 were worth $70,000,000 five years later.

THE CONSOLIDATED RAILROADS

On a memorable day in July 1903, a golden spike was driven into a railroad track at Capestany Farm near Falcón in Las Villas. Cuba had been spanned by rail from Havana to Santiago de Cuba. A few days after this juncture, Don Tomás Estrada Palma, the first

---

the Republic, had later merged with the Western Railroad and the Cuban Central Railway. These in turn merged later with the Sagua and Caibarién Railroads. The second system united the Consolidated Railroads of Cuba with the Cuban Railroad Company, the Northern Cuban Railroads and the lines running from Camagüey to Nuevitas and from Guantánamo westward.

President of the Republic, officially opened the railroad line that spanned the long axis of the nation.

In the years that followed, the system was consolidated with others in the eastern provinces, where colossal sugar mills had been erected, several of them capable of processing over a million bags of sugar each crop year. While the sugar tonnage was satisfactory, there was a dangerous and eventually disastrous decline in other revenues because of the competition of other types of carriers.

The Consolidated Railroads faced a severe crisis in March 1952. As of May 31st of that year, its losses totalled $1,550,000. This made it impossible to maintain wage and salary levels. A wage-cut proposal was submitted to government, which we referred to a Cabinet committee. After exhaustive investigation, the committee rejected the wage cuts, but proposed certain readjustments that temporarily reduced pay rates, but kept employment levels constant. This was authorized by Decree #1535 of June 8, 1955. Later, we were able to have the wages restored to their previous level.

RAILROAD REORGANIZATION

We nationalized a vast rail network by purchase at a price satisfactory to the sellers. There had been no confiscation and no government pressure. Not a single stockholder of the old British company had been deprived of his rights to a proportionate share of his investment even though the Company had paid no dividends and failed to meet its mortgage payments over a number of years. Nor was there any prospect that it would return to solvency.

We did not pay the price initially asked for by the railroad, because it seemed to us excessive. But we paid a fair price. Thus, when we hoisted the national flag on the mast at the Havana Central Station, we had the satisfaction of knowing that it was being done with honor. We would not have had it otherwise in view of the fact that British resources and that illustrious British subject, Mr. Stephenson, had helped Cuba over so many years.

After many years of lagging maintenance, both companies needed total reconstruction of their track and modern locomotives. The old iron horses had to be swapped for Diesels. But the greater weight and speed of the new Diesels would mean immediate replacement of 85-pound rails by 100-pound or heavier ones. We would also have to adopt new mechanized track maintenance methods. All these transitions were well advanced at the time when the Communist hordes spread sabotage and terror, death and destruction, through the Island, uprooting the railroad system as one of their main activities.

Both companies acquired Diesels of up to 240,000 pounds and 1,600 horsepower. We hoped that Cuba would soon become the first country in Latin America with a completely Diesel railroad system. Other improvements were the Budd motor coaches, serving fast, inter-urban timetables, and a vast number of new passenger and freight cars of various models and capacities.

In 1958, Cuba was one of the leading countries in the Americas, and even compared favorably with Europe, in respect to railroad facilities. We had one kilometer of railroad track for every 8.08 kilometers of total area. We had 14,164 km. of track, 565 locomotives, 401 pasenger coaches, 104 box cars and over 10,000 flat cars.[4]

AUTOBUSES MODERNOS

From 1950 to April 22, 1952, Autobuses Modernos, S. A., (AMSA) received the sum of $17,722,885 from the State plus other benefits. The company had been set up by the preceding Administration as successor to the Havana Electric Railway Company, which in turn was the successor to the Havana Urban Railway. The new company was plagued by agitation and gangsterism, which had been tolerated by the previous Auténtico administration. The transfer of its franchise had caused a Senate investigation of the Auténtico Minister of Finance. Eventually, the new firm, headed by financier William D. Pawley, became so much involved in disputes and union demands that Pawley quit in disgust.

Our Administration did its best to bring peace between feuding factions that attempted to impose their will by violence. Many of their leaders had long criminal records. By pursuing their strug-

[4] Of this track, 5,099 kilometers were public carriers, 8,915 kilometers were sugar plantation lines and 149 kilometers were privately owned lines. In one year, 1955, for example, the railroads moved 29 million tons of freight. Sugar haulage provided $23.1 millions of the total railroad revenues of $37.2 millions. Passenger traffic yielded $4.4 millions and miscellaneous income $9.7 millions.

gle against the Government, they helped plunge Cuba into the Red abyss. Nevertheless, the fact remained that, in order to subsist without government aid and meet expenses with its own income, Autobuses Modernos would have to be completely reorganized and its monthly deficit of $300,000 would have to be substantially reduced at once.

The situation deteriorated and we found it necessary to take drastic measures against the radicals who seemed determined to ruin the public transport system and destroy an important source of employment. The measures we adopted consisted mainly of repeated readjustments in pay scales and personnel.

These measures managed to keep the company afloat. However, its income was still insufficient to meet operating costs and still less to service or liquidate the $500,000 loan it had obtained from BANFAIC.

Accordingly, Law #1821 of December 3, 1954 granted AMSA a five-year indirect subsidy in the shape of complete exemption from duties on rolling stock, parts and materials. This too was of no avail.

It was impossible to allow this situation to continue. On July 8, 1958, Congress enacted Law #36 designed to solve the AMSA public transportation crisis. The liabilities of the company were written off; all pending workers' claims were paid off and a pledge was given to the labor unions that the buses would continue to operate. After the termination of government control of AMSA, its stockholders transferred their assets to the Compañía Financiera de Transporte for $6,174,091, assuming the obligation to pay $2,134,949 in past-due notes and $400,000 in debts to the unions.

OMNIBUSES ALIADOS

The growth in the population and area of Greater Havana was not paralleled by the development of modern urban transportation facilities. It seemed that all the subsidies and exemptions we had granted were not enough to meet the needs of the public. Moreover, the relations between labor and management were plagued by conflict.

Within the Omnibus Cooperative (Cooperativa de Omnibus Aliados, S. A., COA), there were irregularities due to the fact that various groups of bus owners were operating under temporary franchises that had been granted by different government officials and which were not consistent as to requirements. We enacted Law #908 of June 12, 1953 to bring order into this situation and regulate cooperatives engaged in intra-urban and inter-urban transportation of passengers. The law illegalized monopoly of routes as we believed that competition would benefit the public. After compliance with basic requisites relating to financial stability and public service, the carriers were given regular franchises in exchange for the temporary ones they had obtained from the officials of the previous Administration. The law also provided that 48.4% of the gross income of the cooperatives must be disbursed as wages and salaries and 7% must go for such social welfare purposes as paid vacations, workers' maternity and retirement funds, etc. This was merely an application of the basic principles of my Administration: to assist business enterprise, protect labor and improve public service.[5]

AVIATION

In March 1953, we established the Order of National Merit in Civil Aviation and proclaimed Civilian Pilots' Day. This was a tribute to the memory of the pioneers of Cuban aviation, Agustín Parlá and Domingo Rosillo, the two heroes of the historic overseas flights of 1913, one of them from Key West to Mariel, the other from Key West to Havana. These flights followed Bleriot's flight across the English Channel in 1909. At the same time, we provided for duty-free import of airplanes for pleasure, sport or educational purposes.

Cuba's flyers have contributed to the milestones in the development of American aviation. The history of air transportation could not be written without a glance at Cuba, nor the history of airmail without reference to Havana.

Law #59 of May 9, 1952 regulated civil aviation as to clearance papers and other requisites for the arrival and departure of passengers and cargo, bringing Cuban practice into conformity with the 1944 International Convention on Civilian Aviation.

---

[5] In 1958, 303 bus companies operated in Cuba with a total 4,459 vehicles, of which 1,919 operated in Havana (1,620 belonging to COA and 299 to AMSA). At the time of the Red takeover, we were planning to coordinate rail and highway transportation, to build a single freight terminal in Havana and establish a piggy-back service.

Law #877 of May 27, 1953 concerned visual aid to navigation and Law #2137 of January 27, 1955 dealt with government subsidy of airlines.

The Compañía Cubana de Aviación (CCA), a successor to Pan American Airways in Cuba, started operations in 1930 with only 925 kilometers of flight (between Havana and Santiago de Cuba), serviced by Ford-powered tri-motor planes. By 1958, Cuban airlines had expanded enough to show their colors in New York, Florida, Mexico, Portugal and Spain. They flew 17,210 kilometers on international routes. Besides Cubana, we had Aerovías Q, Cuba Aeropostal and Expreso Aéreo, all thriving enterprises. We built airports throughout the Island and stimulated private flying and aerial crop dusting of farming areas.

The tremendous expansion that occurred was based on generous government financing of the airlines through BANFAIC and later BANDES during my second Administration. On the 28th anniversary of Cubana Airlines (October 30, 1958), its fleet included inter alia three 86-passenger Super G Constellations, four Britannias with 94-passenger capacity and four 81-passenger Viscounts. For 1960, Cubana planned to add a Boeing 707-120 jet to its fleet, capable of carrying 125 passengers at a cruising speed of 965 kilometers per hour. This ship would have flown from Havana to New York in 2:49 hours and to Mexico in 2:29 hours. The abrupt and tragic end of this expansion program was a great loss to Cuba.

CIVIL AERONAUTICS COMMISSION

Because of the vital importance of air travel, we reorganized the old Civil Board of Aeronautics by Law #1104 of September 30, 1953. The following year (Law #1862 of December 22, 1954), we created the Civil Aeronautics Commission and assigned it the task of ensuring that Cuban aviation complied with the recommendations of the International Civil Aviation Organization.

The CAC was instrumental in general improvement of air carrier regulation. Air travel between Cuba and the rest of the world increased substantially after the 1952 Revolution and the following new international routes were authorized and opened during 1952-58: Miami to Varadero, Santiago de Cuba to Miami, Havana and Santiago de Cuba to Port-au-Prince and Ciudad

Trujillo, Havana to Mexico City, Santiago de Cuba to Kingston, Jamaica, and Havana to New York.

The CAC did a great deal to improve safety of takeoff and landing, a vital necessity as traffic and aircraft speeds increased. Radio beam towers were installed at the Santa Fé airport in Havana and at the Cienfuegos and Punta Alegre (Camagüey) airports. These radio towers not only served as reference points, but provided a long-range guidance system.

The CAC also examined pilots and engineers and certified those who proved qualified. It authorized the use of landing strips and airfields and registered aircraft. It saw that flight routes were verified, that the mechanical condition of aircraft was checked at regular intervals and that the control towers at the airports were properly operated.

AIRPORTS

We built airports at Santiago de Cuba and at the Sugar Mill "Los Caños" near Guantánamo, at Sante Fé, at Bauta, in Pinar del Rio, one at Veradero and still another on the Isle of Pines. Work was under way on the Santa Clara and Banes airports when the Reds took power.

The San Julián airport in Guane (Pinar del Rio), the Navy airport at Mariel, the Air Force bases at Camp Columbia and at San Antonio de los Baños, the Matanzas, Sancti Spíritus, Cienfuegos and Camagüey airports were all enlarged, improved or reorganized. Individuals and companies were encouraged to build innumerable landing strips throughout the Island for business, sport, crop dusting and other purposes.

The International Airport at Rancho Boyero in Havana Province was revamped. Among other things, a hotel for transients was built adjacent to the field. Terrorist gangs bombed and burned some of the new installations, but this merely aroused public anger without interrupting service for a moment. After January 1959, nearly all the Cuban pilots and engineers were driven into exile by the Communists.

To accommodate larger and larger passenger jets and continuously expanding commercial aviation, in which Cuba would play a major role because of her geographical situation, we planned to recondition the former military airport at San Antonio de los

Baños, which had been built by the U. S. Government during World War II and turned over to the Cuban Government thereafter. We built the Midday Expressway (Autopista del Mediodía), a superhighway to serve what was to become our great international airport of the future.

THE NATIONAL TRAFFIC COMMISSION

This organization was created as a branch of the National Transport Corporation to improve traffic conditions and reduce accidents, thus saving lives and property. No solution to traffic problems is possible without the cooperation of the public. Accordingly, we saw to it that the organizations concerned with traffic problems and the appropriate municipal departments were represented on the Board of Directors of the new entity.

Law #1774 of November 2, 1954 empowered the National Traffic Commission to install traffic lights and road signs wherever needed and to promulgate traffic and safety regulations. Local committees were appointed in all municipalities with the mayors as chairmen.

From the very beginning, the Commission adopted measures which rapidly improved the situation. More than 600 automatic lights were installed for motorists and pedestrians. An educational campaign encouraged public cooperation.

THE PARKING METERS

The National Public Parking Organization (ONEP) was created by Law #2068 of January 27, 1955 to solve the problem of overparking on the streets of the cities, a situation that was deteriorating every day. After public hearings at which all interested groups and individuals were heard, the ONEP proceeded vigorously with the installation of parking meters. More than 5,000 of these meters were installed by July 30, 1958. All taxi stands and loading zones needed in the cities had been designated and properly marked by that date.

The income which ONEP received from the parking meters was divided equally among the National Police Retirement Fund, the National Organization of Children's Dispensaries (ONDI), the National Organization of School and People's Dining Rooms (ONCEP), the National Organization for the Administration of

Government Hospitals (ONAHE) and ONEP itself to defray administrative costs.

The Communist movement of the 26th of July made the ONEP one of the chief targets of its campaigns of abuse and defamation and on January 1, 1959, the day of the Castro takeover, all the parking meters in Havana were stolen or destroyed by vandals. The Communists alleged that the meters destroyed the citizens' inalienable right to use the streets. Of course, thinking people realized that while individuals have the right to use the streets for transportation, they are not entitled to occupy them indefinitely and, by so doing, exclude others from their use. Moreover, the parking meter system had been installed only after protracted public hearings at which everyone who wanted to express an opinion was heard. And the system is general in the United States. But reason was not the forte of the Reds, nor rational solutions their purpose. They wished to find scapegoats, arouse hatred and train the mob to destroy the nation's wealth and kill its constructive elements.

AUTOMOBILES AND CUBAN PROSPERITY

Obviously, car registration is an excellent index of living standards and the Cuban figures for 1951-58 show the advances made during my second Administration.

AUTOMOBILES AND TRUCKS IN CUBA

Type of Vehicle	1951	1958	Increase
Private cars	65,439	140,267	74,828
Taxis	18,204	18,886	682
Trucks	34,338	46,569	12,231
Public Buses [6]	4,414	4,248	— 166
All Other [7]	1,781	2,286	505
TOTAL	124,176	212,256	88,080

[6] The decline in public buses was a result of the anarchy and gangster control of public administration during the era of Auténtico power (1944-1952). The buses were in such disrepair that many had to be cannibalized for spare parts.

[7] School buses, hearses, etc., but excluding motorcyles. Official cars are not included. During this period, the number of animal-drawn vehicles dropped from 6,831 in 1951 to 3,652 in 1958.

24

Public Housing and Slum Clearance

In 1952, we inherited a critical problem in the area of urban housing and urban rentals. Emergency laws had temporarily given tenants security and seemingly solved the housing shortage. However, these laws were the source of new difficulties. Ever since March 1949, a lagging building industry had aggravated the housing shortage. Old buildings were rapidly deteriorating due to inadequate maintenance and there was a consequent upward pressure on rents.

The problem dated back to 1939 when the unsatisfactory economic situation had driven urban rents beyond the means of much of the urban working class. Accordingly, on March 23rd of that year, city rents were frozen at the levels of July 1, 1937. This freezing measure was extended later, on three separate occasions: March 25, 1941, September 22, 1941 and January 28, 1944, at which time it was finally decided to keep the rents frozen at 1937 levels until six months after the end of World War II.

We needed legislation that would contribute to the economic upsurge of the nation. Our aims were to protect the interests of people of modest means, but, at the same time, to stimulate investment in residential construction by restoring the profit incentive. The continuing and rapid growth of both population and urbanization made this a problem of utmost urgency.[1]

---

[1] The problem was further complicated by the fact that many buildings under rent control had been leased to business or industry.

We held public meetings on the proposed legislation, encouraging all interested parties to speak out. We wanted a law which would benefit the groups most concerned and which would be accepted by the people.

IN DEFENSE OF THE TENANT

After careful study, Law #440 of October 5, 1952 was enacted, while simultaneously the Government was elaborating a plan to set up an autonomous organization to finance low-cost housing. The new law helped clarify a chaotic situation and had a stimulating impact on residential construction. It had provisions which stayed eviction proceedings except for reasons clearly specified in the statute. It gave priority rights to living space in new buildings to persons evicted by the demolition of the old ones on the same sites.

This was later made more flexible by substituting a cash payment to the tenant who lost his apartment through demolition —sometimes amounting to a few months' rent. The protection against eviction was upheld strictly, however, when the new building was business or commercial. Furthermore, while the new law established reasonable rents, it also granted tax and administrative exemptions as an incentive to the building trades. Rents were readjusted upward when new and improved premises were constructed. It was also stipulated that rent payments must entitle the tenant to certain basic services.

Rent reductions were decreed on dwellings built or licensed subsequent to March 23, 1949 and the frozen rents were applied to premises built prior to that date. For the benefit of the poorer classes, the rents on all tenements and rooms in private houses were cut 30% irrespective of the date when these premises had been built.

One objective of this measure was to destroy a system of collective and promiscuous tenements known in Cuba as *solares*. The rents were made so unattractive that nobody would build any more of them. This was done even though government tax revenues were adversely affected.

Tax exemptions were granted, as a rule, on all construction during the first two years after passage of the law. The period of grace on evictions was lengthened and steps were taken to improve enforcement. Later, Law #888 of June 2, 1952 amended the statute to give it greater flexibility and to mitigate the long protracted litigations between landlords and tenants which were so detrimental to both parties and to business in general.

When these landlord and tenant laws expired in 1958, we again canvassed the groups most concerned and then requested Congress to extend the laws for another year. Meanwhile, a specially designated Cabinet committee would study the situation and try to come up with a more definitive statute that would take into account the sturdy growth of private residential construction.

COOPERATIVES

Law #407 of September 16, 1952, regulating cooperative apartments and office buildings, provided a tremendous stimulus to this sort of enterprise. The statute specified building code requirements such as land area, access to the street, concrete foundations, structural standards, staircases, basements, patios, gardens, elevators, etc., and the way in which each apartment could be used. The management of all cooperative buildings was to be bound by the will of the majority and this was to be stated in the bylaws of the cooperative. *Between 1952 and 1958, $183,379,000 worth of cooperative buildings, providing a total of 42,528 apartments, were built in the province of Havana alone.*

INSURED MORTGAGES

Law #750 of March 20, 1953 authorized a special department of BANFAIC to issue mortgage insurance. Later, this work was assigned to a special autonomous organization, the FHA (Fomento de Hipotecas Aseguradas). After the 1954 election, the three basic laws on housing were consolidated (Law #2066 of January 27, 1955) and the FHA was given $1,500,000 in working capital.

The insured mortgage guaranteed the mortgagor full payment of interest and principal as provided in the mortgage contract. Only mortgages against homes already built or under construction were considered, though mortgage insurance was also made available for additions and improvements and for professional, commercial, industrial or agricultural buildings.

In the case of family dwellings, the insured principal was limited to $16,000, the instrument being a first mortgage with monthly payments covering interest and amortization. Loan applications had to be made through approved credit institutions, subject to examination by the National Bank of Cuba. These institutions handled the mortgages and serviced the accounts.

The FHA was authorized to issue Real Estate Bonds, backed by a Guarantee Fund of $2,000,000, also a Real Estate Fund consisting of the mortgages and property liens assigned FHA by the insured mortgagors and a Sales and Amortization Fund.

The FHA was authorized to set up a Fund of Insured Mortgages, backed by mortgages to the extent of 100%, and to issue bonds against this Fund with the status of a national public issue.

This system provided easy payments and attractive terms for the public. Thousands of medium-income families were for the first time able to realize their dream of owning their own homes. Under the FHA plan, 9,577 homes were constructed, representing a total investment of $78,928,000. The investment in these dwellings was as follows:

No. of Homes	Valuation of Dwellings
1,044	Less than $4,000
2,545	$4,000 to $6,999
2,008	$7,000 to $9,999
2,175	$10,000 to $12,999
1,151	$13,000 to $15,999
654	Over $16,000

Thus, 58.5% of the homes purchased under the FHA plan represented an investment of less than $10,000 and only 6.8% of the total were worth over $16,000. Some 34.7% were homes in the middle $10,000-to-$16,000 bracket.

PEASANTS' DWELLINGS

The road had been cleared for a building boom in the cities under free enterprise and we were simultaneously promoting urban slum removal and public housing. The slums on the outskirts of the cities were an eyesore and a disgrace. We proceeded to remove them under Law #139 of June 17, 1952 to "provide hygienic and comfortable dwellings for underprivileged groups unable to afford to buy or rent them."

Progress was also made in rural housing. During its first year of operations, the National Housing Commission (Comisión Nacional de Viviendas—CNV) built more than 10,000 peasants' homes, either directly or through Local Foundations for the Promotion and Improvement of Peasants' Houses. These were set up in all the municipalities of the Republic and were dependent on the CNV.

We banned farmhouses with sod floors and waived all charges for building permits. All farm and ranch owners who provided quarters for their men were ordered to comply with the standards of construction and hygiene provided in the law. While these alterations were in progress, the tenants were exempted from paying rent. No eviction proceedings were permitted during these periods of alteration.

Income for this plan was provided by Law #1005 of July 28, 1953, which levied an assessment on the net earnings of rural property, but exempted all sugar mills and ranch owners who were willing to build new housing or bring old housing for their workers up to the standards of the statute.

Our minimum standards were: concrete flooring throughout, sanitary toilets, enough bedrooms for the privacy and convenience of the entire family, fiber-cement roofing and drinking water outlets.

The National Housing Commission simultaneously launched a campaign for the reconstruction of the typical *bohio* and, in less than four years, more than 50,000 of these peasant homes were brought up to minimum standards of comfort and health.[1]

The reconstruction of the *bohios* was started along the Central Highway and intersecting roads, where materials could most readily be moved to the work sites. By the end of 1958, we had built some 8,000 new peasant homes, which were healthy and comfortable, along the Highway.

When they seized power at the beginning of 1959, the Communists did not hesitate to take credit for this work and proudly showed these rehabilitated *bohios* to foreign visitors as evidence of their zeal to do something tangible for the common man. These

---

[1] The *bohio* originally meant a Siboney Indian hut, consisting of one small room, generally circular and built of royal palm branches, joined with vines. Palm fronds were used for roofing and packed dirt for the floors. This dwelling evolved in shape and size, but the basic characteristics remained the same. The word itself is of Indian origin.

Communist boasts were applied in fact to all of the 60,000 peasant homes which had been reconditioned, rebuilt or constructed from the ground up by the National Housing Commission under my Administration.

DISASTER HOUSING

Naturally, we gave first priority to the housing of victims of natural calamities. My wife contributed a great deal of time and energy to this program. She was always ready to visit the most remote areas, if disaster had struck them, and did so even when she was an expectant mother and without regard for her own comfort or safety.

More than 2,000 houses, destroyed by a flood which ravaged 13 municipalities in the province of Matanzas, were completely modernized and rebuilt. In the town where I was born, Banes, a model residential project was set up, beginning with 25 one-family dwellings. The beneficiaries were people who had lost their homes because of the flooding of the Banes River. In Jobabo (Victoria de las Tunas) in Oriente, 100 homes damaged or destroyed by tornado were completely rebuilt. The same situation occurred in Cárdenas in Matanzas and here again 100 dwellings had to be reconstructed. Along the Varadero-Cárdenas Highway, 20 new homes were built for underprivileged families. In Morón, Camagüey, when the port of Laguna de la Leche was improved, we built a modern fishing village of 50 homes complete with aqueduct, sewage system and wharves. In Vega Alta, Las Villas, all of the homes destroyed by a tornado were rebuilt.

Hurricane Hilda caused havoc in the Baracoa region of Oriente, leaving thousands homeless. We repaired or rebuilt 5,100 stricken homes and rushed emergency relief to victims of the storm. Throughout the area, we built new houses in better locations, nearer to access roads. Guantánamo, Palma Soriana, Remedios and Caibarién were among the communities which benefitted from this housing program.

SLUM CLEARANCE

In the nation's capital and in various other cities, there were slum districts where vast numbers of people lived in overcrowded conditions which stunted their physical and mental development and constituted a threat to public health. Most of these people had built their own shacks of salvaged materials and were squatting on the land. For humanitarian reasons, it was necessary to eliminate these slums. And also for esthetic ones, since they were eyesores.

Law #130 coped with this problem. A census of the slum districts was taken. Then we proceeded to eradicate the slum dwellings and move their inhabitants to other areas, where job opportunities were better. Simultaneously, we provided retraining for the unemployed in farms and factories, giving them shelter and food during the transitional period.

Through this program, 36 slum districts were eliminated; their shacks were torn down, and the 25,000 people affected were offered better living conditions elsewhere. They were relocated according to family needs, experience and ability. In some cases, they were given land and building materials; in others, they were provided with the tools of their trade. The sick were hospitalized; the children sent to nurseries and schools; the aged sometimes sent to homes and asylums.

Thus, the slum program was solved without protests by any of the groups involved. The slum landlords contributed to the program for humanitarian reasons and because it enhanced the value of their land.

LOW COST HOUSING PROJECTS

Eight years before I took power for the second time, President Grau San Martín had undertaken a low cost housing project in the Aranguren residential subdivision. The project never got off the ground and Dr. Grau's successor, Dr. Carlos Prío made no attempt whatsoever, during his entire term of office, to finish the housing project.

My Administration decided to complete the abandoned project on a long term amortization basis. After having done so and delivered the first 700 homes to buyers, we proceeded to expand the venture into a huge operation under the Social and Economic Development Plan. Some 180 new buildings were constructed, including two apartment houses with 64 units apiece. Ten more were in process of construction when Castro took power. In addition, we built a school center there, the Bernardo Toro Gómez Home for the Aged and the Evangelina Cossío Day Nursery.

Similar housing projects to the one at Havana were undertaken in the provincial capitals: the Calero in Pinar del Rio, the Peñas Altas in Matanzas, the Manuelita in Santa Clara, the Garrido in Camagüey and the Altura de Vista Alegre in Santiago de Cuba. These new housing projects were of modern, functional design, which pointed the way for low-cost housing engineering and architecture.

THE $50,000,000 PLAN

Cuba's international credit rating had become so good that a group of U.S. capitalists offered to invest $50 million over a five-year period at an annual rate of $10 million. An agreement to that effect was signed on November 20, 1958—exactly 41 days before the ominous New Year of 1959—between the Berlanti Construction Company and the National Housing Commission. The project comprised a vast low cost housing development of not less than 11,000 units, including both individual residences and apartment houses. Thus, Cuba was to get additional foreign investment for social purposes of $10,000,000 annually at an interest rate not exceeding 2.5%. The funds were to be handled by the National Bank of Cuba.

However, when the Communists took power, the plan was abandoned immediately and the $10,000,000 on deposit with Bandes was confiscated and later squandered on the so-called agrarian reform.

SOLDIERS' DWELLINGS

After the Revolution of 1933, I began a housing project for servicemen. This was revived in 1952 by Law #816 of April 17th. The Low Cost Housing Administration for Members of the Armed Forces (OVEFA) was organized to work on this problem with FHA facilities and an allocation of $500,000 annually from the State.

OVEFA constructed and improved hundreds of homes for enlisted men and commissioned officers. When the Reds took power, it had reserves on hand of $1,000,000 in the form of BANDES bonds. It was one of the very first targets of Communist rapacity.

SUMMARY

The 1953 population census included questions concerning housing. We found that there were 1,259,641 dwellings in Cuba, which worked out to 4.6 people per housing unit in the country and 3.8 in the nation's capital. It was evident that Cuba needed no less than 50,000 new homes yearly to meet population growth.

Under the stimulus of laws which encouraged private initiative and aided by a dynamic plan to reconstruct rural dwellings, we hoped to solve this problem, which is common to most countries in the modern world.

Between 1953 and 1958, some 56,124 homes were built in the province of Havana alone worth $383,702,216, according to statistics of the National Association of Architects. Of these, 11,905 were individual residences and 42,508 were apartment units. Some 1,651 were other types.

United States Ambassador Arthur Gardner testified as follows on this matter before the Senate Internal Security Subcommittee on August 27, 1960:

"And during the course of the time that I was there, the economy rose tremendously. The building boom was sensational. If you had been in Havana years earlier, as I had, and then saw it the day I left, you wouldn't recognize the city.

". . . I think that the real reason for it was the feeling of definite security that the Cubans themselves had, politically perhaps not, but financially, yes. And they felt that the time had finally come when they could begin investing money in Cuba, rather than putting their money, as they had in previous years, in banks in Switzerland and New York." [2]

Total residential construction in Cuba amounted to $488,057,028 during the entire period 1952-1958, again according to the architects' association. Only about a fifth of this was spent outside Havana Province.

The table that follows shows residential construction in Havana Province and in Cuba as a whole during the 1952-58 period.

[2] Senate Internal Security Subcommittee, *Communist Threat to the United States Through the Caribbean, Hearings,* 86th Congress, 2nd Session, Part 9, August 27, 30, 1960, Government Printing Office, Washington, D. C., p. 664.

Year	Total Residential Construction	Total: Havana Province	Havana: Dwellings	Havana: Apartments
		(figures in millions of dollars)		
1952	49.4	38.0	9.6	13.0
1953	62.7	51.1	11.6	28.0
1954	74.1	60.3	11.7	35.6
1955	69.4	54.2	16.2	29.6
1956	80.4	60.3	18.1	26.8
1957	77.9	58.3	19.4	23.2
1958	74.0	61.5	17.2	27.2
AVERAGE	69.7	54.8	14.8	26.2
1959	33.6	20.4	7.3	4.9

There is little need to stress the thriving condition of the building industry and related industrial fields. Cement consumption increased by over a million barrels from 3,015,901 barrels in 1953 to 4,456,473 in 1957. To meet increasing demand, cement imports rose to 1,519,879 barrels in 1955. However, as soon as the two new plants in Santiago de Cuba and Artemisa started production, imports fell off. By 1957, they were only 540,685 bbls.

We had to import 325,100 tons of steel reinforcing rods during the seven-year period. However, these average imports of 50,324 tons were cut to 21,957 tons in 1957 due to government assistance to the nascent Cuban steel industry. This involved a yearly saving of over $2,000,000 in dollar exchange.

In 1959, the first year of Communist rule in Cuba, housing construction fell by more than 50% in the nation and by about 60% in Havana Province. A flourishing industry, that had provided better housing for the people, that had embellished our cities and that had offered employment for hundreds of thousands of Cubans, had been virtually destroyed.

In 1960, the second year of Communist domination in Cuba, total cement consumption could be provisionally estimated at about 3.6 million barrels, a further decline from 1959, and about 27% below the 1957 level.[3] While this decrease is less pronounced than that shown for housing construction, the reason is that a large portion of cement production was being deflected from such socially beneficial purposes as housing into militarization of the nation as a Soviet satellite. Thus, the extent to which Castro

[3] v. Álvarez, Díaz, *op. cit.*, p. 1,561.

and his Communists had wrecked the housing industry of the Island was statistically masked.

What was really incredible about this sorry picture was the way in which Communist propagandists, their agents, dupes and pawns depicted the supposedly great progress Castro and his Reds were making in the public housing field.

25

The Government Building Program

In the first days of the September 1933 Revolution, I conceived the idea of a Plaza of the Republic, the central theme of which would be a magnificent monument in marble and bronze consecrated to the immortal glory of José Martí and surrounded by government buildings worthy of that nation of which he was the apostle and martyr.[1]

We gave priority to the plan for a palace to house the courts. The Supreme Court, founded in 1899 by Military Governor John R. Brooke—upon the recommendation of the Cuban jurist José Antonio González Lanuza—had been domiciled for 30 years in the Colonial building which had been its cradle. In 1929, it was moved to another Colonial building, called the Palacio del Segundo Cabo, which had been vacated by the Senate when the National Capital was officially opened.

With time, the responsibilities of the Supreme Court increased. There were more courtrooms and more judges. It no longer served merely as an appellate tribunal and interpreter of the

[1] The March 1952 Government commemorated the golden jubilee of the Republic (1902-1952) and the centenary of the birth of Martí (1953) and that of the patriots, Juan Gualberto Gómez, Emilio Nuñez and Martín Moruá Delgado. All the commissions created by law for these commemorations were dissolved by the Communist regime although they had not completed their tasks. In many instances, parks, public institutions, streets and avenues, which had been named by law or by municipal decisions for Cuban patriots, had their names changed to those of various criminals in the service of International communism.

constitutionality of laws. It was called upon to settle administrative and social controversies and to serve as the head of the third power of the State. The Supreme Court, among its other duties, appointed the judges and officials of the courts.

THE PLAZA OF THE REPUBLIC

In late 1944, bids had already been opened on this project, but my term of office was too close to its end to permit us to go ahead. We froze the price of the land which the Government would have to take over for the Plaza at $5.00 per square *vara* (0.836 square meters). This was possible because real estate was cheap and construction activities were lagging in those days. This anti-speculative measure guaranteed completion of the project at a reasonable cost, but my Auténtico successors promptly repealed it.

Land sharks with close connections with high officials of the new Administration bought up the land destined for the Plaza, running its price up from $5.00 to $75.00 per square *vara*. Hence, when I came back into power in March 1952, the enormous area we had planned to devote to the Plaza had to be cut by two-thirds.

THE PALACE OF JUSTICE

One of my first official acts in 1952 was to promulgate Law #25 of April 24th for construction of the Palace of Justice. This law stated that the higher and lower courts "are, as a rule, housed in buildings which are unattractive, inadequate, poorly maintained and unhygienic." By contrast, the other two powers of the State were adequately housed: the Legislature in the National Capitol, inaugurated in 1929, and the Chief Executive in the National Palace, opened in 1920. We were duty-bound, it seemed to me, to treat the Judiciary equally well.[2]

[2] In Cuba, electoral procedures were controlled entirely by the Judiciary, which was completely independent of the Executive and Legislative powers. The Supreme Electoral Court consisted of judges of the Supreme Court and the Havana Circuit Court of Appeals. It had jurisdiction over all matters concerning political parties and political issues. Under its supervision, the municipal election boards prepared rosters of eligible voters, and issued them voting cards, containing photographic and fingerprint identification. These local bodies, chaired by judges appointed by the Supreme Electoral

By Law #1113 of October 20, 1953, the President was authorized to issue $12,500,000 of obligations to construct buildings for the judiciary: $10,000,000 for the Palace of Justice in Havana and the remaining $2,500,000 to build or renovate courthouses throughout the nation.

My co-workers and I had the privilege of formally opening the Palace of Justice on September 1, 1958, thus fulfilling a commitment I had made 15 years previously. Cuban justice was lodged for the first time in a mansion worthy of its dignity, a spacious, modern building, austere in design and functional down to the smallest detail.

NEW COURTHOUSES

A new building was constructed for the Appellate Court, the lower courts, the local electoral court and the other electoral bodies of the judicial district of Holguín, one of the two that comprise the province of Oriente, under the provisions of Law #1113 of 1953. We built 48 courthouses for the lower courts of one-third of the municipalities of Cuba and also furnished and equipped them.

Public opinion was well aware of the fact that my Administration was dedicated to the principle of impartial justice without regard to politics. Some of the judges who participated in the activities of the Castro movement issued biased and clearly incompetent decisions, but my Government never took any action against them beyond reporting their conduct to the investigative departments of the Judiciary.[3] We did not even demand that

Court, regulated election procedure, counted the ballots and issued certificates of election. The Court also had jurisdiction over the National Census Board, which counted, not only the population, but the voters. In Cuba, voting was compulsory for all men and women over 20.

[3] Even in times when the writ of *habeas corpus* was suspended by Congress, the right to the writ was always at least partially upheld by the courts. When the Marxists took power, however, the writ, which protects the life and liberty of the citizens, was unscrupulously ignored and denied. This was done with the assistance of the Professor of Criminal Law at the University of Havana, Dr. José Miró Cardona. This man signed the Communist decrees which applied the death penalty for political offenses and enforced the new criminal laws retroactively, thus unjustly punishing men, sometimes with death, for acts which had not been illegal when committed. In doing these things, Professor Miró Cardona denied and contradicted the principles which he had taught his classes in law school for years.

Judge Manuel Urrutía Lleó be made accountable for his un-mistakably biased activities during the trial of the Castro broth-ers.[4]

THE PALACE OF COMMUNICATIONS

Other departments of the Government had to be rehoused. I have already mentioned the work done in providing adequate domiciles for the revenue collection offices, the postoffices and other public service organizations. Law #16 of December 20th, 1952 authorized the Executive Power to spend up to $3,000,000 for a Palace of Communications. To provide the necessary funds, a special one-cent stamp was issued which had to be placed on every item mailed.

By March 1952, construction had already been started, but the new building did not harmonize with the other edifices planned for the Plaza of the Republic. Obviously we could not stop the project for this reason. We decided to modify the design to make the building less ungainly and more functional. Law #1157 of October 30, 1953 added $2,000,000 to the project and a $5,000,-000 special bond issue was floated for the same purpose on a medium-term basis.

The Palace was completed and in operation in 1957. In quality of materials and workmanship and architectural design, it meas-ured up to expectations. The old St. Francis Monastery, which had been partially restored during my first Administration, was turned into a Colonel Museum and exhibit of the culture and artefacts of the extinct race of Siboney Indians. Ugly additions to the monastery were removed and the dome, carried away by a hurricane a century before, was restored.

THE RURAL POSTMAN

My first administration had introduced major reforms in the Cu-ban communications system. We had created a postal savings sys-

---

[4] When Judge Urrutía applied for retirement, his request was promptly proc-essed and granted. He was never molested or persecuted. Moreover, when he left Cuba to go into exile, he continued to receive his retirement checks punctually. Later, rewarded with the Presidency of Cuba by his friend, Fidel Castro, he was expelled contemptuously a few months later by the despot whom he had protected from the bench in violation of his judicial oath of office.

tem; inaugurated delivery of telegrams by telephone; introduced the money order transmitted by telegraph; brought stamping machines into the country and introduced self-addressed reply envelopes and the international identity postal card.

In my second Administration, we brought postal service to the rural areas. This task required mailmen of a special sort, willing to travel over long routes and poor roads. But it contributed to the national consciousness of rural Cubans and made farmers and peasants better able to participate in the public life of the Republic. Toward the end of my tenure of office, rural postmen were serving 137,048 Cubans and covering 11,000 kilometers of mail routes every day.

HOUSING THE ARMED FORCES

Prior to the Revolution of September 4, 1933, the armed forces of the nation had been quartered in inadequate and unhealthy buildings, most of them improvised and some erected during the latter part of the 19th Century. Still others were temporary wooden barracks which had been built during the U.S. military occupation of 1899-1902.

We introduced Military Cities, the name given to the congeries of buildings which housed regimental commands. These satisfied the physical and morale standards to which the soldiers, sailors and police who defend the nation and uphold law are entitled. Soon they sprang up all over the Republic.[5]

Among the projects completed during my second Administration were the Military City of Matanzas and the Naval District of Oriente. Special attention was devoted to military airfields; landing strips were lengthened and new hangars built. At Ciudad Militar (the former Camp Columbia), the Chiefs of Staff were given more spacious and adequate housing.

---

[5] The Communist demagogues under Fidel Castro attacked these military installations mercilessly. They proclaimed loudly that they were unnecessary and promised to convert them into schools. Once he had seized power, the Red chieftain claimed that he had converted these garrisons into schools. But if so, where had he lodged his Army? And if the children had been militarized and the school teachers forced into the Militia, it would seem that the schools had been turned into barracks! By 1963, it became clear that his real plan was to militarize childhood and the schools and to set up an armed force, under Russian command, sufficiently strong to prevent the people of Cuba from overthrowing his tyranny.

REORGANIZATION

We amended drastically some of the basic laws governing the organization and procedures of the Armed Forces. The Military Penal Code (Law #1930 of 1955) incorporated the latest findings of military penology. Law #2032 of 1955 revamped pleading procedure before military tribunals. The Credit and Insurance Fund of the Armed Forces (CASFA) was created by Law #1051 of 1958 to provide more prompt financial assistance to servicemen in need.

A completely new installation was built for the Army and Navy Club in Marianao Beach by authority of Decree #3852 of December 3, 1957. Financial means for this project were made available in 1954 and the association, which would serve as a liaison center between members of the three branches of the military and between military men and civilians, was given official legal status as the National Association of the Armed Forces of Cuba.

THE NAVY

My second Administration provided the Navy with a new Organic Law (#647 of January 28, 1953) which contained entirely new provisions in such areas as protecting the security of maritime communications and coastal defense.

The Navy's functions were broadened in scope. For example, Law #1597 of August 4, 1954 spared the sands of our northern beaches from indiscriminate dredging from the Canasí River to Punta de Mulas on the peninsular of Hicacos. The Navy was also charged with regulating the felling of trees on the six keys at the entrance to the Bay of Cárdenas. Both measures were designed to protect Varadero Beach as a tourist attraction. Then there was Law #1948 of January 25, 1955 which made all waters between the mainland and the keys, provided the distance did not exceed 10 miles, "inland waterways."

Another improvement was to install a printing plant in the Casa Blanca Naval Yard. This was so well equipped that it issued the publications of the Technical Aid Program for the use of the Navy and in addition was used by the United States Government to print military and training manuals for the use of the signatory nations to the International Technical Aid Program.

During the early months of my second Administration, the Navy printing plant turned out 130 publications with a total of 156,000 copies, distributed among seven countries. This did not include thousands of training booklets for servicemen on such military fields as electronics, radar, navigation, machinery and artillery.

Adjoining the Naval Academy in Mariel, where we enlarged the School for Officers of the Merchant Marine and gave it its own building, a National Academy of Ship's Masters was set up by Law #1171 of October 30, 1953. This was to train ship's masters engaged in the coastal trade, fishing, sports fishing, etc., and coastal pilots and machinist's mates. It was also designed to stimulate the interest of the youth in all matters pertaining to the sea. It contributed to developing national interest in the Cuban merchant marine and in our oceanic industries. At La Dominica near Mariel, there was a school for stewards and cabin boys. Finally, during my first Administration, we had created a Naval Sports Academy under the National Directorate of Sports by Decree #1454 of July 9, 1938.

The growing popular interest in matters of the sea was expressed in 1953 by the organization of the Society of Friends of the Sea, an organization that blossomed out all over Cuba and which was helped financially by funds from the National Lottery.

NAVAL BUILDINGS

During the latter part of my first Administration, a government building, which had been purchased during World War II, was assigned to the Navy as its headquarters. When I took power a second time, I found that the project for a Navy Headquarters was at a standstill. However, six months later, we had the new building finished and on September 4, 1952, the Navy Chief of Staff was permanently installed in it. On the other side of the Avenida del Puerto, we built a dock for the Navy and finished the part of the seawall that had been left undone—from the Pila de Neptuno to the wharves of the Havana Docks Corporation.

New buildings were erected and old ones renovated in the southern Naval District Headquarters in Cienfuegos. In Santiago de Cuba, headquarters for the Naval District of Oriente, a magnificent new building was erected with shops, officers' quarters and furnished houses for enlisted men on 4,500 square meters of land. Part of the adjacent waterfront was filled in and the dock was extended.

The concrete runways were extended at the Naval Air Base at Mariel, which we had build in 1943; new hangars and warehouses were constructed and the control tower was rebuilt. The Casa Blanca Naval Arsenal in Havana was similarly improved.

In all, by the middle of 1958, the Naval construction program had involved the erection of 36 new buildings: 14 in Havana Province, 6 in Pinar del Rio, one in Matanzas, 3 in Las Villas, 4 in Camagüey and 8 in Oriente. The new 10th of March Naval Hospital had been completed and was scheduled for inauguration, but the Communists seized power.

Ever since the incorporation of the Lighthouse and Coastal Lighting Service into the Navy by Decree #226 of February 1, 1944, there had been steady improvement in maintenance, equipment and the number of lighthouses, buoys and channel markers. We concentrated on electric buoys because of their greater efficiency and visibility. We installed them at the ports of Cabaña and Mariel, at Nuevitas in Camagüey and at Nipe, Manatí and Puerto Padre in Oriente. The buoys of the northern coast—from Manatí to Baracia—were totally renovated.

THE VIA CUBA CANAL

One of the most important projects under consideration by my Administration was the draining of the Zapata Swamp so as to use its rich lands for new crops such as fig trees, ramie and kenaf and to plant adjacent areas to rice and peanuts.

This vast agro-industrial plan called for the construction of factories, shops, silos and dams along the projected Via Cuba Canal, which was to cut through the Island from a point east of the Bay of Cárdenas on the north coast to the Bay of Pigs in the south coast in Las Villas Province.

This Canal would have saved ships between ports of North and South America the more than 400 nautical miles involved in following the Cuban coasts to Cape San Antonio or the more than 800 miles if one follows them to Punta de Maisí. The advantages to ships not touching at Cuban ports would have been equally great and, in addition, the Canal would have provided much greater navigational safety. Unfortunately, an effective campaign of vilification of this project by the Communists managed to prevent its being put into operation.

26

Electric Power and Industrial Development

Statistics on electric generating capacity and production and consumption of electricity are universally accepted as indexes of a nation's economic development and prosperity.

Population growth and the prosperity caused by the impact of the Marshall Plan on sugar demand induced the Cuban Power Company (CCE) to launch a $30,000,000 program to expand capacity over the period 1948-1953.

When my Administration took office in 1952, we developed an economic program which required an even greater expansion of electric power production. Power capacity in 1951 had amounted to 183,100 kilowatts. A second expansion program, amounting this time to $75,000,000, was put into motion. This provided for eleven new thermal power plants to boost capacity by 135,000 kilowatts. Of these, two, with a total capacity of 70,000 kilowatts, were installed at Regla; two others at Matanzas provided 30,000 kilowatts; two in Camagüey 10,000; two at Santiago de Cuba 8,000 and one in Santa Clara 15,000.

By December 31, 1955, generating capacity had risen to 297,-200 kilowatts. A third expansion program was then adopted, involving an investment of $60,000,000 in generating facilities in 1956 and 1957. To these programs, the Government contributed $36,000,000 through the *Financiera Nacional* and $24,000,000 was made available by the Export-Import Bank. As a result of this vigorous investment program in greater generating capacity, the power industry of Cuba had 352,300 kilowatts of capacity at the end of 1957, almost twice the 183,100 kilowatts we had inherited from the Auténtico administration.

When the Cuban Power Company was seized by the Communists,[1] its expansion programs were discontinued; all the gains of the workers were wiped out and the once powerful Federation of Electrical Workers (FTPE) was pulverized.[2]

The following table shows electricity consumption in Cuba by major uses and by years in millions of kilowatt hours.

ELECTRICITY CONSUMPTION[3]

(Millions of kwh)

Year	Industrial	Residential	Commercial	Gov't.	Total
1941	89.1	55.9	66.8	103.6	315.4
1942	100.1	57.6	65.4	104.4	327.5
1943	107.6	61.1	67.5	103.5	339.7
1944	117.9	68.4	75.3	109.4	371.0
1945	138.5	77.9	86.0	117.9	420.3
1946	148.3	88.2	97.1	123.7	457.3
1947	140.1	103.8	111.3	130.7	489.9
1948	129.3	128.7	149.2	136.1	543.3
1949	130.8	149.0	165.7	140.1	585.6
1950	144.5	171.3	185.4	143.4	644.6
1951	155.9	203.5	213.6	133.8	716.8
1952	165.5	242.8	246.7	119.4	774.4
1953	175.5	281.2	273.1	121.4	851.2
1954	192.9	312.2	300.5	125.4	931.0
1955	214.7	348.6	334.1	126.5	1,023.9
1956	242.2	393.5	376.0	131.1	1,142.8
1957	270.9	443.9	428.0	139.1	1,281.9
1958	327.8	505.9	478.6	150.5	1,462.8

[1] Cuban Power was by all odds the largest company on the Island. However, some of the smaller companies in the provinces were completing new plants with large capacity such as the one in Salto del Hanabanilla in Las Villas and the projects in La Habana del Este and Toa in Oriente.

[2] The Communist regime also paralyzed the Hanabanilla, Toa and Havana del Este power projects.

[3] Data from the Cuban Power Company, published in *Anuarios Estadísticos de Cuba* of 1952 and 1956; *Cuba Ecómica y Financiera*, Editora Cultural Cubana, S.A., Havana (Various 1958, 1959 and 1960 issues). Also see *Un Estudio Sobre Cuba, op. cit.*, p. 1,170.

Thus, during my second Administration, industrial and commercial consumption of electricity doubled, residential consumption increased somewhat more rapidly, while power use by government rose by only about a fourth. The number of consumers of electricity increased from 259,978 in 1941 to 534,934 in 1951 and 732,413 in 1958.

THE TELEPHONE SYSTEM

In 1909, the Cuban Telephone Company was organized, replacing the old *Red Telefónica de La Habana.* Even though costs had increased considerably, the Company had never had a rate increase. Consequently, it could not afford the expansion and modernization of facilities that the country so desperately needed.

The Company brought its problem to the Government. The expansion program called for an investment of $85,000,000. The capital was to be obtained through the issuance of mortgage bonds but, at current rates, income would be insufficient to meet interest and amortization payments.

The proposed increases would affect 143,000 telephone owners (1957 figures). Accordingly, we put the Company's proposals before various commissions for study. My general policy was to resist such increases as long as possible because of my strong opposition to raising the cost of living. On the other hand, the economic development of the country required more and better telephone service and there were 45,000 persons wanting telephones and unable to get them. This deficit, we estimated, would increase to 75,000 before 1960 unless something was done about the matter.

Arithmetical realities made it necessary to change the rate structure. We authorized this by Law #2083 of February 8, 1955. Then by Decree #945 of March 13, 1957, we effected a modest increase in rates applying only to new installations. To obtain the $85,000,000 of capital needed, the Export-Import Bank advanced $17,500,000; the International Telephone and Telegraph Company put up $7,500,000 and Cuban capital bought $10,000,000 of common stock. Standard Electric Company of Cuba proposed to build a plant to produce telephone equipment in Santiago de las Vegas. The program also called for installing the most modern phone equipment, extending automatic service and opening telephone exchanges in many communities which lacked them. This program was to be completed toward the end of 1960.

By the end of 1958, some 26,362 new phones had been installed and another 20,000 were to be installed next year. However, with the annihilation of free enterprise by the Communists, this expansion program naturally had to be abandoned.

INDUSTRIAL DEVELOPMENT

The industrialization of the nation through the mobilization of investment capital in order to increase output and employment was the main purpose of the Plan of Social and Economic Development. The Law of August 15, 1953 provided the means for this. In the same year, the National Finance Corporation was organized. This was part of the program which culminated in a $350,000,-000 bond issue and the foundation of the Bank of Economic and Social Development (BANDES).

This program was later the target of Communist calumny. A contemporary writer, who sided with my political enemies, refuted these false charges as follows:

"The entire program of industrial development through autonomous organizations suffered from the reiterated charge that only a group of privileged interests benefitted from these financial operations. This created an impression of abject corruption when, as a matter of fact, not the slightest impropriety or mismanagement was ever proved against any official or member of the various Boards of Directors of the autonomous entities . . .

"It was never explained to the people of Cuba that the funds used in BANDES operations were not primarily government money, but private capital obtained by bond issues backed by the projects being financed in accordance with strict regulations and by the funds of BANDES in deposit in private banks . . .

"No one considered the fact that the only possible way to develop the national economy in a democratic system is to create small property owners and new native businesses or else to stimulate 'a mixed economy' with joint ventures of domestic and foreign capital. It is as unproductive to leave the best opportunities to foreign private enterprise as to base economic development on the total socialization of a society." [4]

[4] Dr. Alberto Díaz Masvidal, *Diario de la Marina,* February 25, 1961.

THE SCOPE OF FINANCIAL AID

The figures which follow cover only those operations which were financed directly by BANDES, BANFAIC and the National Finance Corporation or which were supported pursuant to specific laws furthering industrial development such as Law #1531 and Law #1758 of November 2, 1954, covering oil refineries. Thus, hundreds of projects, in which the Government created new industries or brought about the expansion and modernization of old ones, are not included. The period covered is from March 10, 1952 to December 31, 1958.

FOOD INDUSTRIES (28 PLANTS):
Jams and Preserves (9), Tomatoes (2), Purée and Fruit Juices (2), Sausages (1), Chocolate (1), Crackers (1), Soybeans (1), Yeast (1), Fodder (1), Rice Mills (3), Wheat Flour Mills (1), Milk Pasteurization Plant (1), Butter and Cheese Plant (4) $5,292,250

SUGAR INDUSTRY (2 MILLS): $2,000,000

CANE BYPRODUCTS (9 PLANTS):
Cellulose, Pulp and Newsprint (1), Compressed Bagasse Boards and Insulators (1), Paper, Cardboard, Bristol Board and Other Bagasse By-products (1), Corrugated Cardboard and Insulators (1), Pulp and Fiber (2), Other By-products (3) $33,825,000

AGRICULTURAL PROCESSING (1) $833,400

PAPER AND ALLIED INDUSTRIES (6 PLANTS):
Containers (3), Cardboard Boxes (1), Carbon Paper (1) and Printshops (1) $814,635

MINING (14 OPERATIONS):
Iron (3), Copper (3), Manganese (2), Gold (3), Nickel (1) and Other Minerals (2) $77,258,450

METALLURGICAL (10 PLANTS):
Steel (5), Steel Reinforcing Rods (1), Copper Wire (1), Aluminum (1), Sugar Cane Hauling Cars (1) and Other (1) $24,090,720

STONE, CEMENT AND CERAMICS (13 PLANTS):

Quarries (2), Portland Cement (2), Concrete
(4), Shingles (1), Abrasives (1), Glass (1),
Ceramics (2) $14,774,500

PETROLEUM AND PRODUCTS (7 PLANTS):
Research Laboratory (1), Lubricants (2), Refineries (4) $94,333,500

PACKING PLANTS (2) $430,000

MOTION PICTURE (3) $1,096,990

HIDES AND LEATHER PRODUCTS $111,500

LUMBER AND WOOD PRODUCTS $1,170,000

ELECTRICITY AND ELECTRICAL INDUSTRIES (10):
Power Plants (3), Expansion of Telephone System (1), Radios (1), Refrigerators (1), Air
Conditioners (1), Phonograph Records (2)
and Other (1) $267,290,000

CHEMICAL INDUSTRIES (13):
Fertilizer Plants (3), Pharmaceuticals (2),
Glues (1), Plastics (3), Phosphorus (1), Nitro-
gen (1), Glycerine (1) and Acetate (1) $33,876,000

TEXTILE AND CLOTHING (13):
Socks and hosiery (4), Kenaf (3), Rayon (1),
Cordage (2), Brassieres (1), Fabrics (1) and
Other (1) $7,068,645

RUBBER INDUSTRIES (3 TIRE PLANTS) $7,000,000

INDUSTRIAL CITIES (2) $16,000,000

CONSTRUCTION INDUSTRY:

Buildings in Havana (In-cluding $78,298,000 for the FHA)	$383,702,216	
Buildings in the provinces	$104,354,812	
Low-Cost Housing	$50,000,000	
Total		$538,057,028

TOURIST CENTERS (3) $34,000,000

HOTELS AND MOTELS (4) $27,227,000

BANKS (5) $3,174,950

AVIATION $29,947,000

RAILROADS $47,290,000

TRUCKING $31,417,165

MARITIME TRANSPORT $19,568,000

AGRICULTURAL LOANS:	
Rice	$39,979,200
Tobacco	$11,788,500
Coffee	$9,790,800
Corn	$1,076,000
OTHER AGRICULTURAL CREDITS	$52,576,500
LABOR UNIONS	$1,045,650
OPERATING CAPITAL OF BANDES, BCCE & BANFAIC	$21,000,000
MARITIME INDUSTRIAL PROJECTS (12):	
Drydocks (1), Shipyards (1), Wharves (2), Warehouses (1), Fishing Terminal (1), Maritime Terminals (6)	$161,560,820
AUTONOMOUS ORGANIZATIONS (LOANS AND FINANCING)	$14,815,140
AQUEDUCTS (29)	$33,161,295
FOOD MARKETS (3)	$1,543,465
TOLL HIGHWAYS (2)	$40,000,000
TUNNELS (3)	$55,212,290
COMMUNICATIONS: MICRO-WAVE	$10,000,000
SCHOOL BUILDINGS	$20,000,000
TREASURY AND POST OFFICES	$6,000,000
PALACE OF JUSTICE AND COURT HOUSES	$14,400,000
PALACE OF COMMUNICATIONS	$5,000,000
MINISTRY OF STATE BUILDING	$2,200,000
NATIONAL BANK OF CUBA BUILDING	$15,000,000
NATIONAL LIBRARY	$58,000
GRAND TOTAL	$1,834,733,688

Quantitatively, the main elements in this enormous credit and investment program of $1,835,000,000 were the $538 million invested in the construction industry, the $267 million put into power plants, telephone systems and the electronics industry, the $162 million in maritime projects and the $115 millions of agricultural credits. This total does not include grants of $62,348,346 from the National Lottery to aid cultural, charitable and social welfare institutions nor does it include the $48,650,552 contributed by CENPLUC for services to rural areas.

PRIVATE INITIATIVE

The mobilization of government funds for these projects gave a massive stimulus to private enterprise. Without exaggeration, I can say that this dynamic program of investment was renovating the entire economy of the nation. No less than 300 enterprises were directly benefitted. In many instances, the cooperation given industry by the autonomous technical institutions resulted in major improvements in production methods. In other instances, the mere approval of a project by these autonomous entities was considered sufficient reason by the private banking system to approve credit requests.

Cities and towns throughout the country were rapidly changing their appearance. Cuban industry made steady progress. Machinery was modernized; capacity was expanded; business horizons widened beyond the local market to accept the challenge of international competition in the export trade. Cuban workmanship and quality standards measured up to this challenge.

BANDES

This organization operated on such a sound and conservative basis that the problem of bad debts was minimized. BANDES supplied 50% of the capital needed by approved enterprises and projects, provided the other 50% was obtained privately and on condition that BANDES retained the status of preferred creditor. If a project was considered of major importance to the country, but capable management was not available, BANDES would proceed with it, while retaining the right to buy out the private interests and take over at any time. In other cases, projects were financed and then leased to private enterprise at a rent that covered interest and amortization of the loan plus a fair percentage of the profits.

The operation of these institutions created thousands of permanent jobs and contributed greatly to a rise in wage levels which placed Cuba first in this respect in Latin America. Cuba ranked first in Latin America and eighth in the world in the smallness of her percentage of unemployment. In addition, these operations were handled with scrupulous honesty, so much so that, although over a billion dollars was spent, the Communists, after four years in power, were unable to prove financial malfeasance of any sort.

As these lines are written, I am far from my country and must read the one-sided, derogatory and false reports about Cuba under my administration released by some of the wire services. These reports not only distort the truth, but reveal the appalling ignorance prevailing abroad of the economic, social and cultural advances we were able to achieve in the Pearl of the Antilles.

DICTATORSHIP?

It has been said that dictatorship is the concentration of all powers in a single individual. Dictatorship flouts the classic divisions of governmental power in order to place all of it in the hands of the dictator. He commands, the rest obey.

In my two Administrations, I repeatedly waived powers vested in my office in favor of autonomous institutions, directed by strong and capable executives. My purpose was always to decentralize executive power rather than to aggrandize it. I always insisted that governmental power be vested in the people and not in me and I strove at all times to share executive and administrative responsibility with the greatest number of persons and organizations. Thus, I made it a rule never to make a decision without consulting the interested parties.

In other words, my principles and practice were unalterably opposed to the dictatorial centralization of power and in favor of a broad plural power system, involving cooperation of diverse individuals and interests for socially constructive goals. This broad sharing of the challenges and responsibilities of governmment is, in my opinion, the essence of the democratic way of life.

27

Rebuilding Havana

Ruby Hart Phillips, the former head of the *New York Times* Bureau in Cuba and, at the time, a supporter of Fidel Castro, gave a vivid and objective description of Havana in 1952 when I took power.

"People became increasingly impatient," she wrote, "with the slowness of the government to resolve problems which had accumulated over the years. The Prío government had started improvements in Havana, but nothing had been terminated. Havana looked like a bombed-out city of Europe. Streets were torn up. Low lying sections of the city were flooded every time it rained due to lack of drainage. Mosquitoes and flies swarmed over the city and suburbs. Public works projects were started and stopped, leaving Havana more ugly and more in ruins than before the projects had been undertaken. The Grau administration spent four years on one mile of the important highway stretching between Havana and the José Martí International Airport. The Prío government finally did complete this.

"At last, in 1953, work began on projects in Havana." [1]

Our first efforts were directed at finding a permanent solution to these conditions rather than some makeshift, temporary expedients. Thus, long before the end of my Administration, all the old avenues, boulevards and traffic-burdened streets had been rebuilt and solidly paved so they could withstand tropical rain-

[1] Ruby Hart Phillips, *Cuba, Island of Paradox*, McDowell, Obolensky, New York, 1959, p. 264.

storms and heavy traffic. Foundations, surfaces and drainage systems had to meet exacting standards. We applied this rule, not merely to Havana, but to all other cities.

The tremendous and growing volume of vehicular traffic in the city would make any outside observer assume that adequate means of access and egress had been provided and that, specifically, wide, fast-moving access highways would have been built to link the city to the great highway networks east of the capital. Unfortunately, this was not the case.

Despite the fact that Havana was the great center of distribution and consumption of Cuba and an international tourist attraction as well, it had but one narrow, inadequate bridge—the Alcoy Bridge—to handle the tremendous volume of inflowing and outgoing traffic with the east. This constituted a real bottleneck as this bridge was the sole nexus between the metropolis and the Central Highway, at the time the only means of communication with the four provinces east of the capital. Traffic snarls were a daily problem on the Alcoy Bridge.

By the end of my Administration, this problem had been completely solved. Havana had six spacious access highways to the rest of the Island in addition to several inter-municipal highways.[2]

GREAT AVENUES AND HIGHWAYS

When we reconstructed the Central Highway, we provided new access routes into Havana: on the east, to San Francisco de Paula (8 km.) and on the west to Punta Brava (10 km.), in both cases with cloverleaf intersections.

Then there was the Monumental Way. This magnificent highway, which was one of the best in the Americas, incorporated the Avenida del Golfo, then merged into the White Way and proceeded through the tunnel under the Bay of Havana. Brilliantly lighted, it had no intersections or level crossings with other streets or highways. This great artery was to give impetus to the birth of a new city—East Havana. Its historic importance was that it traversed the area where a great battle was fought in the 18th

---

[2] In my *Piedras y Leyes*, *op. cit.*, pp. 362-366, I give details of the streets built, widened, reconstructed and repaired in Havana, Vedado and Marianao.

century between British and Spaniards for possession of Havana, a battle which gave Cuba her commercial freedom.

The 16.7 km. Tunnel Highway, connecting the Monumental Way with the Central Highway passed through the municipalities of Gunabacoa and Santa María del Rosario.

Another nexus highway, also 16.7 km. in length, linked Rancho Boyeros Avenue with La Esperanza Sanatorium and thence with the Central Highway.

The Great Barrandilla Boulevard and the Mid-Day Speedway also made a major contribution to the problem of congestion of traffic at the main access areas to the capital.

COMPLETION OF THE MALECÓN

The Malecón, Havana's oceanfront drive, was begun in 1901 by General Leonard Wood, the U. S. Military Governor of the Island. The project was abandoned when it reached the inlet of San Lázaro opposite the National Children's Home. Years later, President Machado extended the Malecón to the point where he erected a monument to the S.S. *Maine*. My Administration achieved the original plan of bringing the Malecón to the Almendares River in two stages. In my first term, we brought it to G Street in Vedado, where we had to stop construction because of the wartime curbs on the use of construction materials for nonessential purposes. In my second period of office, we brought it to the river. The Malecón, when completed, was one of the most beautiful oceanfront highways in the world.

The final lap in the project made it necessary for us to build new streets and to demolish the old Sports Palace, built in 1944 at the foot of the Avenida de los Alcaldes. We had to construct a second tunnel under the Almendares River to link the luxurious Fifth Avenue drive in Miramar with the Calzada del Vedado at the historic landmark of Torreón de la Chorrera, a coastal watchtower of the era of piracy. Tunneling under the river took sixteen months.

The completion of the Malecón and the new tunnel made it necessary to demolish the old Pote Bridge over the Almendares. This had contributed much to the development of the great residential sections of the city and their magnificent mansions. Its disappearance gave all of Havana a sense of loss.

When the last section of the Malecón was about to be officially opened, violent storms swept the city and proved the solidity of the new avenue.

WATER SHORTAGE

The city was plagued with a water shortage which had become increasingly acute with the rapid rise in its population. The Albear aqueduct and its Vento springs were quite inadequate. During the Administration of President Machado in 1926, new sources of water were discovered near the city at a place known as Aguada del Cura and a second aqueduct was started. However, Marianao, which was growing as rapidly as Havana, also tapped this water source as did Guanabacoa and Regla.

The first step in a massive plan of attack was to reconstruct the network of pipes and conduits, as old as the Albear aqueduct itself, which were costing the city losses of water running into millions of gallons daily. To finance this and to capture and develop the new Cuenca Sur source of water, we floated a $14,000,000 bond issue at 4% interest, maturing in 22 years.

The Cuenca Sur had been chosen by Law #1253 of January 28, 1954 on the recommendation of both foreign and Cuban engineers. With the approval of the National Finance Corporation, the project went forward and was completed on schedule. The new wells turned out to be highly productive. They supplied the city with 100,000,000 gallons of water daily and the shortage disappeared.

The rapid growth of Marianao created a serious water shortage for that city. A loan of $9,000,000 at 4½% and 30 years maturity was arranged with the National Finance Corporation. The new water system was to tap the Cuenca del Ariguanabo and yield 30,000,000 gallons daily.

The development of East Havana, after the new tunnel had been constructed under the Bay, again caused a water shortage. The old Guanabacoa aqueduct was insufficient. New sources were found in the zones of Santa María del Rosario and San José de las Lajas and Aguacate. By Law #2029 of 1955 and Decree #862 or 1957, franchises were granted to tap these sources and the National Finance Corporation was authorized to lend $3,200,000 at 4½%.

For the same reasons, the sprawling Guanabacoa city and

beach resort ran short of water. With financial aid from the Administration, the wells at San Benigno were repaired and modernized and distribution facilities were improved, thus solving the problem.

THE HAVANA TUNNEL

This project was undertaken only after exhaustive study by experts—in particular American concerns with great experience in this area. We had hoped that Cuban firms would be able to do the job, but bids were received from only two firms: Raymond Concrete Pile Company of New York and the Societé des Grands Travaux of Marseille.

Since the French firm was the lower bidder, it received the contract. This did not prevent our political enemies from spreading rumors of corruption, but the low cost and high quality of the completed project refuted them.

Construction work began in September 1955 and the project was formally opened with brilliant ceremonies and blessed by Manuel Cardinal Arteaga y Betancourt on schedule on May 31, 1958.

The cost of the Tunnel was $35,000,000, but it did not cost taxpayers a penny. The Government owned 1,810,328 square *varas* of land on the eastern side of the Tunnel, which it had almost sold in 1910 for 2 cents a square meter. When the Tunnel was opened, the value of this land increased from $9,000,000 to a much higher figure and, when the residential boom in East Havana got under way, the land rose in value to $300,000,000.

This Tunnel was a brilliant engineering accomplishment and the project had general public approval from its inception. The Tunnel of Havana is the sole survivor of the wanton destruction by INRA of the Greater East Havana Project.

TUNNELS UNDER THE ALMENDARES

In 1952, there were only three land connections between Havana and Marianao, and these were quite inadequate. Moreover, deep sea fishing and yachting traffic had increased to a point which made drawbridges impossible. Tunnels were the only solution. We completed the Línea Tunnel, 75% of which had been constructed by the previous Administration, and built the Tunnel of Calzada near the mouth of the river. This project also improved the appearance of the banks of the Almendares River for both native Havanans and tourists.

PORT IMPROVEMENT AND OTHER PROJECTS

Three major projects were completed in the port of Havana: the drydock, the fishing terminal and the maritime terminal. In addition, 427,150 square meters of the Marmilena inlet were dredged to a depth of 36 feet. The 2,970 million cubic meters of bottom dredged in this project were used to fill 585,000 square meters of swamp, for which we built 5,700 meters of bulkheads. The remainder of the muck was pumped through a four km. pipeline to the waste land of Playa del Chivo.

During the rainy season, sections of La Vibora were frequently flooded. We added several kilometers of sewerage. In three years, we build 14 km. of sewerage for the residential sections of La Fernanda, Párraga, La Lira and Gavilán.

PUBLIC BUILDINGS

The Plaza of the Republic included the monument to José Martí, the Palace of Justice, the buildings of the Ministry of Communications, the Court of Accounts, the National Library, the Municipal Palace, the BANFAIC and the National Theatre. The Plaza had splended avenues and was magnificently landscaped.

My Administration furnished and enriched with works of art the Palace of Fine Arts and the National Museum. In addition, we built the following:

The Sports City.

The National Center of Physical Education.

The Carlos III Market with an adjacent building for parking.

The Guanabacoa Market.

The Treasury and Communications Department building in Marianao.

The Municipal Palace of Marianao.

The building for the Chiefs of Staff of the Navy.

Building for the radio-motorized division of the National Police.

A building for the National School of Nurses.

Twelve school centers: four in the capital, four in Marianao, three in Guanabacoa and one in Regla.

Six Navy stations.

A building for the Judicial Morgue and Bank of Human Organs.

Two buildings for the laboratories of the ICIT and the BANFAIC.

SOCIAL WELFARE

During my first Administration, despite limited financial resources, we provided Greater Havana with the Aballí Children's Hospital, the Anti-Polio Institute, the Children's Municipal Hospital, the Military Hospital in Marianao and the Police Hospital in Havana.

In my second Administration, we built, among others, the National Hospital, the General Hospital of the ONDI, the Municipal Clinical and Surgical Hospital, the Naval Hospital, the ONRI Hospital, the Cristo de Limpias Home for the Mentally and Physically Retarded and the new buildings for the Nuestra Señora de la Mercedes and the Juan Bruno Zayas Radium Institute Hospitals.

We also erected a building for the Havana Nueva Day Nursery in Vedado, a Hospital for the League Against Blindness (made possible in considerable part because of donations made by Mrs. Batista from her personal funds), improvements in the Curie Hospital for cancer patients and an animal clinic for the Organization of Mercy to Animals.

THE CONSTRUCTION BOOM

The three basic urban laws of my Administration were the Rent Control Law, the law regulating cooperative ownership of real property and the FHA law. These caused a great building boom throughout the Island, especially in the nation's capital, and to such an extent that in five years the entire appearance of Cuba was drastically changed. The city of Havana, which previously had grown by spreading out horizontally, now grew vertically. Skyscrapers began to rise everywhere. Some of them, like the FOCSA Building in Vedado, which was 34 stories high, were reminiscent of New York. Between 1952 and 1958, a total of 14,-572 cooperatively owned apartment buildings were constructed in Cuba.

28

The War Against Christianity

During the latter part of my Administration, at a time when Marxist-Leninist materialism was striving to undermine the religious faith of mankind, Cuba testified to her firm adherence to the moral principles of Christianity and to her faith in God. Thus, conventions of Cubans meeting to draft a new Constitution for the nation invoked the blessings of God in their preambles. And it was no accident that Article 35 of the 1940 Constitution, upon proclaiming the freedom of religion and the right to worship as one pleases—principles which my Government invariably respected—recognized Christian morality as the standard which should govern all human relationships.

THE CHRIST OF HAVANA

It was in accordance with these sentiments that a monument to Christ was built on the eastern side of Havana Harbor at the highest point of La Cabaña. Its conservation in perpetuity was ensured by an autonomous foundation, amply endowed with capital by the Government and through private donations.

This monument was the realization of an aspiration which I had had for a long time. When the 1954 elections were over, work began. The sculptress was sent to Italy, after preliminary planning and design, where she undertook this colossal work of engineering, art and reverence. Finally, on the 24th of December 1958, just seven days before the triumph of the forces of the Anti-Christ in Cuba, the statue of Our Savior was solemnly unveiled in all its sacred splendor with the blessings of His Excellency, Manuel Cardinal Arteaga. Brilliantly illuminated, the monument to Christ could be seen from many parts of Havana and from miles out to sea.

But then the Communist hordes descended on us. They came disguised as believers in His mission, wearing beards as He did and carrying rosaries and crucifixes. This was a sacrilegious mockery. While the Communists spread hate and terror, dug common graves with bulldozers and piled them with the corpses of their innocent victims, hypnotized mobs of normally peaceful people to demand blood and more blood and to scream for the execution wall, imposed a death penalty that Cuba had abolished, applied it retroactively to actions which had not been offenses when committed, perverted the minds of children so that they informed on their parents and proceeded with a relentless persecution of the Church, they found men of substance, not merely in Cuba, but elsewhere, who extolled them, served as their fawning apologists, called black white and tried to anesthetize the human conscience.

There were even people who compared Castro to Simón Bolívar and, for that matter, to the Christ. Thus slavery was equated with freedom, murder with justice, evil with good, filth with cleanliness, the liberation of peoples with their enslavement to a foreign despotism. In some instances, these propagandists were simply agents of the Communist conspiracy against mankind; in others, they were motivated by resentment of those who were not psychically crippled. In still other instances, we were dealing with the shallow, glib politician, who confuses words with thought and oratorical afflatus with truth. These men had the right to applaud Castro and thus show the world their incapacity to distinguish between human bondage and human freedom, but they had no right to blacken and falsify the vision of Bolívar or to invoke the authority of Christ for their love affair with incarnate evil.

It has always been my view that those who knowingly and willingly serve as the apologists for crimes against humanity are themselves guilty of crimes against humanity.

A CHRISTIAN PEOPLE

To deny Christ is to deny our dearest tradition, to deny life itself. An essentially and profoundly Christian nation, Cuba saw some of the pioneers of her independence and the creators of her nationality spring from the ranks of the clergy. In the Colonial era, such outstanding Cuban clergymen as His Excellency, Don Santiago Joseph Echevarría, the last Bishop of the Diocese of Cuba before it was divided, governed the spiritual life of Cuba, Florida, Louisiana and Jamaica with wisdom, virtue and intellectual merit.

Two Cuban clergymen sat among the deputies to the Courts of Cádiz in 1810: Dr. Juan Bernardo O'Gavan and Félix Varela of Havana, "the first to teach us how to think." In addition to being a distinguished philosopher, Varela was a patriot who had a vision of independence and protection of the rights of the people. Before his time, residents of Cuba were classified as *peninsulars* and *creoles*. Whenever the word *peninsular* appeared, Varela would write *Spaniard* and, when he saw the word *creole*, he would write *Cuban*. Thus, he began to create our national consciousness and served as precursor of the convulsive struggles for independence of the 19th Century.

Other clergymen, such as Brother Jacinto María Martínez, fought equally well for human rights. When Bishop of Havana, Brother Jacinto was expelled from his diocese by Spanish volunteers because of his stern opposition to the despotic abuse of power.[1] Then there was the group of Havana priests who were banished to the island of Fernando Po in one of the most dramatic episodes of the Ten Years' War. We should also remember Father Batista who received Carlos Manuel de Céspedes, "the Father of the Republic of Cuba," under the pallium in 1868.

When Cuban independence was finally attained at the cost of the sacrifice of such of its heroes as Father Guillermo González Arocha and Father Manuel Dobal, our first Constitution was based on José Martí's formulation of "triumphant love" and on its

---

[1] The volunteer corps were organized by Spanish merchants during the War of 1868 to help the garrisons in the forts, but they were rarely used in combat. They fired and hired the Captains General, as in the case of General Arsenio Martínez Campos, during the early stages of the struggle. Their passionate zeal caused many dramatic incidents, such as the hanging of eight medical students in 1871.

new banner was written his phrase "with all and for the good of all." These precepts taught respect for the full dignity of man and gave the nascent democracy a solid foundation of freedom. And among these freedoms, was that of religion.

At the end of my second Administration in 1958, the Catholic population of Cuba was estimated as 5,665,000 or 94.2% of the total.[2] Our hierarchy comprised a Cardinal-Archbishop, two archbishops and six bishops.

We had 723 priests: 240 of them diocesan and 483 religious; 815 churches and 210 parishes in 126 municipalities. There were 126 monasteries with 984 monks and 209 nunneries with 2,225 nuns. As for education, there were 130 Catholic boys' schools with 33,691 pupils and 194 Catholic girls' schools with 34,335 students. Seventy-five charitable institutions helped 90,919 people.

Cuba had one priest for every 8,644 inhabitants, one church for every 7,669 and one parish for every 29,762 Catholics. One of every 92 Cubans received education at a Catholic school.

DIPLOMATIC RELATIONS

Late in 1929, when the Treaty of Letrán was signed, ending the anomalous political relationship between the Papacy and Italy, a new state was born. It was the smallest in the world in territory, but the greatest in spiritual force for it contained the Cathedral of Peter with its Michelangelo dome and was the spiritual guide of one-fifth of mankind.

Five years later, on my recommendation, Cuba established diplomatic relations with the Vatican. Since then Havana has had a Papal Nuncio and a Cuban Ambassador has represented us in Vatican City.[3] This in no way changed the principle of separation of Church and State proclaimed by Cuba's liberators. But this separation was not used as the pretext for the implacable hostility to religion apparent in certain other states and the funds from the National Lottery, for example, were made available impartially to religious and lay institutions, benevolent organizations and civic groups, irrespective of creed, race or origin.

[2] These figures are from the 1961 *Pontifical Yearbook*.
[3] The first Nuncio was Monsignor Jorgé Caruana, a man of faultless behavior who was remembered with affection. The first Ambassador was the Cuban journalist Nicolás Rivero y Alonso, brother of the unforgettable "Pepín" Rivero, managing editor of the *Diario de la Marina*.

These charitable grants, that ran into millions of dollars during the 1934-44 revolutionary era, were again bestowed on a large scale in 1952-58. Churches, schools, retreats, asylums, communities and clergymen received economic aid. A score of Negroes' clubs and associations were given improved or new buildings. Veterans' centers and Masonic lodges were subsidized. The Cathedral of Havana was restored to its former glory; the Cathedral of Matanzas was saved by reinforcing its foundations; the reconstruction of the Cathedral of Santiago de Cuba was started. When the Lottery could not meet all of these demands, the CNAP and PANADE, under my wife's guidance, came to the rescue.

THE GREAT PRECEPT

"Render therefore unto Caesar the things which be Caesar's and unto God the things which be God's." [4] This great precept of Christ correctly defines the relationship between Church and State.

How then could anyone justify the conduct of those clergymen who joined the cause of the enemies of the Republic and of the Church itself? Propaganda and terror may have combined to prevent some of them from seeing what was clear as daylight— the cloven hoof of communism behind the false veneer of nationalism in the 26th of July Movement. But how could priests justify violating the sacred rules against murder and the use of the name of God in vain?

The Communist terror, during the civil struggle, resulted in the near destruction of the National Sanctuary of Our Lady of Charity in El Cobre. [5] This we quickly rebuilt. Sacred images were stolen, for instance, that of the Virgin of Regla and Saint Mark the Evangelist in Artemisa.

The pious were sometimes deceived by the false promises of Castro and his Communists. These included millions of dollars for yearly "crusades," compulsory religious teaching in the public schools, a brigade of chaplains, etc., etc. All of these pledges were widely publicized and many honest people were fooled. Satan won his battle by promising "all of this shall be yours if you kneel and worship me."

[4] *Luke*, xx:21.
[5] Built by my Administration. Only a few glass windows, imported from Italy, remained to be installed in December 1958.

INTERVENTION BY THE HIERARCHY

When the civil struggle became more intense, the hierarchy attempted to mediate. I welcomed this effort as did the leaders of those opposition political parties which favored an electoral solution to the crisis. However, Castro and his Reds rejected mediation in favor of the seizure of power by violence.

Washington then imposed an arms embargo on the legitimate government of Cuba, an inexplicable move which made Communist victory almost inevitable. After that, came the reign of blood.

At the beginning of the era of circus trials, frenzied mobs and firing squads, some Church dignitaries forgot that their duty was to follow the teachings of the Gospels, condemn violence and preach love among men. Instead, in their sermons and writings, they justified the crimes and moral enormities of the traitor.[6]

First came the extermination of those Cubans who believed in freedom and the decimation of the officer corps of the Armed Forces. After our leadership had been truncated, the middle class was destroyed and the proletarian classes enslaved. Then, as the country was driven toward economic disaster, it was sold to Castro's Russian masters. When complete ruin had descended on Cuba, the regime showed its true face, waged war on the Church and worked with might and guile to eradicate Christian morals and religious faith from the conscience of the people.

Now the rosaries, which the Rebels had carried when they came down from the mountains to deceive the people, were thrown aside and the true face of the conqueror became visible. With few exceptions, exceptions which the Cuban people will always remember, the princes of the Church, the priests and the lay organizations which supported Christianity reacted as might have been expected when the masks were discarded. From the pulpits, on the streets, in the prisons, everywhere, they denounced the crimes and oppression of Cuba's Anti-Christ.

An old legend says that when Jupiter lit his torches and the rumbling of his arms thundered in the sky, it was a sign that the sins of mankind had provoked his anger. And the legend seems to have been true for a bolt of lightning descended upon the hier-

---

[6] Who they were and what they said can be ascertained by reading the issues of *Bohemia* in Cuba, appearing subsequent to January 1, 1959.

atic head of the Christ of Havana, a premonition of the sorrows and scourges that were to be visited upon the unhappy people of Cuba.

Epilogue: Slavery and Its Apologists

My Administration was overthrown by force and violence exactly 54 days before the scheduled inauguration, on February 14, 1959, of a President-elect who had been chosen by the Cuban people in democratic elections and whose victory was acknowledged even by his political opponents at the joint session of Congress at which the ballots were counted. The victorious candidate was of my political party. He was unacceptable to the Rebels in the mountains because Dr. Andrés Rivero Agüero was unwilling to sell his country to the Soviet dictatorship.

The Administration of March 10, 1952 had been internationally acknowledged as legitimate on two occasions: first, by the diplomatic recognition of my Government by non-communist countries after the Revolution of the 10th of March and, second, upon my inauguration on February 24, 1955 as the constitutionally elected President of Cuba for a term of four years. On that latter occasion, 51 nations sent their envoys extraordinary to attend the solemn ceremonies and thus show their good will toward our new Administration. Of course, no Communist countries were represented as, several years before, I had severed diplomatic relations with the Soviet Union. The diplomatic envoys present represented all 19 Latin American nations, Canada, the United States, 19 European countries (among them the Vatican), 10 Asian countries, Egypt and Indonesia.

The extremist movements, which are carrying the plague of

violence through Latin America, which spread havoc and blood-shed in the Far East, in Laos, in the Congo and elsewhere are undoubtedly communist-dominated or communist-influenced. Whenever eruptions of this sort occur, the long arm of the Kremlin is likely to be the moving force. Sometimes, the Reds act directly and openly; on other occasions, they display their "neutralist" face. In either case, their propaganda and action is adjusted to the peculiarities of the nation they seek to destroy. Their purpose in every case is to weaken democracy and Western Civilization and to make a contribution to the Soviet conquest of the world.

The Communist propagandists show an extraordinary ability to use the most effective media. Thus, they have friends within the great international news agencies who lose no time in transmitting any items that may further the cause. Any story, no matter how unimportant, will circle the globe in a matter of minutes if it is grist to the mills of communism.

There were two incidents of this sort in Cuba during my second Administration which were instructive. The first occurred several years ago. Clever agitators made a bet with some drunken U. S. Marines that the latter would not dare to climb the statue of Martí in Havana's Central Park. A team of press cameramen suddenly appeared from nowhere and photographed this trivial incident. Their picture was flashed around the world with the caption: "American Soldiers Desecrate the Statue of Cuban Patriot José Martí." Obviously, the stage had been set in advance; the bet was a ruse by the Communist instigators of the plot and the purpose was to arouse popular anger against the United States. Fortunately, the people of Cuba did not fall for it.

The second instance occurred when, in the midst of a resounding propaganda campaign against my Administration, a certain South American delegate to the United Nations proposed that a telegram be sent to me as President, requesting that a certain "Rebel" be spared from the firing squad. He was perhaps unaware that in those days the death penalty did not exist in Cuba. Nevertheless, the "news" of this man about to be executed by "tyranny" girdled the globe and had the desired effect.

The same impressive tactic was repeated when reporter Herbert L. Matthews visited Cuba and secretly interviewed Castro in the Sierra Maestra; when anarcho-communist banners of the 26th of July Movement were displayed high on the Eiffel Tower, mocking the dedication of France to liberty; or when American and Canadian civilians and Marines were kidnapped in Oriente to blackmail the United States into declaring an arms embargo against the legitimate government of Cuba.

The presence of a foreign hand can be sensed in everyone of these "episodes." It is a long hand, the directing brain of which was carrying out a plot, not primarily against my Administration, but rather against the free institutions of the Americas.

Well trained in mass psychology, the Reds have advanced everywhere by brainwashing, frightening the cowardly and impressing the ignorant. They are aware that the despotism which strangles prostrate Poland, turns Hungary into a land of martyrs and imposes its system of blood and terror through Asia, Africa and the Americas may well provoke a reaction from the West and from the world in general either because of solidarity with the human cause or for purely political reasons.

To minimize the possibility of a strong reaction of this sort, the Reds constantly dope the masses with their slogans against war and in favor of international peace. Within the great nations of the West (the United States, England and France), they utilize the so-called liberals to head their campaigns against the cold war.

THE BLACK LEGEND

My Government fought against terror and communism in the interests of the peace, progress and freedom of the people. We respected the rights of all. We even commuted Castro's prison sentence so he could seek political power via the polls rather than through violence and terror. We left no stone unturned in an effort to achieve the most for the Cuban people. We multiplied the autonomous organizations so that a larger number of Cubans could take part in governmental responsibilities and work for the promotion of social welfare. We never deprived anyone of his property or his rights.

Legends of non-existent tortures and abominable persecutions were ceaselessly spread and repeated by the Communists, their agents and dupes. Rumors sprouted like mushrooms of mass assassinations and summary trials that never took place. Propaganda presented these baseless rumors as sober facts and even went so far as to support them with the false testimony of indoctrinated physicians and intimidated lawyers.

Wherever possible, the fog of confusion was spread over the distinction between political persecution and the legitimate duty of the State to defend itself. The armed forces were obligated both to obey the law and to enforce it. If they ever reacted with outbursts of violence, as has been charged, this was not because they derived any morbid pleasure from physical assault, but because they were provoked, sometimes to the limits of human endurance, by the carefully contrived campaign of hatred, violence and murder launched against Cuba by the forces of international communism.

Was it meritorious to murder a soldier or policeman while he was performing his duty to defend his country or to enforce the laws? Should terrorists be praised when they threw bombs into crowded places, tearing apart the bodies of workers, teachers, government employees, women and, for that matter, children, splattering blood, tissue and human organs in all directions? Many Cubans paid with their lives for performing their duties as the citizens of a democratic regime. Some were murdered by the Communists of Fidel Castro for voting at the polls; others for even lesser reasons.

I wondered how it was possible for influential foreign correspondents and shapers of public opinion in the Free World to remain silent when Cubans who defended law and order, justice, democracy and free institutions, performing their duty in doing so, were branded as "war criminals." I wondered how these people succeeded in closing their eyes, their ears and their mouths to the massacres and frightful acts of persecution and cruelty which characterized the Communist regime in Cuba from its very inception. These men who denounced crimes that never occurred and then explained away the enormities that did occur at least pretended to be spiritually part of Western Civilization. They were ultra "liberals," to be sure, but they had seemed not to be devoid of human decency.

Why wasn't at least a minimum of pity or ordinary Christian feeling shown when a soldier, in the performance of his sworn duty to protect his country, was murdered by an enemy who wore no uniform, lurked in ambush or attacked only from behind, sometimes wearing women's clothes to do murder with impunity?

THE SILENCE OF THE "HUMANISTS"

The revulsion of the civilized and Christian world to incredibly long lists of assassinations, tortures and extortions by the Castro regime has at last become general. It has taken years for this to happen, but, as the proverb says, "God for a witness and time for the truth."

The cold-blooded assassination of over a hundred innocent Cubans by Raúl Castro in the first days of Red victory (they were machinegunned and toppled into bulldozed ditches) was the first act of a carefully planned operation. The destruction of the Army and its villification by propaganda was essential to the Communist plan of imposing a Red force commanded by Russian officers. The Castro brothers shrewdly recognized that the professional corps of officers and soldiers could not be corrupted and would never acquiesce in the sale of their country to a foreign power.

Thereafter, the creation of popular militias converted every school into a garrison and placed the people at the mercy of armed gangs of frustrated people with an uncontrollable lust for plunder and blood.

Another virtue which was attributed to the self-styled "liberators" was "honesty and efficient administration." Yet the man who calls himself the Tropical Robespierre has never accounted for eleven million dollars extorted by his revolutionary forces nor has he ever attempted to account for the vast income of INRA to the Court of Accounts, to which my Administration reported in full and in accordance with the Constitution and the laws. Nor has he ever made this accounting directly to the people, either in his marathon televised harangues or otherwise. As for the "efficiency" of the new Administration, the shortest answer is that Cuba is in ruins, its economy destroyed, its political life under as primitive a type of absolute personal rule as can be found in modern history.

The native Cubans who mistook the bearded leader for a Moses destined to lead them to the promised land, suffered in their property and flesh the penalty for their error. At first, they blamed the colossal blunder of "agrarian reform" on inexperience. They neglected to urge mercy for the men sent before firing squads or to rot in filthy prisons by courts of illiterate and vengeful representatives of the "revolution." Some would justify their moral inertia by confessing fear of being labeled "Batistianos"; others morbidly acquiesced; still others joined the mobs. The reaction came too late and was on a global scale only when the corpses of innocent victims were piled high.

Where were the national organizations of self-styled humanitarians? They kept silent during the reign of terror, closed their eyes to the total violation of human rights, then joined the clamor of denunciation from the safety of exile when it was fashionable to do so. Many of them, still unrepentent enemies of democracy, private property and personal freedom, were presented as heroes of "Fidelismo without Fidel." That is to say, endorsing the events of the past, eliminating Castro individually and themselves supplanting him as the gravediggers of civilization in Cuba.

Thus, a political ideology arose that took under its banner all the frustrated and rejected neurotics, the resentful lawyers without clients, the doctors without patients and the vast mass of drifting opportunists, the men without trades, professions or competence. They were supported, while in exile in the United States, by glib men who felt sympathy for the mass of radical resentment, frustration and incompetence that had been rejected even by the Communist dictatorship. To gain an audience, this new group repeated all the old lies of the Communists, including particularly the denial that Cuba, when free, had made great advances in science, culture, the arts, and social justice.

For over three years, the OAS was concerned about the conditions of political prisoners in every American country except Cuba.

The International Red Cross, which had previously been so receptive to the false charges of the outlaws of the Sierra Maestra, remained silent and inert while brutal violations of human rights were perpetrated daily against the people of my unfortunate country. Yet, under my Administration, the Red Cross had been given every facility to investigate the charges leveled by the Marxists, even when they were absurd and obviously designed to impress the naïve and enrage the ignorant. The press is full of the enormities perpetrated in Communist Cuba. How can the International Red Cross reconcile its zeal of yesterday with its callous indifference of today?

THE AMERICAN WHITE PAPER ON CUBA

A White Paper on Cuba was published by the United States State Department in April 1961, a few days before the disastrous and half-hearted attempt of the Administration to overthrow the Castro dictatorship by spending Cuban lives, while withholding American arms and avoiding official responsibility.

The *New York Times,* which was exceptionally well-informed concerning the inner workings of the New Frontier, reported as follows on April 4, 1961 concerning its origins:

"According to informed sources here, the idea for the pamphlet was President Kennedy's. He has long been concerned at the lack of popular understanding in Latin America of the United States attitude toward the Castro regime . . .

"The pamphlet was written largely by Mr. (Arthur M.) Schlesinger with the cooperation of Richard Goodwin, a Presidential assistant dealing with foreign aid,[1] and in consultation with the State Department.

"However, according to these informants, President Kennedy devoted many hours to the pamphlet, personally going over it with Mr. Schlesinger."

The nature of this analysis of the Cuban tragedy can be gathered by the following excerpts from a brilliant speech delivered by Spruille Braden before the Cuban Chamber of Commerce in the United States on May 17, 1961. A former U. S. Ambassador to Argentina, Colombia and Cuba and at one time Assistant Secretary of State for Latin American Affairs, Mr. Braden has a keen understanding of the realities of inter-American affairs.

"That abysmal ignorance in Washington concerning this whole Cuban situation endures, even at this late date, is clearly apparent in the so-called White Paper issued by the Department of State on April 3rd.

"This document begins by giving approval, i.e., encouraging

---

[1] Richard Nathan Goodwin was one of the most powerful White House advisors on Latin American affairs during the first years of the Kennedy Administration. His qualifications for this job, so important to the security of his country, were that he had never been to Latin America prior to 1961, spoke no Spanish and was under thirty. However, he was from Harvard and a socialist or a liberal extremist of one brand or another.

what it calls the 'authentic and autonomous revolution of the Americas,' that is to promote more Fidelismo but without Fidel. For my part, I prefer to see the sound evolution of the Americas without the violence, abuse and waste inherent in all revolutions. Nor do I consider it wise or proper for my government to advocate 'authentic and autonomous revolutions' all over the American continents. This is an outright intervention which may prove very costly and disastrous for everyone concerned, and especially for the U.S.A.

"The State Department continues with an apocryphal history of the Castro revolution, with many half truths and outright errors. It is ignorant of the fact that the 26th of July Movement was a child of the Buro del Caribe, which in turn was the off-spring of the Comintern. It repeats the old fantasy about Fidel being a 'traitor to the revolution.' His revolution was Communist-planned and inspired from the beginning; he was a traitor to God and country, but never to his Communist bosses and beliefs. It damns Batista as a tyrant and impugns the honor and reputation of anyone and everyone who even remotely had been connected with him. It implies that the Cuban nation as a whole, until the advent of Castro, suffered from want, lack of medical care, housing and other social needs. In an unbelievable display of ignorance, it praises David Salvador, a notorious Communist, as fighting for a free labor movement and childishly accepts Pardo Llada's absurd allegation recently that he was anti-Communist . . .

"As most of you know, Batista and I, as Ambassador during his first term, had some pretty severe, head-on collisions. Clearly, I am not prejudiced in his favor. But, as a matter of simple justice, I should like to call certain facts to the attention of the authors of the White Paper . . . To speak, as the White Paper does, of the 'rapacity of the leadership' and damn such splendid characters as Saladrigas and hundreds of others like him, is calumny, cheap demagoguery and a despicable act, unworthy of a responsible government and foreign office.

"The White Paper's direct and implied animadversions as to the poverty and bad economic conditions of Cuba, prior to the coming of Castro, are inaccurate and evidence the socialistic prejudices of its drafters.

"How false is the picture drawn by the White Paper can be shown by a few brief citations: Cuba, previous to 1959, enjoyed the largest per capita income of any Latin American republic. Gross national income was $2,834,000,000 and bank clearings $6,908,000,000 in 1958. There was a massive construction of hospitals, schools of all grades, houses for the poor and middle class, highways and feeder roads. The standard of living was rising; there were 4 to 5 persons for each radio, 13 to 18 for each television set, and 39 to each automobile. I remember the long-shoremen getting $27 per day even when I was in Cuba.

"Of course, there still existed much corruption, poverty and illiteracy; and there was the perennial problem of 'el tiempo muerto' (the dead season). Yet, right on Manhattan Island, not to mention in the rest of the city, there are comparable conditions of poverty, illiteracy, and crime. And a trip to the West Virginia, Kentucky, and Tennessee hills may be edifying in respect to bad rural conditions.

"To sum up, the White Paper is one of the most indefensible documents I ever have seen issued by a presumably responsible foreign office. The best that can be said for it is that it displays such ignorance and lack of understanding as to explain in considerable measure the tragic bungling of the catastrophe in Bahía de Cochinos."

NEGLIGENCE OR TREASON?

Testifying before the Senate Internal Security Subcommittee on June 12, 1961, former U. S. Ambassador to Mexico, Costa Rica and El Salvador Robert C. Hill testified that, in his judgment, the *New York Times* and the State Department contributed to the seizure of Cuba by Castro and the Communists. He added that in May 1959 "the Russians themselves identified Raúl Castro as a Communist" in an official Communist document duly reported by the U. S. Embassy in Moscow to the State Department.[2] Mr. Hill stated that this report was called to the attention of the Department, but was evidently ignored. Hill noted that Ambassador to Cuba Earl E. T. Smith was instructed by the State Department to be briefed by Herbert L. Matthews of the *New York Times,* who "has always been an enthusiastic supporter of Fidel

---

[2] Dispatch #666, May 22, 1959, "Soviet Attitude Toward Latin America," American Embassy, Moscow, to Department of State.

Castro"[3] and added: "Individuals in the State Department and individuals in the *New York Times* put Castro in power."[4]

Mr. Hill and several other former United States Ambassadors laid blame for decisions favorable to Castro and adverse to the interests of the United States on a certain William Arthur Wieland, alias Montenegro, who was in charge of Caribbean and Mexican affairs during the time that free Cuba was undermined, betrayed and destroyed. Hill testified concerning a session on board an airplane with Dr. Milton Eisenhower, the brother of the President and an influential policy maker on Latin American affairs. Ambassador Hill and his staff tried to warn Dr. Eisenhower of the fact that Castro was a Communist or Communist tool, but they were incessantly interrupted by Wieland. When Wieland stated that "there is no evidence of Communist infiltration in Cuba," Colonel Glawe, the U. S. Air Attache, retorted: "You are either a damn fool or a Communist."[5]

Hill testified that, at a conference of American Ambassadors in El Salvador in 1959, Philip Bonsal, who had just been named U. S. Ambassador to Cuba, insisted that nothing be put in the communique which might seem critical of Fidel Castro as that "would make his (Bonsal's) job in Cuba very difficult." When Hill objected, Bonsal replied: "If you cannot be a team player, why not resign?"[6]

Hill also testified concerning the existence of a pro-Castro cell in the American Embassy in Havana and a "CIA representative in Havana who was pro-Castro."[7] He told U. S. Ambassador to Cuba Earl E. T. Smith that he was sorry for him because:

"You are assigned to Cuba to preside over the downfall of Batista. The decision has been made that Batista has to go. You must be very careful."[8]

Hill added that this decision had been made at a low bureaucratic level, not by top officials, but by subordinates. Nonetheless, it was a firm decision and nobody entering the State Department

[3] U. S. Senate, Senate Internal Security Subcommittee, *Hearings, Communist Threat to the United States Through the Caribbean, Part 12, Testimony of Robert C. Hill,* June 12, 1961, p. 815.
[4] *Ibid,* p. 821.
[5] *Ibid,* pp. 806-807.
[6] *Ibid,* pp. 816-817.
[7] *Ibid,* p. 821.
[8] *Ibid,* p. 807.

271 *Slavery and Its Apologists*

could be unaware of the fact that Castro's rise to power was being plotted.[9] Among other things, FBI officials in Mexico, who were sent there with the full cooperation of the Mexican Government, sent reports on the Communist connections of Castro and his movement to the State Department. However, these reports were sidetracked "at the desk level" and "had not reached the upper echelons of the State Department." [10]

CONCLUDING

Thus, the testimony of American Ambassadors who believe in freedom and patriotism has helped reveal some of the machinations of "ultra-liberals" and pro-Communists who, from the shelter of the government departments they had infiltrated, managed to make possible the creation of the first Soviet state in the New World. Simultaneously, an audacious propaganda of lies was used to brainwash the people. Despite Cuba's obvious prosperity and advanced labor, educational and social welfare institutions, it was alleged that her underdeveloped condition called for a revolution.

This came as an unbelievable shock to those of us who love peace, who have always worked for fair relations between men and peoples, who strove to provide the homes of our neighbors with the same happiness and security that we wanted for our own homes, who battled continuously for better health, more education and culture, and higher living standards for the people, and who defended our nation's sovereignty and worked for conditions of order and due process of law in which all men of good will could live without fear. We found that everything we had struggled for was swept aside in the savage chain of crimes and moral enormities that followed that ominous New Year's Day of 1959. In addition, we found ourselves and our life's work villified as that of despots, killers and men indifferent to the needs and welfare of the people.

When he was contemplating the horrors of fratricidal war, Abraham Lincoln once said his greatest consolation was his knowledge that "even this shall pass." On another occasion he told a wounded soldier, "Remember, Dick, to keep close to the peo-

9 *Ibid*, p. 808.
10 *Ibid*, p. 819.

ple—they are always right and will mislead no one." [11] A consolation for us is the knowledge that, despite the cruelties of the Red terror and the confusing and false propaganda of its agents, admirers and dupes, the common people of Cuba have a greatness of capacity, comprehension and courage that their oppressors cannot imagine.

The chains of slavery will not for long bind a people which has offered so many blood sacrifices for its liberty.

Now I am finished. I have tried to give a factual account of the services which my associates and I performed, or tried to perform, for our country. The purpose of this book has been to present the Cuban story as it is in a setting of hard facts and stubborn realities. The truth, like liberty against slavery and light against darkness always and in the long run wins its battle against lies and slander.

As Milton wrote in *Areopagitica:*

"Though all the winds of doctrine were let loose to play upon the earth, so Truth be in the field, we do injuriously by licensing and prohibiting to misdoubt her strength. Let her and Falsehood grapple; who ever knew Truth put to the worse, in a free and open encounter."

It cannot be otherwise in Cuba.

[11] Quoted in Carl Sandburg, *Abraham Lincoln: The War Years,* Harcourt Brace & Company, New York, 1939, Vol. III, p. 384.

Appendix

AUTONOMOUS ORGANIZATIONS

Rice Stabilization Administration	AEA
Coffee Purchase and Sale Administration	ACVCAFE
Corn Stabilization Administration	AEM
Cooperative Agency of Distribution and Supply	ADASCA
Rural Credit Associations	ACR
Cojimar Tourist Center	ACETCO
Varadero Tourist Center	ACETVA
Cuban Bank for Foreign Trade	BCCE
Bank of Social and Economic Development	BANDES
National Bank of Agricultural and Industrial Development	BANFAIC
National Bank of Cuba	BNC
National Garments Bank of Cuba	BNCC
Credit and Insurance Funds of the Armed Forces	CASFA
Child Guidance Center	COI
José Martí Centenary Commission	
General Emilio Nuñez Centenary Commission	
Juan Gualberto Gómez Centenary Commission	
Martín Morua Delgado Centenary Commission	
Civil Aeronautics Commission	CAC
National Executive Committee of Agricultural and Mining Cooperatives	CENCAM

Executive Committee on Forest and Agro-Pecuarian Restoration	CEREFA
National Executive Committee of Local, Urban and Rural Foundations	CENPLUC
National Development Commission	CFN
National Sports Commission	CND
National Housing Commission	CNV
Malaria Commission	C de la M.
National Commission for Public Beaches	CNPP
Commission to Regulate the Shoe Industry	CRIC
National Commission for Smallpox Vaccination	CNVAV
Directing Council to Construct the Palace of Justice	CDCPJ
Permanent Directing Council of the Archives of Cuba	CDPAC
National Economic Council	CNE
National Council on Education and Culture	CNEC
National Council for Tuberculosis	CNT
National Corporation of Public Assistance	CNAP
National Transport Commission	CNTC
National Organization to Construct Toll Roads and Bridges	ENCOP
National Finance Corporation	ONFC
Insured Mortgages Bank	FHA
Depositors' Insurance Fund	FDS
Home for the Physically and Mentally Handicapped	HIFM
Cuban Institute of Cartography and Cadastral Survey	ICCC
Cuban Sugar Stabilization Institute	ICEA
Cuban Coffee Stabilization Institute	ICECAFE
Cuban Statistical Institute	ICE
Cuban Reinsurance Institute	ICR
Cuban Institute of Tourism	ICT
Cuban Institute of Technical Investigation	ICIT
Military Technological Institute for the Youth	IMJT
National Cardiological Institute	INC
National Institute to Develop the Motion Picture Industry	INFIC
National Institute of Hygiene	INH
National Institute of Fishing	INP
Technical Institute of Rural Sanitation	ITSR
National Planning Board	JNP

Autonomous Jurisdiction of Topes de Collantes	JATC
National Organization for the Administration of Government Hospitals	ONAHE
National Organization of Mobile Public Libraries	ONBAP
National Organization of School and People's Dining Rooms	ONCEP
National Organization of Children's Dispensaries	ONDI
National Organization of Public Parking	ONEP
National Parks and Green Areas Administration	ONPAV
National Organization for the Rehabilitation of Invalids	ONRI
Low Cost Housing for Members of the Armed Forces	OVEFA
Matanzas Airport Foundation	PAM
Foundation for Aid to Children, Old, Destitute and Sick Persons	PANADE
Foundation for Children's Homes	PACI
Administrative Foundation for the City of Balneario de San Diego	PECBSD
Foundation for the Veterans' Home	PHV
Foundation for the Economic Rehabilitation of Baracoa	PREB
Foundation for Fine Arts and National Museums	PBAMN
Association for the Prophylaxis of Leprosy, Skin Diseases and Syphilis	PLECS
First Hydroelectric Center of Cuba	PRICHEC
National Society of Cuban Authors	SNAC

Statistical Appendix

TABLE 1: RANK OF LATIN AMERICAN COUNTRIES IN 24 INDEXES
OF ECONOMIC, SOCIAL AND CULTURAL PROGRESS *

| | | Number of Times in: | | | |
Rank	Country	First Place	Second Place	Third Place	Total Placements:
1	CUBA	9	3	12	24
2	Argentina	6	5	2	13
3	Uruguay	4	6	—	10
4	Venezuela	6	1	2	9
5	Mexico	—	4	2	6
6	Costa Rica	—	2	2	4
7	Dominican Republic	1	2	—	3
8	Panamá	—	—	2	2
9	Brazil	—	1	—	1
10	Paraguay	—	1	—	1
11	Chile	—	—	1	1
12	Colombia	—	—	1	1
13	Bolivia	—	—	1	1
14	Honduras	—	—	1	1
15	El Salvador	—	—	1	1
	TOTALS	26	25	27	78

* These 24 Indexes are shown in Tables 3-26 inclusive.

TABLE 2:   RANK OF LATIN AMERICAN COUNTRIES IN 23 INDEXES OF ECONOMIC, SOCIAL AND CULTURAL PROGRESS [*]

Rank	Country	*Summation of Reciprocals of Rank in the 23 Series*
1	CUBA	13.29
2	Argentina	10.09
3	Venezuela	8.08
4	Uruguay	7.21
5	Mexico	4.13
6	Costa Rica	2.86
7	Panama	2.64
8	Chile	2.61
9	Brazil	2.57
10	Dominican Rep.	2.35
11	Colombia	1.64
12	Peru	1.14

[*] These 23 indexes are shown in Tables 3-25 inclusive. The method of scoring is to count 1 for first place, ½ for second place, ⅓ for third place and 1/nth for nth place.

(A) INTERNATIONAL COMPARISONS

TABLE 3:   INCOME PER CAPITA IN U. S. DOLLARS

Rank	Latin American Country	Year	Income per Capita
1	Venezuela	1958	868
2	Costa Rica	1958	361
3	CUBA	1958	334
4	Chile	1958	291
5	Mexico	1958	260
6	Uruguay	1957	253
7	Panama	1956	246
8	Dominican Republic	1957	239

TABLE 4:   PERCENTAGE OF ILLITERATES TO TOTAL POPULATION IN LATIN AMERICA IN 1958 *

Rank	Country	Percent Illiterate
1	Argentina	8
2	Costa Rica	21
3	Chile	24
4	CUBA	24
5	Puerto Rico	26
6	Panama	28
7	Uruguay	35
8	Colombia	35
9	Mexico	38
10	Ecuador	44
11	Peru	50
12	Brazil	51
13	Dominican Republic	57
14	El Salvador	58
15	Nicaragua	60
16	Paraguay	60
17	Venezuela	60
18	Honduras	65
19	Bolivia	69
20	Guatemala	72
21	Haiti	90

* Data from the *United Nations Statistical Yearbook,* 1959. The Communist leader, Antonio Nuñez Jiménez, claimed in 1959 that the Cuban illiteracy rate was only 22.8%.

TABLE 5:   PERCENTAGE OF NATIONAL INCOME DEVOTED TO PUBLIC EDUCATION IN 1959 *

Rank	Country	Percent
1	CUBA	3.4 †
2	Argentina	3.1 ‡
3	Costa Rica	3.1
4	Peru	3.1
5	Chile	2.6
6	Guatemala	2.3
7	Brazil	2.3 §
8	Colombia	1.9 §

* Pan American Union, *America in Figures,* 1960, Washington, D.C. The comparable U.S. figure for 1957-58 was 4.3%.
† 1957-58.   ‡ 1959-60.   § 1957.

TABLE 6:   INHABITANTS PER UNIVERSITY STUDENT (1958)*

Rank	Country	Inhabitants per Student
1	Argentina	135
2	Uruguay	199
3	CUBA	273
4	Mexico	334
5	Panama	387
6	Paraguay	496
7	Costa Rica	514

* UNESCO, *Annuaire Internationale d'Education*. The comparable figures are 61 for the United States and 210 for Canada.

TABLE 7:   INHABITANTS PER PHYSICIAN IN ACTIVE PRACTICE*

Rank	Country	No. Inhabitants	Year
1	Argentina	760	1956
2	Uruguay	860	1957
3	CUBA	1,000	1957
4	Venezuela	1,700	1957
5	Chile	1,900	1953
6	Mexico	1,900	1956
7	Paraguay	1,900	1957
8	Brazil	2,500	1954

* Pan American Union, *America in Figures*, 1960.

TABLE 8:   MORTALITY RATE PER THOUSAND PERSONS (1958)*

Rank	Country	Mortality Rate	Rank	Country	Mortality Rate
1	CUBA	5.8	12	Peru	10.3
2	Uruguay	7.0	13	Paraguay	10.6
3	Bolivia†	7.7	14	Honduras	11.1
4	Venezuela	7.8	15	Mexico	11.6
5	Argentina	8.1	16	El Salvador	11.7
6	Canada	8.1	17	Chile	12.1
7	Dominican Rep.	8.4	18	Colombia	12.8
8	Nicaragua	8.7	19	Ecuador	15.2
9	Costa Rica	9.0	20	Brazil	20.6
10	Panama	9.0	21	Guatemala	21.3
11	United States	9.4			

* *Statistical Abstract of the United States*, 1960.
† Probably due primarily to underreporting.

TABLE 9: INFLATION IN LATIN AMERICA
(U.S. Department of Commerce data)

Rank	Country	*Percent Increase in Consumer Goods Prices in 1958*
1	CUBA	1.4
2	Dominican Republic	1.9
3	Honduras	2.9
4	Guatemala	3.3
5	Ecuador	3.5
6	Costa Rica	4.3
7	Venezuela	4.7
8	El Salvador	5.9
9	Panama	6.2
10	Nicaragua	6.9
11	Mexico	7.8
12	Uruguay	9.1
13	Colombia	9.6
14	Peru	12.4
15	Brazil	15.4
16	Argentina	19.8
17	Chile	35.7
18	Paraguay	43.8
19	Bolivia	63.0

TABLE 10: FOREIGN TRADE: VALUE OF IMPORTS IN
DOLLARS PER CAPITA (1958)*

Rank	Country	*Value of Imports*
1	Venezuela	2,380
2	CUBA	1,320
3	Panama	1,042
4	Costa Rica	865
5	Argentina	590
6	Chile	550
7	Uruguay	537
8	Nicaragua	531

* Pan American Union, *America in Figures, 1960.*

TABLE 11: GOLD RESERVES PER CAPITA IN U.S. DOLLARS*

1	Venezuela	156.5
2	Uruguay	73.0
3	CUBA	55.3
4	Panama	45.5
5	Costa Rica	17.4
6	Dominican Republic	15.1
7	El Salvador	14.5
8	Guatemala	12.8

* Pan American Union, *America in Figures, 1960.*

TABLE 12: NEWSPAPERS PUBLISHED PER THOUSAND INHABITANTS (1952-1958)*

Rank	Country	Number of Units	Year
1	Uruguay	180	1958
2	Argentina	180	1958
3	CUBA	129	1956
4	Panama	124	1957
5	Venezuela	102	1956
6	Costa Rica	102	1958
7	Nicaragua	90	1957
8	Peru	76	1957

* Pan American Union, *America in Figures, 1960.*

TABLE 13: NEWSPRINT CONSUMPTION IN KILOGRAMS PER CAPITA (1958)*

1	Uruguay	11.1
2	Argentina	8.5
3	CUBA	5.0
4	Venezuela	4.5
5	Chile	3.5
6	Brazil	3.2
7	Costa Rica	2.9
8	Mexico	2.4

* Pan American Union, *America in Figures, 1960.*

TABLE 14: CONSUMPTION OF ELECTRICITY (IN KILOGRAMS OF COAL EQUIVALENT PER CAPITA 1958)*

Rank	Country	Kg. Per Capita per Annum
1	Venezuela	2,458
2	Argentina	1,077
3	Mexico	813
4	Chile	757
5	CUBA	726
6	Uruguay	683
7	Panama	456
8	Colombia	446

* Pan American Union, *America in Figures, 1960.*

TABLE 15: TELEPHONES PER 100 INHABITANTS (1959)*

1	Argentina	5.99
2	Uruguay	5.01
3	CUBA	2.62
4	Venezuela	2.47
5	Chile	2.25
6	Panama	2.37
7	Colombia	1.81
8	Brazil	1.46

* Pan American Union, *America in Figures, 1960.*

TABLE 16: AUTOMOBILES PER THOUSAND INHABITANTS (1957-58)*

1	Venezuela	40.8
2	Argentina	31.8
3	CUBA	31.5
4	Panama	21.0
5	Mexico	19.5
6	Costa Rica	18.5
7	Chile	15.3
8	Brazil	11.8

* Pan American Union, *America in Figures, 1960.*

TABLE 17:   NUMBER OF TELEVISION BROADCAST STATIONS (1957)*

		No. of Stations
1	CUBA	23
2	Mexico	12
3	Colombia	8
4	Brazil	6
5	Venezuela	4
6	Argentina	1
7	Dominican Republic	1
8	Uruguay	1
	TOTAL	56

* Pan American Union, *America in Figures, 1960.*

TABLE 18:   TELEVISION SETS PER 1,000 INHABITANTS (1959)*

1	CUBA	56
2	Venezuela	29
3	Argentina	19
4	Mexico	17
5	Brazil	13
6	Colombia	10
7	Uruguay	5
8	Dominican Republic	5

* Pan American Union, *America in Figures, 1960.*

TABLE 19:   MOVIES: TICKETS SOLD PER CAPITA PER ANNUM (1958)*

1	CUBA	9.0
2	Mexico	8.5
3	Venezuela	8.2
4	Brazil	5.3
5	El Salvador	4.5
6	Colombia	4.1
7	Argentina	3.9
8	Guatemala	2.9
	U.S.A.	12.5

* Pan American Union, *America in Figures, 1960.*

TABLE 20:   KILOMETERS OF RAILROAD TRACK PER THOUSAND
SQUARE KILOMETERS OF NATIONAL TERRITORY

Country	Railroad Track (Km.)	Area in Thsds. Sq. Km.	Km. of Track per M Km. of Area
Argentina	43,956	2,775	15.8
Brazil	37,967	8,510	4.5
CUBA	4,784	114	42.0
Mexico	23,360	1,968	11.9
Peru	4,023	1,284	3.1

TABLE 21:   RADIO RECEIVERS PER THOUSAND INHABITANTS (LATE
1950s)*

U.S.A.	925
United Kingdom	285
Germany (Federal Republic)	276
France	239
CUBA	176
Japan	159
Italy	126
U.S.S.R.	163

IN LATIN AMERICA:

1	Uruguay	261
2	CUBA	176
3	Argentina	158
4	Venezuela	126
5	Panama	124
6	Chile	99
7	Mexico	84
8	Brazil	76
9	Costa Rica	73

* UNESCO, *Basic Facts and Figures, 1959.*

TABLE 22: INFANT MORTALITY IN LATIN AMERICA 1958: (DEATHS
DURING FIRST YEAR PER THOUSAND BIRTHS—SOURCE:
Statistical Abstract of the United States, 1960)

Rank	Country	Infant Mortality Rate
1	CUBA	37.6
2	Paraguay	55.3
3	Panama	57.9
4	Argentina	61.1
5	Honduras	64.4
6	Nicaragua	69.3
7	Uruguay	73.0
8	Dominican Republic	76.6
9	El Salvador	79.3
10	Mexico	80.0
11	Peru	88.4
12	Costa Rica	89.0
13	Bolivia	90.7
14	Venezuela	91.2
15	Colombia	100.0

TABLE 23: AVERAGE SIZE OF FARMS IN CERTAIN LATIN AMERICAN
COUNTRIES (1958)

Country	Average Size of Farms in hectares
CUBA	56.7
United States	78.5
Mexico	82.0
Venezuela	335.0

TABLE 24: CALORIES CONSUMED PER PERSON PER DAY IN LATIN
AMERICA IN 1958 [*]

Rank	Country	Calories
1	Argentina	3,106
2	Uruguay	2,991
3	CUBA	2,682
4	Brazil	2,353
5	Chile	2,344
6	Peru	2,077

[*] Food and Agriculture Organization of the United Nations.

TABLE 25:   U.S. INVESTMENTS IN LATIN AMERICA

(in millions of dollars)

	Country or Area	1956	1958	Increase or Decline
	All Latin America	7,059	8,730	1,671
1	Venezuela	1,829	2,722	893
2	Brazil	1,218	1,345	127
3	CUBA	777	1,001	224
4	Mexico	690	781	91
5	Chile	676	736	60
6	Central America	630	737	107
7	Argentina	466	517	51
8	Peru	343	429	86
9	Colombia	298	289	— 9
	All Other	132	173	41
	Percent represented by Cuba	11.0%	11.5%	13.4%

TABLE 26:   HONEY AND BEESWAX

Rank	Country	Production	Exports	Consumption
		(Millions of Pounds)		
1	Argentine	62.1	30.9	11.2
2	Mexico	28.6	22.0	6.6
3	CUBA	8.8	8.2	0.6
4	Guatemala	5.1	4.6	0.5

TABLE 27:   HIGHER EDUCATION STUDENTS PER THOUSAND INHABITANTS, A WORLD COMPARISON (1957-1958)*

Country	Population in Millions (1957)	Students in Higher Education	Students per Thousand Inhabitants
U.S.A.	171.2	3,037,000	17.7
CUBA	6.4	86,500	13.5
U.S.S.R.	200.2	2,110,860	9.5
Japan	90.9	626,736	6.9
France	44.1	180,634	4.1
Italy	48.5	154,638	3.2
Germany	51.5	153,923	3.0
U.K.	51.5	96,128	1.9

* UNESCO, *op. cit.*

TABLE 28: NEWSPRINT CONSUMPTION PER CAPITA (LATE 1950s)*

Country	Kg. of Newsprint Consumed per Capita per Annum
U.S.A.	36.3
United Kingdom	20.0
France	10.6
West Germany	8.0
Japan	6.0
CUBA	5.0
Italy	4.4
U.S.S.R.	1.6

* UNESCO, *op. cit.*

TABLE 29: PHYSICIANS PER THOUSAND INHABITANTS, A WORLD COMPARISON (LATE 1950s)*

Country	Physicians (thousands)	Population (millions)	Physicians per 1,000 Population
Italy (1958)	69.9	48.5	1.44
West Germany (1959)	72.8	51.5	1.41
United States (1958)	217.1	171.2	1.27
Japan (1960)	97.3	90.9	1.07
France (1959)	44.4	44.1	1.01
CUBA (1960)†	6.4	6.4	1.00
United Kingdom (1959)	42.5	51.5	0.83

* Figures for physicians from *Statistical Abstract of the United States, 1962,* pp. 935-936. Population data from UNESCO, *op. cit.*
† The ratio of physicians to population was exactly the same in 1957.

(B) OTHER TABLES

TABLE 30: CONSTRUCTION IN CUBA (MILLIONS OF DOLLARS)*

Year	Total	Havana Province	Other
1952	49.4	38.0	11.4
1953	62.7	51.1	11.6
1954	74.1	60.3	13.9
1955	69.4	54.2	15.2
1956	80.4	60.3	20.1

1957	77.9	58.3	19.7
1958	74.0	61.5	12.5
TOTALS	488.1	383.7	104.4
Increase			
1952-1957	28.5	20.3	8.3

* According to the National College of Architects.

TABLE 31:   GAINFULLY EMPLOYED POPULATION OF CUBA (1958)

Category	No.	Percent
Agriculture, hunting & fishing	818,706	41.5
Mining and quarrying	9,618	0.5
Manufacturing	327,208	16.6
Construction	65,292	3.3
Public utilities	8,439	0.4
Commerce	232,323	11.7
Transport & communications	104,003	5.0
Service	395,904	20.1
Other	10,773	0.9
TOTAL	1,972,266	100.0

TABLE 32:   CONSOLIDATED OPERATIONS OF CUBAN BANKS
(Millions of Dollars)

Year	Capital	Savings	Demand Deposits	Loans
1951	37.1	113.6	667.7	394.7
1952	41.7	141.2	656.0	461.1
1953	40.8	159.6	629.0	427.8
1954	45.4	178.6	635.0	466.1
1955	49.3	212.2	704.0	532.5
1956	67.0	293.5	948.0	666.1
1957	74.2	395.8	1,089.9	784.5
1958	77.3	443.7	1,076.7	836.3
INCREASE BETWEEN 1951 and 1958:				
	40.2	330.1	409.0	441.6

TABLE 33:   HOSPITAL FACILITIES IN CUBA

	Hospitals	Beds
Built before 1933	36	6,893
1933 to 1944	18	6,732

1952 to 1958	43	7,516
TOTAL PUBLIC	97	21,141
TOTAL PUBLIC AND PRIVATE		35,000

NUMBER OF PERSONS PER HOSPITAL BED (1958)

CUBA	190
United States	110*

* *Statistical Abstract of the United States, 1962.* In 1958, there were 1,578,-000 hospital beds in the United States, serving 174,057,000 people.

TABLE 34:   HIGH SCHOOLS, SPECIAL SCHOOLS AND UNIVERSITIES

Type of Institution	Total in 1958	Created by Batista	Created by Others
Universities	13	9	4
High Schools	21	15	6
Schools for Teachers	19	11	8
Home economics schools	14	8	6
Commercial schools	19	10	9
Art Schools	7	2	5
Technical Schools	22	15	7
Schools of Journalism, etc.	6	6	0
TOTALS	121	76	45
PERCENTAGES	100%	63%	37%

TABLE 35:   SUGAR PRICES, PRODUCTION AND EXPORTS

Year	Crop (Mils. Long Tons)	USA Price ¢	World Price ¢	Exports ($ Mils.)
1954	4.75	4.93	3.49	431.5
1955	4.40	4.80	3.42	472.6
1956	4.60	4.86	3.31	523.2
1957	5.51	5.33	5.12	645.0
1958	5.61	5.22	3.45	587.5
1959*	5.99	5.40	2.96	491.7
1963†				

* The first year of the Communist regime in Cuba.
† 1963 = 3 Mils. or so.

TABLE 36:   NATIONAL OWNERSHIP OF THE SUGAR INDUSTRY

Year	Cuban Mills No.	Pct.	U.S. Mills No.	Pct.	Other Ownership No.	Pct.
1939	56	22.4%	66	55.1%	52	22.5%
1954	116	57.8%	41	41.0%	4	1.2%
1958	121	62.1%	36	36.7%	4	0.3%

TABLE 37:   SUGAR OUTPUT IN CUBA, U.S.A. AND U.S.S.R.

Year or period	Sugar Production in Thsds. Short Tons:		
	USA	USSR	CUBA
1935-1940 average	1,901	2,761	3,183
1950-1955 average	2,351	3,010	6,078
1955/56	2,313	4,200	5,229
1956/57	2,529	5,000	6,252
1957/58	2,735	5,800	6,372
1958/59	2,820	6,100	6,600

SUMMARY OF LABOR LEGISLATION IN CUBA

1878   Law restricting child labor.
1909   Arteaga Law, requiring that wages be paid in legal tender, not in scrip.
1910   Law authorizing construction of houses for workers.
1910   Regulating closing hours of stores.
1913   Commission to study an Employment and Social Security Code.
1916   Worker's Compensation Law.
1921   Regulation of hours for banks and pharmacies.
1924   Labor commissions set up at Cuban ports.
1931   Establishment of an unemployment fund.

AFTER THE REVOLUTION OF SEPTEMBER 1933:

1933   Law requiring that 50% of every labor force be Cuban.
1933   Trade Union Law.
1934   Law protecting women workers.
1934   Law of collective labor agreements.
1934   Law establishing the right to paid vacations.
1934   Law protecting workers and employees against arbitrary discharge.
1934   Law affirming the right to join unions and the right to strike.
1934   Eight-hour day law.
1934   Health and maternity protection for workers.
1934   National Minimum Wage Commission.
1935   Employment Exchanges Law.
1936   Superior Council on Social Security.
1936   Organization of an institute to retrain disabled workers.
1936   National Institute of Prevention and Social Reforms.
1937   Central Board on Maternity and Health.
1941   Compulsory Arbitration Law.

1943 National Commission of Social Cooperation.
1945 Regulation of working hours in summer.
1948 Law requiring banks to close on Saturdays.
1948 Law on health standards in places of employment.
1952 Financing of Palace of Labor.
1953 Labor-Management Technical Committees.
1953 Compulsory payment of union dues provided by checkoff.
1955 Law eliminating Communists from the trade unions and from public employment.

DURING THE FIRST YEAR OF CASTRO COMMUNISM:

1959 Abolition of the right to organize unions.
1959 Strikes outlawed.
1959 Minimum wage laws repealed.
1959 Collective bargaining abolished.
1959 Right to job security terminated.
1959 Paid vacations abolished.
1959 Compulsory work for the State instituted.
1959 Payment of wages in scrip authorized.

DISABILITY, OLD AGE, RETIREMENT AND DEATH BENEFITS

Category	Number of Funds in 1958	Beneficiaries in 1958
Workers	21	1,400,000
Professionals	20	8,000
Government employees	11	140,000
TOTAL		1,620,000
Percent of Cuban labor force insured		90%

SOCIAL SECURITY: CONSOLIDATED DATA FROM 21 RETIREMENT FUNDS

	$ Millions
Collections in 1955	56.6
Collections in 1958	68.0
Increase	11.4
Consolidated Balance 1955	99.0
Expenditures	74.1
Contribution to Capital	14.9
Total Assets in 1955	212.2

TRADE UNIONS IN CUBA: CONFEDERATION OF CUBAN WORKERS (CTC)

	Oct. 1944	Dec. 1958
Number of Industrial Unions	30	33
Number of Union Locals	1,560	2,490
No. of Collective Contracts in Force	2,624	7,638*

* Havana Province only.

TABLE 38:   LATIN AMERICAN MONETARY RESERVES OF GOLD AND CONVERTIBLE FOREIGN EXCHANGE IN MILLIONS OF DOLLARS

	Country	1958	1960
1	Venezuela	1,050	558
2	Brazil	465	428
3	CUBA	373	144
4	Mexico	372	393
5	Uruguay	205	213
6	Colombia	160	153
7	Argentina	129	658

TABLE 39:   CUBA AS A MINERAL PRODUCER (1958)

	Cuba's Position in:	
Mineral	The World	Americas
Cobalt	First	First
Nickel	Second	Second
Chronium	Eighth	Second
Manganese	Eighth	Second
Copper	Eleventh	Sixth

Index